1992

THE WAR IN INDO-CHINA 1945-54

Jacques Dalloz

THE WAR IN
INDO-CHINA
1945–54

TRANSLATED BY
JOSEPHINE BACON

Gill and Macmillan
Barnes and Noble

PUBLISHED IN IRELAND BY
GILL AND MACMILLAN LTD
GOLDENBRIDGE
DUBLIN 8
with associated companies in
Auckland, Delhi, Gaborone, Hamburg, Harare,
Hong Kong, Johannesburg, Kuala Lumpur, Lagos, London,
Manzini, Melbourne, Mexico City, Nairobi,
New York, Singapore, Tokyo
First published in France in 1987 by Éditions
du Seuil as *La Guerre
d'Indochine 1945–1954*
© Éditions du Seuil 1987
© English translation Gill and Macmillan Ltd 1990
Translation and manufacture of
this book arranged by Martello Editions Ltd,
Dublin under licence from Gill and Macmillan
Translated by Josephine Bacon/Pholiota Translations Ltd,
7 Caledonian Road, London N1 9DX
Typeset in 10/12 Ehrhardt
in the Republic of Ireland by
Officina Typographica, Galway
Printed in Great Britain by
The Camelot Press, Southampton

BRITISH LIBRARY CATALOGUING IN PUBLICATION DATA

Dalloz, Jacques
    The war in Indo-China 1945–54.
    1. Indo-China. Guerrilla wars, 1946–1954
    I. Title II. Guerre d'Indochine 1945–54. *English*
    959.704'1
    ISBN 0–7171–1723–5

PUBLISHED IN THE UNITED STATES 1990 BY
BARNES AND NOBLE LTD.
8705 BOLLMAN PLACE
SAVAGE, MARYLAND 20763
ISBN 0–389–20897–3

Contents

List of Maps

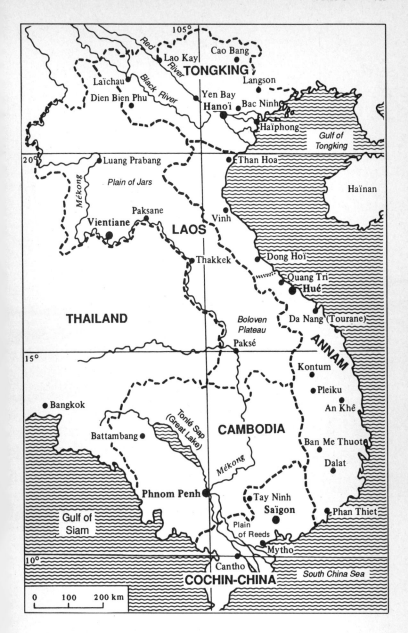

I. GENERAL MAP OF INDO-CHINA

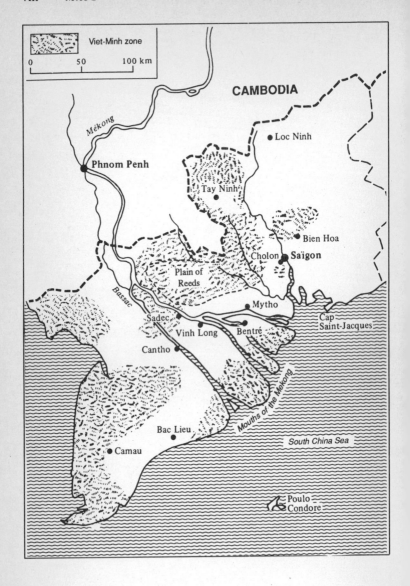

2. COCHIN-CHINA IN MID-1949

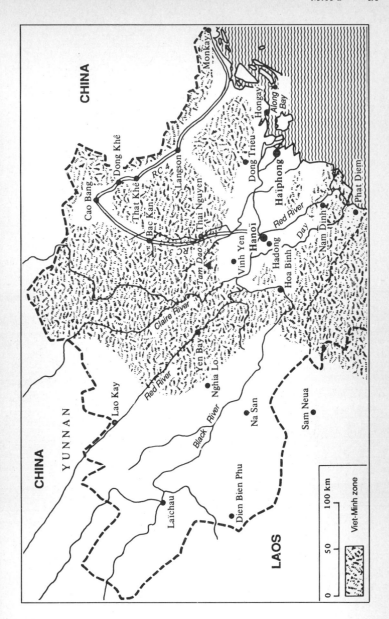

3. TONGKING IN MID-1949

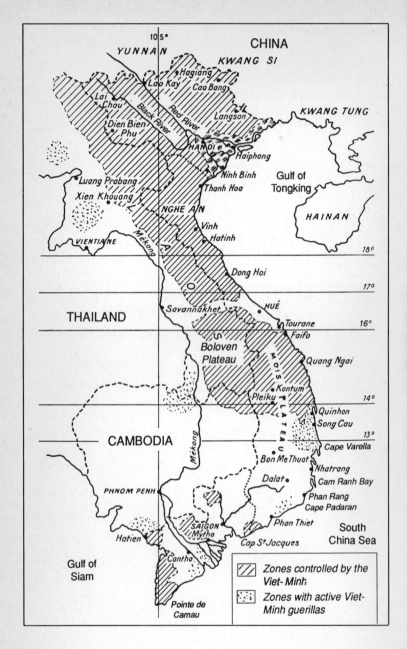

4. THE MILITARY SITUATION IN MAY 1954

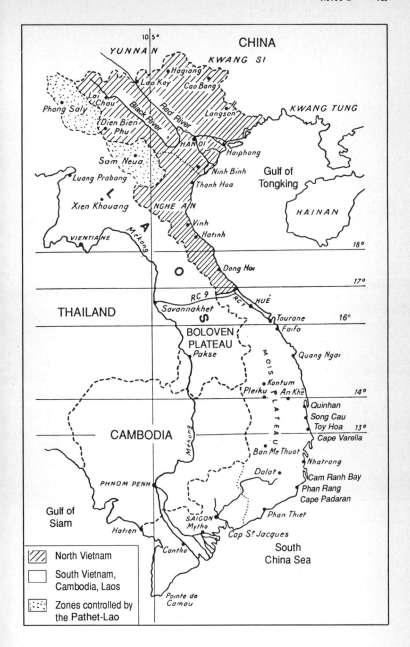

5. AFTER GENEVA

Abbreviations and Glossary

ANZUS	Australia, New Zealand and the United States. 1951 pact linking these three countries.
APV	Armée populaire vietnamienne.
BACBO	Tongking.
BISHOPRICS (THE)	The dioceses of Phat Diem and Bui Chu on the south-eastern stretch of the Red River.
BTLC	Bureau technique de liaison et de coordination. Information service of the French colonial office.
CAI	Annamite overseer.
CANBO	Officer in the Viet Minh.
CGT	Confédération Générale du Travail.
CHU LUC	Regular forces of the Viet Minh.
CONG	Communist.
DAI VIET	Right-wing nationalist party.
DEUXIEME BUREAU	French intelligence service.
DOC LAP	Freedom, autonomy, independence.
DONG MINH HOI (DMH)	Abbreviation of Viet Nam Cach Menh Dong Minh Hoi, a Vietnamese revolutionary league controlled by China.
DRV	Democratic Republic of Vietnam.
EDC	European Defence Community.
EMGDN	General chief of staff of the National Guard.
FLN	South Vietnamese Liberation Front.
FUNC	United National Front of Cambodia.
GCMA	Mixed airborne commando groups. Anti-guerilla units set up by the French.
GPRF	Provisional government of the French Republic. The formal title of the government from the Liberation to the establishment of the Fourth Republic.

GRA	Gouvernement revolutionnaire annamite.
HUYEN	Province.
ISARA (LAO)	Free Laos.
ISSARAK (KHMERS)	Free Khmers.
KY	Region: the "three *Ky*s" are the three regions of Vietnam.
LAO DONG	Abbreviation of Dang Lao Dong Viet Nam, The Workers' Party of Vietnam. Communist party, founded in 1950
LIEN KHU (LK)	Interzone
LIEN VIET	Abbreviation of Hoi Lien Hiep Quoc Dan Viet Nam, Nationalist Popular Front of Vietnam.
MAAG	Military Aid and Advisory Group.
MRP	Mouvement Républicain Populaire. The French Christian Democratic Party.
NAMBO	Cochin-China
NHA QUE	Peasant.
OSS	United States Office of Strategic Services. Fore-runner of the CIA.
PAM	Programme d'aide militaire.
PATHET LAO	Literally, the Lao state. The Laotian revolutionary forces.
PCI	Communist Party of Indo-China.
PHU	District.
PHUC QUOC	Abbreviation of Viet Nam Phuc Quoc Hoi. League for the restoration of Vietnam.
PRACHACHEON	People's Party. Cambodian Communist Party.
QUOC NGU	The transcription of Vietnamese into Latin characters.
RC	Route coloniale.
RPF	Rassemblement du Peuple Français. Ultra right-wing Gaullist party, 1947–53.
SANGKUM	Abbreviation of Sangkum Reastr Niyum, Popular Socialist Community. A party set up by Norodom Sihanouk in 1955.
SDECE	Overseas information and counter-espionage department.
SEATO	South East Asia Treaty Organisation.
SFIO	Section Française de l'Internationale Ouvrière. The full title of the French Socialist Party.

TA DIEN	Tenant farmer.
TDKQ	Tieu Doan Kinh Quan. Light battalions of Bao Dai's army.
THIRD FORCE	Coalition of political parties who excluded both the Gaullist RPF and the Communists and formed the government of the Fourth Republic from 1947 to 1951.
TLD	Tong Lien Doan Lao Dong. The Vietnamese workers' confederation.
TU VÉ	Militia.
UBKC/HC	Uy Ban Khang Chien/Hanh Chinh. Administrative and resistance committee.
UDSR	Union démocratique et socialiste de la Résistance. Small centre-left party.
USIS	United States Information Service.
VIET BAC	North Tongking.
VIET MINH	Abbreviation of Viet Nam Doc Lap Dong Minh. Vietnamese independence league.
VNQDD	Viet Nam Quoc Dan Dang, Nationalist party of Vietnam, founded in 1927.
XA	Village.

I

Colonial Indo-China

A FRENCH CREATION

Gesta Dei per Francos. The Christians and missionaries in the Annamite empire were first persecuted in 1858, providing France with an excuse for military intervention. Napoleon III's regime was thus able to assuage Catholic opinion whilst simultaneously preparing to lay siege to a country that would open up the way into South China. The conquest, which began under the Second Empire, was continued by the Third Republic and, within the space of a third of a century, France had established a foothold in the Far East. Even though its borders largely corresponded to the boundaries that the Emperors of Annam had given their territories, Indo-China was a colonial creation linking countries with different traditions. The Union of Indo-China was established in 1887 and was eventually organized on a permanent basis by Doumer, who arrived as governor-general ten years later, just after the signature of the peace treaty.

The territory measured one and a half times the size of France and contained a wide variety of inhabitants. This was particularly true of the central chain of mountains and the highlands in the north. These sparsely-populated, malaria-ridden regions contained only three or four inhabitants per square kilometre, but were something of an ethnological museum. First, there were Indonesian-type races of extremely ancient origins, known to the Vietnamese as Mois or savages. Later, these were joined by newer and more highly-developed races who had infiltrated from Yunnan in China, for example the Thais (of whom there were about one million in the period between the two world wars), Mans (100,000), Meos (the newest comers) and others. The frequent mingling of these races did not prevent each from retaining its own specific characteristics. The Thais were more numerous in the north and the Mois in the south. Because the country was broken up by mountains, each group was divided into sub-groups offering the widest possible variety. Thus among the Mois there were differences of language[1] and varying degrees of economic development. For example, some cultivated their rice in irrigated fields. There were also differences in their inheritance laws (maternal or paternal) and so on. Although they were so varied, the mountain races normally had some features in common, such as tribal structure, extensive grubbing out of land to make space for crops, ignorance of the written word and animist beliefs.

The geographical nature of the cordillera made it impossible to establish any political structure there. The Laos, who were one of the Thai groups, managed to set up principalities such as Luang Prabang in the mid-Mekong basins of the west. Further south, the Khmers founded a kingdom on the plain surrounding the Great Lake. The ruins of Angkor bear witness to its past splendour. But the kingdom, threatened by Annam on one side and Siam on the other, went into total decline in the nineteenth century. It had once covered all the plains of the lower Mekong, but by this time it had already lost the delta region to the Annamite empire—in other words, that part of Cochin-China which still had 600,000 Cambodian inhabitants in 1939. The protectorate established by Napoleon III undoubtedly saved Cambodia from disappearing altogether. Laos and Khmers are similar to the Siamese in their language, art and religion. The religion is Theravada Buddhism, the Lesser Vehicle. Hindu culture made a futile attempt to penetrate the Annamite cordillera. The mountains served as a dividing line not only between the rival expansionist aims of Annam and Siam, but also between the two great areas of Far Eastern civilization, the Hindu and the Chinese.

Annam: the pacification of the South. This was what the Chinese called their march southwards. During the period when the Annamites, in other words the Vietnamese, fell under the rule of the Middle Kingdom, they were concentrated mainly in the Red River delta, an area the size of two French *départements*. The year 1939 marked the thousandth anniversary of the country's liberation from Chinese rule, and the liberator Ngo Quyen was commemorated as a national hero. Although Annam later paid tribute to the Celestial Empire, the Chinese never managed to re-establish control over what they called the pacified South, partly because the latter was protected from its powerful neighbour by a high, broad mountainous barrier. Being a nation of paddy-field rice-growers, the Vietnamese shunned the wooded slopes of the Annamite central mountain chain. For centuries, they expanded along the coasts, creeping slowly southwards and occupying the ever-narrowing coastal plains of the region known during the French occupation as Annam. Eventually, they reached the Mekong delta, where they found a vast area in which to settle. Their march southwards took centuries and was achieved at the expense of the Hindu population. By 1939, the Chams, who had created the kingdom of Champa, had disappeared almost entirely. Only a few thousand of them were left.

As for the Khmers of Cochin-China, they had already been supplanted several decades previously when the French annexed the region. Although Vietnam is nearly 2,000 km long, its total area is only just a little over 70,000 sq km. It stretches from the Chinese border to the Pointe de Camau on the Gulf of Siam and is broken up into a series of plains, some of which are isolated from each other by the central Annamite chain. The plains only broaden out at the two deltas. Geographically, the country is shaped like a pole with a heavy basket balanced at each end and consequently it was readily represented during the colonial era as a yoke borne on the shoulders of a Vietnamese native. There were obvious differences between the Red River delta, which had been carefully cultivated over a period of centuries, and Cochin-China, a colonized region in which pioneers had driven back the Cambodian minority and progressively developed a vast amphibious area. The French and the Americans both capitalized on these differences. It did not matter that these were the same people speaking the same language, albeit in a variety of dialects. Furthermore, China's influence was strong. The Middle Kingdom no longer dominated Vietnam politically but the mark of Chinese civilization was still there. Its influence was everywhere, in agricultural methods, in the use of ideograms, in religious and ideological trends (starting from Mahayana Buddhism, or the Greater Vehicle) and even in the social and political systems.

The capital was moved from Hanoi to Hué at the beginning of the nineteenth century. The court of Hué was modelled on that of Peking in its taboos, etiquette and bureaucratic structure. The Emperor, who was known as "the Son of Heaven", served as a mediator between heaven and his subjects. In the spring, he would perform the ritual ploughing of the first furrow, which symbolized this role. The Emperor was said to have the mandate of heaven. However, this mandate could be lost. The clergy were experts at interpreting signs portending such an eventuality, such as disasters, social problems or moral decline. In such a case, revolution and a change of dynasty were in order.

One should not be misled by the term "feudalism" used by some writers.[2] The feudal system as understood in western Europe and Japan did not exist in China or Vietnam. The monarchy relied on a hierarchy of officials known as mandarins, who were recruited by a complex system of three-yearly competitive examinations. One could enter for these examinations up to quite an advanced age and if one passed them the honour reflected upon the whole village or clan. Like the Emperor, the mandarins contributed towards maintaining harmony in the world. Like him, they also had absolute power over their subjects. They were described as "fathers and mothers of the people". Not all scholars became imperial officials. Many of them lived in the villages where they used their influence and taught children to read. But whether they were mandarins or not, all the scholars were subject to the same disciplines and conventions. They constituted the only social group to possess a real national awareness, a fact demonstrated by their role in resisting French invasion, and they were the guardians and defenders of a set of values commonly known as Confucianism.[3]

Confucianism was a traditionalist philosophical, political and moral system which exalted the past and took a cyclical view of history, thus ignoring the idea of progress. It was a brand of humanism aimed first and foremost at achieving social harmony through adherence to the rules laid down in its canon law books. Although humanist, Confucianism had ritualistic trappings. There was actually a Minister of Rites in Hué, who was responsible for court etiquette, the compilation of the calendar and the famous three-yearly examinations. Confucianism was the official ideology of China and it had an acute sense of hierarchy. The relationship between inferiors and superiors and between young and old was strictly codified. Social groups were classified. Scholars came at the top, followed by peasants, craftsmen and, finally, traders. So in this agrarian society, scholars and those who worked the land were exalted while commercial activity was despised.

Young intellectuals came to regard Confucianism as a pernicious brand of traditionalism because it always harked back to the same texts and because it justified domination by a single class of society which accumulated all the knowledge and power. They also condemned it for looking backwards towards a mythical golden age, despising science and technology and trying to enmesh society in a restrictive network of rituals. The type of cultural revolution that occurred between the two world wars was aimed primarily at abolishing Confucianism in all its immobility.

The three-yearly examinations were abolished in Vietnam in 1919, the same year that China was shaken to its foundations by the uprising of 4 May.[4] By 1939, the image of the mandarin with his long fingernails, transported in his painted wooden palanquin while people fell prostrate before him, was a thing of the past. But the serious, sententious scholar who wore a black turban was not, nor were the customary formulae and precepts of Confucianism. Thus numerous traces of the ideology of old Vietnam survived, although some members of the intelligentsia were simultaneously developing great enthusiasm for the ideas of the Vietnam of the future. Actually, there is not such a great discrepancy as might be imagined between Marxism and the type of Confucianism that linked knowledge with power and justified the one as well as the other, disdaining the after-life and concentrating upon man within the community. According to this theory, the individual's most important task is to perform his social duties correctly; it thus demands exemplary moral conduct of those in positions of politica! responsibility. Furthermore, the Chinese world was used to contradictory thinking: the Taoist tradition led the way to acceptance of dialectical materialism. Even the religion, which was a vague syncretism rooted in popular consciousness intermingled with Buddhist influences and elements of Taoism, constituted no obstacle to the spread of Marxism.

In old Annam, which thought in terms of groups rather than individuals, the two most widely practised religions were linked to the two basic social units. The family practised ancestor worship, whilst the village worshipped its own guardian spirit. Families and communities were ruled by their oldest members. It was the head of the family who presided over the cult of ancestors. Thus there was hierarchy in the family, hierarchy in society and in the state and hierarchy in the cosmos. All this was intregrated into the Confucian system, in which filial piety was a cardinal virtue. There was a proverb, "The power of the Emperor stops at the bamboo hedge", a reference to the protective hedge that surrounded every Annamite village. The autonomy of individual communities was one of the political realities of old Vietnam that the colonists respected to a large extent. Communities were governed by councils of elders. Central government dealt with these councils, not with individuals, particularly when it came to taxes. So at the bottom end of the system there were hundreds of villages protected by hedges and sheltered from the sun by fruit-trees, tiny gerontocratic republics. At the top, an absolute ruler assisted by a bureaucracy of mandarins ruled over all. Yet the power of both these institutions was tempered and justified by Confucian morality. That, in a nutshell, is the Annamese system of government prior to the colonial era.

Vietnamese political unity disappeared under French rule, although the French had helped the Nguyen dynasty to re-establish it in the late eighteenth century.[5] The colonists, eager to erase the memory of the old Empire, divided it into three parts, Cochin-China, Annam and Tongking, each of which had a different status. They also added two peripheral regions, Laos and Cambodia. Although official documents sometimes distinguished between Hindu and Annamite regions, nothing in colonial terminology ever recalled the unity of the past. Only the central part of the country (i.e. the pole in the image) retained the old name of Annam. Furthermore, the new name, Vietnam,[6] which was being bandied about by the revolutionaries, was banned as subversive. The first country to succumb to France was Cochin-China, and it was made into a so-called incorporated colony. This made it an integral part of the French Republic[7] and its inhabitants were considered to be French, even though the vast majority of them did not enjoy French citizenship, being merely French subjects. Cochin-China was ruled by a governor. Cambodia and Annam were given the status of protectorates. European power there was based on treaties signed by their sovereigns. In fact, the French found reason to intervene more and more in the internal affairs of these countries, greatly exceeding the rights granted to them by the original agreements. To all appearances, both Annam and Cambodia were governed by absolute monarchs who ruled according to the traditional laws, pomp and ceremony. They were represented in the provinces by officials appointed by the sovereign. However, in actual fact, the monarchy existed alongside a colonial administration which governed the country under the authority of a resident minister. The administration even chose the sovereigns, and deposed them if necessary.[8] The French gradually infringed upon the ruler's prerogatives until they reduced Annamite imperial power to a minimum. It reached its nadir around 1930, before Bao Dai reached adulthood. At this point, the Emperor was no more than a revered idol. A brochure compiled for the colonial exhibition of 1931 explains the situation nicely.[9]

> The local native administration represents the conservative, quasi-ritualistic element of government. The basic role of the French administration is to ensure that it functions properly, to review and apply all kinds of reforms and to administer directly any service requiring European specialist and technical knowledge. This judicious formula of the separation of powers and jurisdiction seems to be the best model for a protectorate.

The passage refers to Laos, but it applies to all French-style protectorates. However, both Laos and Tongking were governed by mixed regimes. In the case of the former, only the tiny kingdom of Luang Prabang had the status of a protectorate, the rest of it was governed directly. Tongking, on the other hand, was a most unusual kind of protectorate. Apart from the fact that the largest towns, Hanoi and Haiphong, were French territories, the resident minister was soon granted permanent authority over the region by the sovereign of Annam and so, protector as well as protected, he found himself representing both the Emperor and the Republic.

No matter what the official status of each country, everything was run by a governor-general who, in turn, was responsible to the French Colonial Office. This arrangement is a clear demonstration of the French concept of a protectorate.[10] The general government in Hanoi directed a hierarchy of provincial officials via the governor of Cochin-China and the four resident ministers. It was backed up by numerous departments and allotted a large budget supported by indirect taxation. Customs duties and taxes on salt, opium and alcohol formed the basis of the resources for the general budget. It was a situation that certainly fuelled the anti-colonialist arguments. The colonial powers imposed heavy taxes on products such as salt, alcohol and rice which were essential to the native lifestyle. They benefited from the sale of opium, the consumption of which was strictly forbidden in France. They also slapped heavy taxes on imported foreign products, thus making the cost of living very high.[11] Many of the accusations of immorality and inexperience in the French system are based on these examples. The high direct taxes used to fund local budgets were also called into question. Furthermore, these taxes were insufficient to cover costs because the general budget had to subsidise the budgets of the five countries. In the case of Laos, the most underprivileged country, the subsidy amounted to more than the taxes received and the Cochin-Chinese members of the Colonial Council complained that the Federation was milking their region.

In the early twentieth century, France became anxious to reassure the taxpayers back home concerning the cost of its imperialist ventures. The principle was thus introduced of financial autonomy for each colony, or group of colonies in the case of the Federation. As a result, Indo-China received nothing at all from the French budget and had to rely on its own resources. Certainly, the Union could still finance its infrastructures by borrowing from France, but then it would have had to pay interest, so it resorted to taxation. The taxes in question were paid almost exclusively by the native masses and it became the main task of the colonial administration to collect them. They were out of all proportion to levels of taxation in pre-colonial times. However, in this way, the responsibility of the state was reduced to a minimum.[12]

Indo-China stood apart from the rest of the Empire on account of its complexity. It consisted of one colony, two protectorates and two regions ruled by mixed regimes, all of which came under the authority of a governor-general. However, these legalities will not be dwelt on in great detail, since the same principles applied everywhere. Indo-China was subject to the omnipotence of authoritarian, paternalistic French officials. The Federation was ruled by about 400 civil servants who received their orders from the proconsul of Hanoi, the latter being more powerful than the majority of government ministers in Paris. Even though assemblies were set up between the two world wars, the system of representation remained poorly developed. The Colonial Council of Cochin-China was appointed by a dual electoral system weighted heavily in favour of the French. The basic function of this council was to vote on the local budget. In the protectorates, the various assemblies had no more than a consultative role. The *Grand Conseil des intérêts économiques et financiers* (Great Council for Economic and Financial Interests) established in 1928 at a federal level was great in name only. A proportion of its members were nominated by the administration and the rest came from regional asssemblies. This method of appointment, plus the limited nature of its duties, meant that it only counterbalanced the power of the governor-general in a very small way. Finally, an extremely small minority of natives enjoyed the same rights as the French settlers. These were the 3,000 or so "naturalized" subjects, most of whom lived in Cochin-China. F. Harmand (1845–1921), who knew the country well, wrote in *Domination et colonisation*, "A society that has been dominated will not submit gladly and trustingly to the conqueror's rule. That is why domination cannot easily be reconciled with the egalitarian principles of democracy. It is impossible to transfer the principles of democracy to a dominated society."

For the colonizer, domination was largely justified in terms of what was achieved, and this was ritually extolled by the administration. The *pax gallica* brought order and security, although the only inhabitants who could appreciate this at all were the very old who could remember the robber bands who had once roamed the countryside. France saw herself as a conduit of enlightenment and prided herself on her achievements in education.

The education system encouraged the study of French, made it easier to study the Vietnamese language, now transcribed into Latin characters,[13] and opened the minds of the young natives to the modern world.[14] Institutions of higher learning were opened in Hanoi, although in some subjects studies had to be completed in France. In a country accustomed to selection by competition, on account of the Confucian tradition, the French education system produced many brilliant successes. Of the few colonial subjects that achieved qualifications in higher education, a significant number came from the Federation. The future Prime Minister

Xuan, who graduated from the *École polytechnique*, is one example of republican meritocracy that government circles liked to quote officially.
Colonization equipped the country with intellectual resources of a high
calibre. For instance, there were departments of geography, meteorol-
ogy and geology and, most important of all, the *École française d'Extrême-
Orient* (French School of Far Eastern Studies) which produced some
notable works on Indo-Chinese civilizations. Knowledge of the past
went hand in hand with the preservation of ancient sites; the *Beaux-Arts*
restored numerous monuments, beginning with the temples of Angkor.

The health of the population improved greatly. Hospitals and dispen-
saries were built and innoculation campaigns launched. The fight
against malaria began with the distribution of quinine and the cleaning
up of plantations and work places. One of the least controversial advantages to emerge from colonization was the Pasteur Institute, which
played a vital role in reducing mortality. Although progress was obvious,
it is difficult to quantify it. There are no statistics for the pre-colonial
period, and the only valid figures for the period leading up to World War
II cover the large towns and cities. The mortality rate in Hanoi and
Saigon was about thirty per thousand. In the capital, infant mortality fell
from 44 per cent in 1925 to 19 per cent in 1938.[15] The birth rate remained at its traditional level, and so the country experienced an increase in population, a fact which the colonial regime claimed as one of
its first proofs of success.

Major water projects were undertaken from the very beginning of colonization. In Tongking, human civilization went back so far that it was
possible to make only a few minor adjustments to the existing system. In
Cochin-China, however, active attempts were made to conquer the
delta, and the area covered by rice fields increased sixfold. As a result,
Cochin-China was able to provide the bulk of the Federation's exports.
Plantations were established on the hills and plateaux, particularly on
the 'red earth' areas of southern Indo-China, which were excellent for
growing the Para rubber plant. Rubber accounted for 20 per cent of the
country's exports. Many mineral deposits were exploited, particularly in
Hongay and Tongking. One of the images used to illustrate the
economic development of the Empire was the Hongay coalfield with its
vast seams and its 30,000 employees.[16]

A rail network was constructed and 3,000 km of railway line was built
in Indo-China. Work began with the building of the famous Yunnan line
which ascended the Red River valley and brought South China under
French influence. The Trans-Indo-China railway was completed in
1937, making it possible to travel from Saigon to southern China via

Hué and Hanoi. New tracks and roads were also opened. In pre-colonial times, the main route through the Annamite empire was no more than a narrow track, slashed by rivers which had to be traversed by boat, and mountains which were negotiable only by means of steps cut out of the rock. The new *route mandarine* made it possible to travel from one end of the country to the other along a road six metres wide with no ferry crossings, for the last ferries had recently been abolished. Colonization brought few new towns, though Haiphong is an exception to the rule. However, the existing towns, particularly the two capitals, Hanoi and Saigon, were modernized. In order to revive the Indo-Chinese economy, the colonial administration took active charge of all work on communications and services, getting the Federation deeply into debt in the process.

Much had been done, but much still remained to be done. This was how the colonial authorities tended to evaluate the whole venture, presenting it overall in positive terms. "Indo-China could not wish for a better destiny. Half a century of French peace has brought its nations a miraculous degree of economic prosperity and political security."[17] Albert Sarraut became the bard of French-style colonization. Sarraut was a former governor-general of Indo-China and several times Minister for the Colonies. He was a radical politician and a champion of long terms of office for government ministers. In one chapter of his book, *Grandeur et Servitude coloniales* (Colonial Greatness and Servitude) published in 1931, he demonstrated that there was a reverse side to the coin. Advances in medicine had led to an increase in population, thus giving rise to serious social problems; the development of education had caused ill-feelings and errors of judgment, and so on. Yet, despite all this, the venture was an exciting one and the Republic owed it to itself to carry on.

COLONIAL SOCIETY

Indo-China, which the French considered as a colony for "exploitation" as opposed to a "settlement" colony, was dominated by a small European minority. The 1937 census provided the following statistics: 42,000 "Europeans and similar persons" 36,000 of whom were "French by birthright" and 3,000 of whom were "naturalized French subjects".[18] Within the French community, 59 per cent of the working population were in the army and 19 per cent in the colonial administration. Civil servants and army officers were sometimes attracted to the colony because it could offer them financial benefits or help them to advance their careers, or because they had a taste for things foreign or because they were disillusioned with the mother country or because it could offer them greater scope for action. If the 600 or so missionaries are added to these figures, one is left with a very small number of actual settlers. The latter were happy to call themselves Indo-Chinese and their particularism was a constant source of amazement to French visitors to the colony, especially when it tended towards separatism.

There was a considerable variety of status within the small society of colonists. There were officials as opposed to settlers and the tiny minority of country dwellers as opposed to the town dwellers, and so on. However, they presented a united front towards the native population. It was an accepted fact that Europeans were at the top of the social hierarchy. Mandarins kowtowed to them ceremoniously. European prestige was such that it was not done for a Frenchman to have to submit to the orders of an Annamite under any circumstances.[19] Hence the excitement when the governor-general, Varenne (1925–8) recommended the promotion of native officials. A tiny minority of people, such as missionaries and military commanders, who were stationed in remote spots had jobs which obliged them to understand the natives. However, for much of the time, French society was self-contained and enjoyed the affluent colonial lifestyle. People entertained, hunted, played tennis and spent holidays in mountain resorts during the rainy season. They employed numerous servants, who were often called "boys". A few old colonists would look back nostalgically at the period prior to the arrival of European women, contrasting the days of the pioneers—who lived with native mistresses, if necessary—with the new period of the remittance men. Colonization encouraged the growth of another minority. In 1939, there were over 300,000 Chinese living in the peninsula. Their guilds and trade associations were extremely powerful. For example, the Chinese dominated the rice trade in Cochin-China. They slotted easily into local life and happily intermarried with the natives. The French recruited most of their purchasing agents from among them. Merchants, craftsmen, property owners and money-lenders, the Chinese accounted for a large proportion of the Indo-Chinese middle classes. Their wealth and their network of business connections aroused mixed feelings, reminiscent to a certain extent of those aroused by the Jews in other parts of the world. As in France, the Chinese community was largely urban, and all the big cities had a Chinese quarter. The largest of these was Cholon which was actually a separate town from Saigon until 1932.[20]

On the other hand, 90 per cent of the Vietnamese themselves lived in the country. Colonization did not eradicate native craftsmanship, because the standard of living of the masses was so low that the peasants could not afford to buy the manufactured goods that came from France and had to make do with traditional products.[21] The Vietnamese peasantry was basically composed of smallholders, many of whom owned their own land. However, there was also a minority of day labourers, especially in the South. In Tongking, the majority of farmers had no draught animals. Furthermore, 50 per cent of the peasants owned less than a hectare of land. A pre-war writer, Y. Henry,[22] quoted the following example. When the Forestry Department wanted to create a nursery of 2.5 hectares in the Red River delta it had to negotiate with sixty-seven landowners.

As the population increased, the land problem grew worse on the most densely-populated plains. The smallholders, in particular, found themselves in difficulty during the slack period between the time when the previous harvest had been consumed and the new one had not yet been gathered. If freak weather conditions occurred, or if there was an unexpected event such as illness or an accident, the whole family was threatened with starvation.[23] In such cases, families resorted to borrowing from prominent people, i.e. from the Chinese. The usurer was a scourge common to the peasantry of all Far Eastern countries, and usury was traditionally rife in Indo-China. It was normal to pay interest rates of around 4 per cent a month. Many peasants were unable to repay, so they parted with their plots of land instead and became tenant farmers.[24] At the same time, much of the common land was divided up. This was done with the help of mandarins and notables and naturally favoured the most well-to-do. Large estates grew in number although it must be borne in mind that in Tongking one only had to own ten hectares in order to be classed as a large estate owner. It was a far cry from the Radziwills and the other great landed gentry of central Europe. Thus, the colonial era caused great changes within peasant society.

The phenomenon was particularly evident in Cochin-China, where 50 per cent of the land was owned by 2.5 per cent of the population,[25] and most especially in Transbassac, the western part of the colony. The irrigation projects carried out there made it possible to establish vast estates. Some of these were conceded to the French, who took over 300,000 hectares of rice fields and employed day labourers to cultivate them. However, for the most part, the new lands were acquired by Cochin-Chinese dignitaries. They leased them to tenant farmers, known as *ta dien*, each of whom took on between five and ten hectares and often employed day labourers. Thus these tenant farmers were not among the poorest members of the Vietnamese peasantry. The large landowners were often paternalistic and had protégés, even though they scarcely ever visited their estates except at harvest time. The Vietnamese bourgeoisie, which was often extremely acquisitive and was part of the mandarin system, lived off ground rents and also owned urban real estate and shares. However, its role in terms of modern capitalism was an extremely limited one. Big business was in the hands of the French and three groups in particular, the Bank of Indo-China,[26] the Rivaud group and the Rothschild-de-Wendel group. As far as trading was concerned, the Vietnamese middle classes had to contend not only with colonists,[27] but also with the Chinese and even the tiny Hindu community. Although Indo-China was the foremost French colony from an industrial point of view, the Vietnamese only controlled small businesses. They did not own any firm employing more than 200 workers. In addition to this bourgeoisie proper, there was another middle class created by colonization, namely members of the liberal professions, minor officials and so on. All these groups had a tendency to become gallicized. The ambition was to marry into a French family or to become "naturalized".[28] It was the bourgeoisie who purchased most of the French goods imported into the country. As far as young people were concerned, the zest for modern life as represented by the colonial system and the thirst for new knowledge were not without their drawbacks. They often felt cut off from the historical and social reality of their country, yet they were not fully integrated into the French community which kept itself firmly at the controls of the country.

Indo-China was the "pearl of the Empire" and its growth was assured.[29] Yet, as befits a colonial society, the capitalist economy was merely superimposed on the traditional one and ignored vast sectors of it. Since the Annamite region was privileged by comparison with the western regions, the Indo-Chinese working class was almost exclusively Vietnamese.[30] This small but concentrated proletarian group numbered about 200,000 in 1939, or 5 per cent of the Indo-Chinese population (a count based on families). However, this percentage may be questionable, particularly if one takes into account the fact that this new class was unstable and that its members often retained links with the land. Some of them went back to it, in fact. The figure of 200,000 must certainly be taken as a minimum. The working class was divided into four groups, plantation workers (especially on the rubber plantations), large numbers of miners as is typical of colonized countries, transport workers (the 14,000 railway workers constituted a very distinct group) and workers in the processing industries. This last sector consisted mainly of small firms, the majority of which handled agricultural produce and manufactured goods for local needs. However, in 1939, the largest factory in the Federation, namely, the cotton mill at Nam Dinh employed over 5,000

workers and the *Distilleries de l'Indochine* at Cholon employed over
4,000. The pressure of population meant that workers were paid much
less in the north than in the south. Working conditions were particularly
bad in the mines of Tongking (people talked of the Hongay hell) and on
the rubber plantations. The latter were situated on sparsely-populated
plateaux and employed large numbers of workers under contract. Consequently, thousands of coolies were sent south by a certain type of un-
scrupulous recruiting officer who made illiterate workers sign harsh and
totally binding contracts. To quote the words of Roubaud, "However
horrible the truth is, it must be written: the Annamite worker signed a
contract committing him to three years of slavery."

Whatever their status the workers, who were from the countryside,
had to be broken in so that they would meet the demands of their new
employment. Annamite overseers known as Cais were entrusted with
this task, and the employers often paid the wages directly to them. If
necessary, these overseers imposed fines or even resorted to corporal
punishment. Governor-general Varenne ordered an enquiry which was
carried out by the Inspectorate of Works. It resulted in the powerful De-
lammare report. An improvement in working conditions followed,
particularly after the Popular Front came into being.[31] Labourers constituted only a fraction of the urban lower classes, and the small
craftsmen, domestic servants and the large underclass should not be
forgotten.

Just as colonization caused the emergence of new social classes it also
enabled the spread of new religions. Obviously, the French presence
meant Catholicism. Missionaries had been active in Indo-China before
the French military invasion and, to some extent, provided a pretext for
it. Catholics amounted to less than 10 per cent of the population and
were mainly concentrated along the Annamite coasts, where they
formed extremely tight communities. As the religion of the colonizer,
the status of Catholicism was such that conversion to Christianity was
one means of assimilating. Catholicism led vigorous campaigns against
Vietnamese tradition. Catholicism constituted such an integral part of
the French system there that republican anti-clericalism never touched
the Federation, any more than it did the rest of the Indo-Chinese Empire for that matter. The religious link was borne out by the presence of a
mission tent at the 1931 Colonial Exhibition. As for the local Catholic
press, it extolled the imperial venture and dwelt upon the need to look to
Christian inspiration for guidance in the work that went on there. However, Rome was anxious for the future of these young churches and insisted that religion and colonization should be kept separate from one

another. The encyclical *Maximum illud* of 1919 warned that missionaries were in the service of the Gospel, not of this or that western power. The document passed more or less unnoticed at the time, but more attention was paid to the developing native clergy. The first Vietnamese bishop, Monsignor Tong,[32] was consecrated in 1933. Despite the sympathy of the administration, Catholicism experienced a period of relative stagnation just before the war. Instead, this period was one of a revival of the sects.

This was a phenomenon that really only affected Cochin-China, and served to emphasize its distinctive nature. Cochin-China was the southernmost region of Indo-China, belatedly colonized by the Vietnamese, so Annamite tradition had become superimposed on the original Cham or Khmer tradition. It was also an incorporated colony, and annexation to France meant that it had been cut off from the traditional state religion for decades. The Cadaoist sect[33] was founded in 1926 by the entrepreneur and colonial adviser Le Van Trung and grew progressively over the years. Based on Buddhism, Cadaoism consisted of much spiritualism, a touch of freemasonry and a whiff of Taoism or Confucianism, using an ecclesiastical structure inspired by Catholicism. The combination was a ragbag. Basically a spiritualist cult, it was superficially intellectual. The sect attempted a renewal of Buddhism but at the same time it preached foreign cultures. It borrowed widely from France, drawing on Allan Kardec (from a spiritualist point of view), Joan of Arc, Victor Hugo and others, and it combined a pope and bishoprics with masonic symbols. This syncretic sect is just one of numerous colonial cultural movements linked with European domination, for example, Chinese Taipings, Black African Christs, etc., in all their political ambiguity. Cadaoism became a force the administration had to reckon with, on account of its hundreds of thousands of followers, its capital Tay Ninh, its able "pope", Pham Cong Tac and its strict hierarchy. It was a movement founded by prominent French-speaking natives connected with the colonial system, but it began to worry the French authorities during the pre-war period, because it was moving towards pro-Japanese anti-colonialism. However, this led to no more than a series of retractions.

The Hoa Hao sect was a later phenomenon, founded in 1935. It was also more localized and sketchy. None the less, it spread throughout the countryside of Cochin-China. It presented itself as a revived form of Buddhism. Huynh Phu So, the illiterate young peasant who founded it, began to interest the authorities when he started to predict in his preachings that the colonial power would be unseated by the Japanese and its system of domination would collapse. Dubbed the "mad bonze" by the French, he was imprisoned in August 1940.

The vast majority of the population of Indo-China were Vietnamese. On the eve of World War II, they accounted for 17 million of the Federation's 22 million inhabitants. The plains on which they lived bore the brunt of the drastic changes brought about by French intrusion. The interior of the Peninsula had not been transformed to such a great extent. Consequently, in 1939, Laos with its 230,000 sq km and its population of one million, had only 500 French inhabitants and one secondary school, the *Collège Pavie*, which had about 100 pupils. Less than half of these were Laotians. The only industry was the tin mines of Nam Pathene. Furthermore, the 6,000 miners who worked them were all Vietnamese. This is a typical example. Laos and Khmers did not participate in the few modern activities that took place within the two kingdoms, and it was from the Annamite minorities that the Indo-Chinese Communist Party later drew its first recruits. Christianity did not manage to penetrate the area west of the cordillera and the religious life of Laos was hardly changed at all by colonization. The administration was content just to move the focal point of local Buddhism from Bangkok to Phnom Penh by setting up first a *Pali* school,[34] then the *Institut d'études Bouddhiques* (Institute of Buddhist Studies). Cut off by the mountains, Laos looked towards Siam and seemed to turn its back on the Federation and the colonial authorities who wanted to make it a definite part of Indo-China despite its geography and history. So it had to be de-isolated. A road was built linking the Annamite coast with Thakkek on the Mekong. There was talk of adding a branch of the Trans-Indo-China railway to cross the Mu Gia Pass but, for the time being, the country had no railways at all and only 28 kilometres of asphalted road.

Thus, the Lao population of the Mekong basin was hardly disturbed at all by the French. The latter made their presence felt only in the mountains along the borders with Cochin-China and Cambodia. In 1934–5, the general government carried out military operations to crush the Moi tribes of this difficult region. Thus peace was achieved just after the birth of conquest ended at a time when the process of decolonization had already begun.

THE NATIONALIST MOVEMENT
On the eve of the World War II, the French people still knew very little about the Empire, and even less about its problems. Mandates, protectorates, incorporated colonies, most of them were no more than large pink areas on the map. Films, periodicals and literature gave the public

its share of exoticism in which the colonist was often glorified. Sometimes, however, he was shown as rather inferior like Raffin Su-Su, the administrator of Laos, portrayed in the novel of the same name by Ajalbert,[35] the image of the human wreck as opposed to that of the empire builder. Officially, France's mission was seen as a civilizing one and its achievements were extolled. The glorification of the Empire at the 1931 colonial exhibition in Vincennes, for example, or in the propaganda of the early part of the war served to instil confidence and show that France was still a world power.

In admitting that western civilization was not the ultimate in civilization and in calling for mutual enhancement between cultures, "colonial humanism" actually justified the principle of colonialism. Senior officials such as Hardy and Delavignette, theologians and Catholic intellectuals such as Folliet, the author of *Droit de colonisation* (The Right to Colonization) published in 1931, and politicians such as Sarraut all agreed that the most advanced nations had a right, even a duty, to bring progress to backward nations. Once European domination had been justified in this way, it was doomed to disappear. It remained to be seen where the final process of de-colonization would lead. Two opposing solutions were possible, independence or assimilation, as well as various forms of federation. But the prospect of achieving any of these solutions seemed very far off. Albert Sarraut became a spokesperson for those in favour of cultural assimilation. His prolific, grandiloquent writings and speeches are full of suitable quotes on the subject. Instead, however, let us examine a more obscure document. This is how one official pamphlet,[36] published in 1930, saw the future of Indo-China:

> Just as ripe fruits detach themselves from the tree but stay at the foot of it, beneath the shelter of the branches, so adult colonies may, quite justifiably, wish to loosen the ties of filial gratitude that bind it to the mother country without presuming to repudiate them. Thus, the venerable Republic of France must continue to spread its protective shade over the face of the earth and bring its offspring scattered all over the world together under a new federal regime based on a common past, educational system and interests. France and Indo-China must collaborate in setting up this new order, united in the same ideal of infinite justice and progress. Certainly, the time is nigh when Indo-China will feel it has reached the age of majority and aspire to a degree of intellectual emancipation from France. This will be received in the same progressive and rational way that a wise mother goes about satisfying the impatience of her grown-up children. For France is

not afraid to set the world yet another example of her wisdom and generosity.

Anti-colonialism was rare. It was espoused only by the left, certainly not by the Radical Party, which was quite happy with the idea of assimilation into the Republic and saw the imperial venture as a feather in the cap of the regime. The SFIO (*Section française de l'internationale ouvrière*) (French section of the Workers' International) condemned abuses and pointed out the need for change, but few socialists thought that colonization ought in itself to be condemned. Thus, ex-governor-general Varenne was more representative of the party's view than was Challaye. The former can be ranked as one of the champions of colonial humanism. Challaye was unable to make his views prevail at the 1931 conference of the League of Human Rights, which took colonization as its theme. So anti-colonialism was basically represented by the Communist Party, which pledged itself to the cause right from the start in accepting Lenin's twenty-one conditions.[37]

The Second Congress of the Communist International laid down its doctrine on colonialism a few months before the birth of the French Communist Party. It rejected the ideas of the Indian, Roy, who considered that world revolution depended primarily on revolution in dominated countries. Instead, it adopted those of Lenin, who felt it was important to keep hold of both ends of the chain. The working-class struggle in industrial countries must take place alongside the liberation of colonized nations. The congress explained that the fight against imperialism would deprive the developed states of the immense profits they reaped from exploiting dominated countries, and they would no longer be able to corrupt their proletariats by offering them the crumbs of benefits accumulated overseas. The struggle against colonialism was brought to the fore within the plan of action laid down by the European communist parties (an obligation which was reiterated at subsequent Communist International congresses) and collaboration was urged between communists and the "national bourgeoisie". Finally, the theory was put forward that, through their struggles, the colonies could pass directly from feudalism to socialism without having to go through the capitalist phase. Until the Popular Front came to power, the French Communist Party waged a ceaseless war on French imperialism. *L'Humanité* described the pomp and ceremony of the colonial exhibition in Vincennes as "the apotheosis of crime". Denouncing the provocative anti-colonialist campaigns of the SFIC (French section of the Communist International), Sarraut made the resounding statement, "*Le communisme, voilà l'ennemi*" ("Communism, there's the enemy") in Constantine in 1930, while Gautherot published his *Bolchevisme aux colonies* (Bolshevism in the Colonies).

The hand of Moscow was apparent everywhere in communist activities. Eventually, the USSR realised the threat posed by Nazism and Japanese expansionism and thereafter the struggle against fascism took precedence over all other issues. The French Communist Party moderated its initial anti-colonialist stance somewhat, a change of attitude that was evident at the Arles Congress in 1937, where Maurice Thorez recalled the words of Lenin, "the right to divorce in no way implies an obligation to divorce" and called for the creation of "suitable conditions for a free, trusting and fraternal union between the colonized nations and the people of France."

Journalists and writers played their part in the struggle against colonialism, and not just within the *Ligue contre l'oppression coloniale et l'impérialisme* (League against Colonial Oppression and Imperialism), an organization founded in 1927 and influenced for the most part by the communists. Suddenly, there was an outpouring of writings denouncing French activities in Indo-China. An outstanding example is the book *Indochine SOS* published in 1935 with a preface by André Malraux, himself the author of a number of scathing articles that appeared in Indo-Chinese newspapers. Also worth mentioning are *Les Forceries humaines* (The Human Forcing Houses) by Garros, *La Route mandarine* (The Mandarin Road) by Dorgeles, *Les Jauniers* (The Yellowizers) by Monet and *Souvenirs de la colonisation* (Memories of Colonization) by Challaye. In his book *Viet Nam*, the journalist Roubaud conducted an extremely critical enquiry but concluded by ritually extolling the virtues of the Empire.[38] So there was anti-colonialism and anti-colonialism.

A young revolutionary responded to Louis Roubaud's hackneyed argument about the French contribution in the following manner, "You have done many useful things, particularly for yourselves, with our money and our labour." This pithy quotation captured the feelings of the nationalists nicely. They challenged every single aspect of the Empire's achievements. "In the eyes of Annamites the conquerors simply wanted to ensure their own convenience and comfort. They needed roads so that they could drive their cars, schools so that they could train qualified personnel for their own ends and hospitals so that they could cure themselves and prevent the spread of epidemics that might affect them. All this was paid for very heavily by the Indo-Chinese workers."[39] As for the supposed progress in education, there were now hordes of illiterates in a country that had been quite well educated before the arrival of the French. What of the increase in agricultural production? Even here, there was plenty of scope for denouncing the injustice of the system. Malnutrition and famine were rife, though the Federation was one of the largest exporters of rice. Furthermore, this rice was basically used by the French to feed their livestock. Certainly, industries and plantations had been created. But at what human cost? And for the benefit of whom? Far from representing progress, colonization was a retrograde step. "No country has a monopoly on modern culture. It spreads through its own inbuilt powers of expansion, and colonization is merely a means of harnessing this power and channelling it for the benefit of selfish interests."[40]

Thus the contrast between present mediocrity and past splendour, which nostalgia tended to enhance, the examples of the struggles of neighbouring countries and the feeling that there was a culture to be preserved despite European contempt for it, all served to add fuel to the struggle of a minority. Furthermore, this minority could actually draw on the ideology of the colonizer, contrasting the ideas of the Enlightenment and the republican tradition with the realities of the colonial system. Young Indo-Chinese intellectuals particularly disliked the contempt displayed towards them by young whites, and the unfair privileges which the latter enjoyed, not to mention the tendency of many French residents to think of all natives as "boys". Furthermore, they were bitter that despite their personal attributes and qualifications they had no access to positions of responsibility. Moreover, the colonists distrusted the spread of education amongst the natives. Sarraut, like the good radical that he was, set himself up as the champion of republican education and meritocracy and was frequently criticised for this.[41] In 1930, the *Courrier de Saigon* newspaper wrote, "The route taken by France is the route to anti-France". Annamite students studying in France added their voices to the unrest that swept the peninsula that year, prompting the French authorities to expel the most militant of them. This is how Trotskyism reached the colony.

Today, the Museum of the Revolution in Hanoi glorifies the struggle of all Vietnamese patriots, bringing together different styles of nationalism in an effort to show the long-standing continuity of the struggle against the French. It even gives pride of place to the literary figures who defended the Confucian tradition and led the resistance to the colonial invaders in the late nineteenth century. Their failure did not mark the end of nationalism. Having realized how powerful France was and the futility of trying to restore the old order, the nationalist movement then had to feel its way. The life of Phan Boi Chau (1867–1940) bears witness to this process. As a young mandarin, Phan Boi Chau took part in the scholars' revolt. At one stage in his life, he became fascinated by Japan. Its victory over the Tsar's army in 1905 proved that white supremacy was not inevitable. So, he dreamed of a revival of the Annamite Empire brought about by an enlightened prince. The similarities between the old Chinese order and the old Vietnamese order made him an enthusiastic student of the events and convulsions experienced by Vietnam's larger neighbour and caused him to follow the fortunes of the Kuomintang with great interest, being on the left wing of the movement. He hoped for a Meiji-style monarchy for his country, and then for a Sun Yat Sen-style republic. Finally, having plotted the overthrow of the colonizers for so long, Phan Boi Chau ended up by stepping aside.[42] In the 1930s, this former revolutionary returned to Indo-China and became an enthusiastic supporter of Franco-Annamite cooperation.

The Constitutionalist Party, founded in 1923, preached precisely this type of cooperation. It was largely influenced by the thinking of Phan Chu Trinh, who came from the same social background as Phan Boi Chau. Rejecting Confucian teaching, Phan Chu Trinh became an advocate of science and technology and a champion of modernity. His brand of nationalism purported to be legalist and stood up for a kind of cultural revolution. It aimed to appeal to French democracy.[43] The Constitutionalist Party expressed the views of the Cochin-Chinese bourgeoisie and called for greater freedom and more Annamite participation in the government and running of the country. By the end of the 1930s, it was beginning to be superseded by a new organization of the same kind, Dr Thinh's Democratic Party, which advocated a gradual development towards dominion status.

Hopes began to be raised in Hué in 1932 when Bao Dai returned from his studies in France and ascended the throne of Annam. There was talk of a return to the spirit of the Protectorate. The new monarch appealed to men of talent who were also known to be patriots, for example, the young Catholic mandarin, Ngo Dinh Diem, and the publicist, Pham Quynh. A famous critic of the colonial system, Pham Quynh was a product of both Vietnamese and western education. In his *Essais franco-annamites* (Franco-Annamite Essays), he tried to establish the right conditions for a national revival. He not only advocated restoring the country's sovereignty as far as possible, but also returning to the past to some extent. For although he did not deny the need for a modern contribution to society, he warned against acculturation.[44] The French administration was not deaf to his argument. Worried about the activism of the country's westernised youth, it began to find virtues in the tradition it had previously decried. "To the West its ingenuity, to the East its wisdom." However, the colonial authorities had no intention of relinquishing the power they had progressively usurped from the Annamite monarchy. In 1938, when Bao Dai visited France and requested autonomy for Annam and Tongking, Mandel told him that in view of the international situation the time was not right. The disillusioned sovereign consoled himself for his powerlessness by spending his time in the hunting field. As for Diem, he soon resigned. Pham Quynh stayed and consequently came to be regarded as a yes-man by the revolutionaries.

In 1927, a group of young, middle-class Tongkingese founded the VNQDD,[45] which was modelled on the Kuomintang. It took the same name, which it simply translated into Vietnamese, the same structure, based on the communist model, and the same platform. Like their great neighbour to the north, the countries of Indo-China had three main problems. There was the national problem, since they were subject to foreign domination; the political problem, or the need to replace the Confucian monarchy; and the social problem, the most pressing aspect of which was peasant poverty. The response of both the VNQDD and Kuomintang to these issues comprised the three principles of Sun Yat Sen, nationalism, democracy and socialism.[46] Socialism was defined in vague terms. Democracy was a declared aim, but a transitory period of dictatorship on the part of the elite was deemed permissible. In fact, the organization's main platform was nationalism. Everything else depended on liberation from European domination, even more so in Vietnam than in China, because foreign rule was exercised more directly in Vietnam.

Since the VNQDD was a revolutionary party, it embarked upon a programme of propaganda, organization and carefully-timed action aimed primarily at triggering off a general uprising and overthrowing the French. A young man called Pham Hong Thai who threw a bomb at governor-general Merlin, and died in the act, was extolled by the party as an example of a national hero. In 1929, Bazin, who was head of the *Office général de la main-d'oeuvre* (General Department of Labour) and therefore a prime example of colonial exploitation, was assassinated on the orders of the VNQDD. The repression exercised on this occasion by the *Sûreté* (Criminal Investigation Department) prompted the organization to act in a hurry. On the night of 9 to 10 February 1930 the Annamite riflemen in the Tongkingese garrison in Yen Bay massacred their French officers. This mutiny was followed shortly afterwards by a series of lesser incidents. A general uprising was threatening. The colonial administration struck quickly and hard and the Yen Bay mutiny was suppressed on 10 February. The *Sûreté* made a number of arrests. Most of the leaders, including party leader Nguyen Thai Hoc, were executed. So in 1930 the bourgeois revolution lost both its historic leader, Phan Boi Chau, who was discredited by his new moderate stance, and its partisan movement, the VNQDD, which was crippled by effective police repression and almost ceased to exist. The way was now clear for the communist revolution. Phan Boi Chau and the VNQDD made their exit from history just as Ho Chi Minh and the Indo-Chinese Communist Party came on the scene.

Ho Chi Minh was still called Nguyen Ai Quoc[47] when he created the Indo-Chinese Communist Party in 1930. Born in 1890 in Nghe-An in the north of Annam, his family were scholars who were hostile to the French occupation. He left his home country before World War I and travelled for a while, eventually settling in Paris. There, he scratched a living in various odd jobs and frequented socialist circles where he discovered Marxism. Wilsonian idealism raised his hopes to some degree at the end of the war and he presented a plan to the Peace Conference for liberating his country. Needless to say, this plan, which seems extremely moderate by today's standards, was ignored. At Christmas 1920 he represented Indo-China at the Tours Conference. A lost figure among the illustrious representatives of French socialism, he spoke in favour of colonized nations.

He also became a member of the Communist Party. Faced with a major power such as France, the Indo-Chinese revolution would have no chance of success without international support and the communist movement turned out to be a boon for dominated countries. As a member of the SFIC Nguyen Ai Quoc was a militant anti-colonialist at first and put forward his ideas in on the subject in his newspaper *Le Paria* ("The Tribune of the people of the colonies") and in the militant treatise entitled *Le Procès de la colonisation française* (The Case against French Colonization). Even then, the future Ho Chi Minh was reproaching the communists of the SFIC for not prosecuting the anti-colonialist struggle with sufficient vigour. He repeated this accusation at the fifth congress of the Communist International, saying:

> Comrades, pardon my boldness but I feel compelled to say that after listening to the arguments of the French comrades I was under the impression that they wanted to kill the serpent by tapping it on the tail. As you all know, the sting and life force of imperialism are currently centred in the colonies rather than in the mother countries. The colonies provide them with raw materials and soldiers to man their armies. The colonies are the basis of the

counter-revolution. But, when you speak of revolution you dismiss the colonies.[48]

In 1923, Nguyen Ai Quoc left Paris for Moscow. He stayed in the communist Mecca for only a year. In January 1925, he went to Canton at the request of the International to assist Borodin. Borodin was its representative in the Kuomintang, which was then linked to the Communist Party within the United Front. In the space of a few years, Nguyen Ai Quoc became familiar with the ways of the Soviet, Chinese and French communist parties, and these three related organizations all influenced Vietnamese communism.

In 1925, the city of Canton was not only the capital of the Chinese revolution, but also of the Vietnamese revolution. The latter found refuge in the shelter of the former. A number of young exiles had been drawn to Canton by the presence of Phan Boi Chau because it was where the assassination attempt on governor-general Merlin had taken place. The grave of the person responsible for it had become a place of pilgrimage for Annamite revolutionaries. So it was in Canton in 1925 that Nguyen Ai Quoc founded the Thanh Nien youth movement, for whom nationalist themes prevailed over Marxist-Leninist dialectic. It was a sort of preliminary to the creation of a true communist party. The best activists were sent to Moscow or to the Chinese military academy in Whampoa to complete their training. The first group included Tran Phu, who later became the first Secretary-General of the Indo-Chinese Communist Party. The second group included Pham Van Dong, a young mandarin whose father had been Emperor Duy Tan's principal private secretary.

The split between Chiang Kai-shek and the Chinese Communist Party in 1927 forced Nguyen Ai Quoc to leave Canton. Deprived of its leader and exposed to the mistrust of the Kuomintang (although fear of the French tempered the latter's hostility to the suspected Marxist group), Thanh Nien soon became prey to deep divisions. It fell to the future Ho Chi Minh to restore unity when he returned to China having wandered around Europe and Asia for several months. He created the Vietnamese Communist Party in Hong Kong in February 1930, no doubt at the instigation of the Third International. That autumn it became the Indo-Chinese Communist Party.

In October 1930, the central committee adopted the political principles drafted by Secretary-General Tran Phu.

At the present moment the only revolution possible is an agrarian and anti-imperialist one. The bourgeois democratic revolution is the period of preparation for socialist revolution.... The bourgeois democratic revolution basically consists of the abolition of feudalism and pre-capitalist forms of exploitation and the full implementation of agrarian reforms on the one hand, and overthrowing French imperialism so as to ensure the complete independence of Indo-China on the other. The two aspects of the struggle are closely linked, for only by overthrowing imperialism can you abolish the landowning class and carry out the agrarian revolution successfully and only by doing away with feudalism can you overthrow imperialism.

So the Party, which combined nationalist and militant elements shaped by the International, also had to combine the anti-colonialist struggle against France with the class struggle against "feudalism". It was not easy to strike a balance between socialism and nationalism, neither was it always easy to reconcile the demands of the International for world-wide strategy with the Party's need to carry on the struggle at home and its aim of dominating the national movement. The Comintern had insisted that the Party should cover the whole colony and call itself the Indo-Chinese Communist Party, not the Vietnamese Communist Party. It was obliged to carry on its struggle against the French without sliding into chauvinism as the proto-communist group, the Thanh Nien, had tended to do. In 1932, the Indo-Chinese Communist Party took issue with Nguyen Ai Quoc's lingering nationalism. One of the leaders of the communist regime, Tran Huy Lieu,[49] deplored this in 1960, saying: "Instead of being enthusiastically supported as it should have been in a colonized country, nationalist feeling was sometimes considered archaic and contrary to the spirit of proletarian internationalism."

As it became better organized, the Party began to plan mass actions. There were plenty of motivating circumstances, not so much due to the repressive measures against the VNQDD, but more because of the economic difficulties the country was experiencing from the severe effects of the world crisis[50] and the aftermath of bad harvests. On 1 May 1930 a series of strikes began. They were protests against taxation, action against mandarins and notables and raids on government buildings. The movement was particularly strong on the narrow plains of north Annam, one of the country's most under-privileged regions. Things came to a head there in September-October 1930, when a group of peasants ousted the local mandarins and notables and organized themselves into "soviets". It was not until the following spring that order was fully restored, after the administration had suppressed the leadership and offered help and pardon to the rest. Although there were no French deaths, the movement was none the less a violent one. The native guard fired on the crowd, the air force was sometimes called to the rescue and mandarins and notables were assaulted, tortured and killed. The struggle had both a national and social aspect and was aimed at both the foreign intruders and the social classes associated with them. Furthermore, the solidarity that existed between the colonial administration and these social strata greatly assisted police operations.

The Nghe-Tinh[51] soviets were glorified after the Vietnamese revolution. Yet at the time they existed, Yen Bay still overshadowed French public opinion and the movement went unnoticed. Besides, it was a period when no one knew who was who and the rebellion was simply put down to Marxist groups. On 14 February 1930, the president of the Chamber of Deputies made the following announcement when he opened the session: "I have had four questions from the floor. The first was from M. Pierre Taittinger about the events of Yen Bay, which prove that there is growing communist activity in our overseas territories...."[52] The campaign conducted by the French Communist Party further contributed to the general confusion. It was during this period that Louis Aragon wrote in *Front rouge*:

> Yen bay, what is the meaning of this name which reminds us that you can't gag a people, you can't kill them with the executioner's curved sabre. Yen Bay. Our message to you, yellow brothers, is that for each drop of your lives the blood of a Varenne will flow.

However, the local authorities most certainly knew what was going on. The reports, written by civil servants and military officers, were extremely lucid in weighing up these incidents.[53] The *Sûreté* managed to capture the leaders of the Indo-Chinese Communist Party. Tran Phu died in hospital, no doubt as a result of torture, and most of the others were sent to Poulo Condore prison where they set up a kind of red university. Nguyen Ai Quoc was sentenced to death in his absence and arrested by the Hong Kong police. For once, the *Sûreté* were misinformed and reported that he had died in a British jail.[54]

The SFIC set up an amnesty committee and led a campaign asking for a board of enquiry to be sent to Indo-China. The action of the French communists prevented the Indo-Chinese Communist Party from going under completely until such time as the creation of the Popular Front brought about a revival. The Blum government, whose Minister for the Colonies, Marius Moutet, had participated in the Committee for the Defence of Indo-China, freed a number of political prisoners and granted unprecedented rights. As an incorporated colony, Cochin-China had traditionally enjoyed more freedom than the rest of the Federation.[55] The change brought about by the Popular Front made an immediate impression there. Amid an atmosphere of seething political and trade union activity, the Indo-Chinese Communist Party became legitimized, retaining a clandestine organization in accordance with the Twenty-one Conditions. Under the leadership of Giau, the communists led a series of strikes in co-operation with the Trotskyists, with whom they also co-published the Saigon newspaper *La Lutte* (The Struggle), which first appeared in 1933. Publication was permitted because the newspaper was in French. The communists also led the movement to press for an Indo-Chinese congress, a task which involved preparing general reports and drawing up lists of requests or complaints to submit to the board of enquiry which Paris was promising to send.[56] Numerous committees, of which bourgeois reformists were also members, were formed for this purpose.

The Indo-Chinese Communist Party established a vast network of the most diverse organizations. It boosted the development of the Democratic Front.[57] "This consists not only of Indo-Chinese but also of progressive French elements. It embraces both the working people and the bourgeoisie" (Nguyen Ai Quoc). This line, which followed the new strategy of the International, did not please the Trotskyists and a split occurred between the two movements in June 1937. Ta Thu Thau and his friends retained control of *La Lutte*, and their intransigence won them electoral successes. They gained four out of five of the electoral college's votes at the 1939 elections to the Colonial Council of Cochin-China. On the eve of World War II, the Third and Fourth Internationals were the scenes of heated debates. The Trotskyists rejected any kind of compromise with colonialism and opposed the idea of participating in the war under French command. Instead, they preached revolutionary defeatism. As a result, the Indo-Chinese Communist Party labelled them "the servants of fascism". Its own stance was one of conditional support for the military effort and it encouraged its sympathisers to join the army as much to set up communist cells in it as to defend the country against Japanese imperialism.

When war actually came, France found that the only threat to the Federation was the external threat from Japan. The Japanese had been attempting to conquer China since 1937 and their expansionist aims had found various collaborators within Indo-China, such as the Cadaoists—the supporters of Prince Cuong De—who had been in exile in the archipelago for many years. It was a sign of the times that a military man, General Catroux, was appointed to the post of governor-general for the first time since the invasion. But, for the time being, the country remained calm and French residents could safely go anywhere unarmed.

The economic situation had improved since 1934.[58] The Trans-Indo-China railway had just been completed and duly extolled by the administration as a new achievement, a contribution to unity and progress. These were the last of the good times for French Indo-China.

In September 1939, a few days after the outbreak of war with Germany, the Daladier government banned the French Communist Party, judging it to be defeatist. The colonial power had already taken advantage of the decline of the Popular Front in order to resume its former authoritarian ways. Now it was able to exercise relentless repression against Marxist groups. The Trotskyist Party was almost completely disbanded and its leader, Ta Thu Thau, suffered a spell in prison which left him half-paralyzed. Most of the key members of the Communist Party in Cochin-China were arrested, including Giau. The communist leaders in the north were able to withdraw into China. Until that point, the Vietnamese communists had had close ties with the French and Soviet communist parties without being in a position of total allegiance to them. The Indo-Chinese Communist Party consisted entirely of native members and so, unlike the Algerian Communist Party which consisted largely of Europeans, it was always more than a mere satellite of the French party. As for the relationship between the Soviet Communist Party and the Indo-Chinese Communist Party, it was certainly closer than that between the Chinese Communist Party and the Soviet party. However, the marginal position of the Vietnamese communists enabled them to apply the International's directives in their own way. They obeyed, but they did so in such a way as to avoid compromising their dominant position within the nationalist movement. Neither the reformist notables, nor the Trotskyists of Saigon nor the VNQDD, which survived only in the form of rival groups under the protection of the Kuomintang, could ever challenge this position. The war and anti-communist repression in France and throughout the Empire severed communications with the other major parties and left the Vietnamese communists to themselves. The period from 1939 to 1941 was a particularly difficult time for the party, but it emerged with a new face, that of Ho Chi Minh and nationalism.

2

Indo-China Under the Japanese

DECOUX'S INDO-CHINA

The Japanese occupation of the island of Hainan in February 1939 highlighted the threat hanging over Indo-China. The Siamese government to the west was sympathetic to Japan. Ever since General Luang Pibul Songram's coup d'état, Bangkok had, in fact, been seeking an alliance with Tokyo. The country had changed its name to Thailand as a demonstration of its expansionist policies. On the eve of the war in Europe, the defence of the French colony had to be organized in the light of this double danger. The "génésuper"[1] commanded the land forces under the authority of the Governor-General. If the auxiliary forces (local guard) were included, there were 50,000 troops. Mobilization would increase it to 90,000. It was not a motorized army; it had limited radio equipment, rusting armoured equipment and no anti-tank weapons. In the air and at sea the picture was the same, even though the FNEO (Far East Naval Forces) could be called on when necessary. Of minor importance operationally, Indo-China was neglected in favour of the European front. Its army remained a colonial army, capable of maintaining domestic order but incapable of confronting an external enemy in modern warfare.

When the conflict broke out in Europe, the Japanese, who held Eastern China—the strategically useful country—had still not resolved what they referred to as the China Incident. They had been unable to curb the resistance of Chiang Kai-Shek, whose army was being supplied with arms via three routes, Russia, Burma and the Yunnan railway, the latter being the fastest and the safest. Tokyo had been complaining to Hanoi and Paris since 1937 and, in an effort to keep the peace, the French government had undertaken to prohibit the supply of arms to Nationalist China. But this gesture did not satisfy the Japanese. Firstly, there was no guarantee that the French promises would be kept, and secondly the agreement applied strictly to arms. A vital commodity such as fuel was allowed to circulate freely.

The collapse of the French military forces in June 1940 gave the imperial government the ideal opportunity to make its presence felt. The threat was clear to governor-general Catroux. The three divisions of the Cantonese army were putting pressure on the Tongking border and naval and air attacks on the Chinese could be launched from the bases. On 16 June, Catroux took the initiative of prohibiting the supply of fuel to Kunming.[2] In spite of this, three days later, the Japanese sent an ultimatum to Hanoi: the transport of all goods to China was to be stopped and the Japanese controllers posted at the border and in Haiphong were to be entitled to carry out checks.

Catroux conceded just as Britain was agreeing to intercept the traffic on the Burmese route. Circumstances had forced the governor-general to make his decision without consulting the government, which was now installed in Bordeaux. His weakness in the face of the Japanese and his lack of deference to the Ministry led to his dismissal. The favoured Admiral Darlan chose one of his peers, Decoux, commander of the FNEO,[3] to replace him.

The transfer of powers took place on 22 July. In the meantime, however, a Japanese military mission had arrived in Hanoi. Catroux was forced to engage in new talks about such matters as the right of the imperial troops to cross Tongking. That summer, while the Mikado's boats and planes were yielding to minor but numerous encroachments by the French, new demands were being put forward. The result was an agreement in principle, signed on 30 August, between the governments of Vichy and Tokyo. In return for the recognition of French sovereignty over Indo-China, the privileged position and prevailing interests of the Japanese Empire in the Far East were to be ratified. A military convention would apply the terms locally. Decoux played for time, with the result that on 19 September Tokyo issued a new ultimatum: unless the convention was signed by midnight on 22 September, the Cantonese army would force its way through.

There were several hours of acute tension during which a trial of strength was expected.[4] Agreement was reached at the last moment. Japan was given the use of three aerodromes and permission to station 6,000 troops north of the Red River. Japanese forces were authorised to pass through Tongking to Yunnan, but the total number of imperial troops present in Indo-China must never exceed 25,000 men. Finally, if put in a difficult position by the Chinese, the Cantonese army could transfer to Haiphong and re-embark, but a special document was to be prepared to fix the terms of this particular eventuality. The agreement, signed on the afternoon of 22 September, did not deter the Commander of the Cantonese army from engaging in hostilities that same evening. For four days, there was heavy fighting in what could be called the New Langson Incident. There was misinformation from the Deuxième Bureau (French intelligence), which had described the Japanese forces as demoralised and harassed. In fact, massive defection of native troops and the enemy's superior equipment created total disorder (the artillery was firing on the French positions). It was altogether an unhappy state of affairs for the Indo-Chinese army. On 26 September, just after Langson had fallen, the colonists suffered a new blow—troops landed in the Haiphong region. This time, Decoux decided to avoid direct confrontation. Humiliating though it was, this double show of strength did not jeopardize the agreement of 22 September. Drawing its own conclusions from what was happening, the government of Thailand put forward territorial claims and then opened hostilities. This war, although it consisted mainly of skirmishes, was to confirm the weakness of the French forces, although they did finally manage to secure a remarkable naval victory. The outcome was a forced mediation by Tokyo: the peace treaty of 8 May 1941 cut off Laos and Cambodia from their western provinces.[5]

An alliance with Siam was now vital to Japan, whose imperialist plans had been decided. Expansion would no longer be to the North (Siberia) but to the South, to the detriment of the colonial empires of the defeated or struggling Western European powers. Tokyo's new demands for concessions in Indo-China were indicative of this change of direction. Whereas the ultimata of 1940 were seen only in the context of the China situation, the stationing of Japanese troops in Cochin-China was proof that the peninsula was to serve as a base for the conquest of the southern territories. Under the terms of the Darlan-Kato agreement of 29 July 1941, Vichy undertook to accept these new demands. In addition to the articles setting out the stationing of Japanese troops, the treaty contained a rather scabrous passage on "joint defence".[6]

Tokyo had not only established a military hold over Indo-China, it was also exerting economic control. The agreement of 16 May 1941 is of particular significance in this connection. It conceded a most-favoured nation clause to the Japanese and handed over the mining, agricultural and hydraulic concessions to Franco-Japanese Indo-China companies. At the same time, the parent state was cut off and by the end of 1941 the British blockade was total. The virtual monopoly of France over the economy of the peninsula was thus over.

Thanks to the position France was in and the situation of its forces in the Far East, these concessions could only be avoided through external intervention. So whenever the opportunity arose, steps were taken to solicit the support of the United States. On 18 June 1940, Catroux sounded out the Americans' intentions through the embassy in Washington. But Welles, the Under-Secretary of State, made it quite clear that his country would not enter into a war against Japan in the event of aggression against Indo-China. Hanoi and Vichy renewed their demands for aid in August of the same year. Washington advised firmness, but also issued a warning to the imperial government. When Decoux tried to purchase weapons and planes from the US during the war against Thailand, the Americans refused to deliver, fearing that the equipment would one day fall into the hands of the Japanese. In July 1941, alerted by Vichy of the full extent of the Japanese demands, Roosevelt again put off any military involvement but imposed sanctions on all US trade with Japan. The President's subsequent proposal to the Mikado's ambassador for the neutralisation of Indo-China was not taken seriously by Tokyo. Britain was also approached on several occasions, but given the state of Anglo-French relations at the time and the military situation on the Euro-African front, it was unlikely that any help would be forthcoming from this quarter.

In the aftermath of Pearl Harbor, the Japanese government requested and obtained clarification of its interests through a new ultimatum. However, the country's involvement in the war did not fundamentally affect the agreements already made. Most of the Japanese in power were satisfied with a system which maintained the old colonial supremacy. An experienced administration maintained order in this kind of rear base, while the country's integration into the "Asian co-prosperity sphere" meant that the Indo-Chinese economy was contributing to the war effort against the Anglo-Americans. This *modus vivendi* was to last for more than three years. From the governor-general's point of view, the "Liaison Committee", now the "General Commission for Franco-Japanese Relations", was involved on a daily basis in resolving the many difficulties created by the uneasy cohabitation of the two imperial powers. However, in spite of the concessions it had made, France retained a workable policy, a large[7] and free army and its officials continued to run the country; kings and emperor continued to swear allegiance to the governor-general. French sovereignty was not under threat. Decoux's overriding preoccupation was to maintain this balance, which was difficult but vital for the maintenance of the status quo. It meant not defying the Japanese, while keeping a check on any encroachments. It also meant keeping Indo-China out of the conflict in the Pacific as far as this was possible, in other words, leaving it in the eye of the cyclone.[8] It has to be said that the Admiral carried out what could be termed his foreign policy with courage and skill.

From the outset, there were Japanese who were opposed to the colonial system being continued in Indo-China. Had not the Mikado declared that the Empire would free the people of the Far East from white supremacy? This theme had been abundantly developed in the propaganda of the New Order. Why make this such a blatant exception? Many members of the Vietnamese nationalist movement were hoping for some Japanese action. During the Langson Incident, nationalists of varying persuasions, in particular Prince Cuong De's partisans, had penetrated Tongking in the vehicles of the invading army. The swift settlement of this affair had put an end to the activity of these groups. Many of their members had been arrested and were often executed by the French when the latter had recovered the region; the rest returned to China. In December 1940, the annihilation of the rebel gangs was complete. The Japanese authorities were subsequently careful not to give official support to adversaries of the colonial system. But in Tokyo, the Association for the Expansion of Asia kept in contact with Prince Cuong De and pressed for the removal of white power. In 1943, the president of the Association, the retired General Matsui, travelled to Indo-China. His ill-timed declarations in Saigon caused Decoux to protest to the Japanese government which made an official retraction.

On-the-spot officials, servicemen and some ordinary individuals were, however, in contact with Vietnamese nationalists. The sects were ideal targets for Japanese propaganda. Support for the Japanese among the Cao Dai led the government to close down some sanctuaries and arrest some of its dignitaries. In August 1941, Pope Pham Cong Tac was exiled. But in spite of the repression, contacts were maintained and at the end of the war the links between the Cao Dai sect and the Kemptetai (Asian Gestapo) were public knowledge. Members of the Hoa Hao sect were also supplying information to the Japanese, who placed its leader under their protection. In Cambodia (more than in Vietnam) the Japanese played the card of Buddhist solidarity, attracting the sympathy of some of the bonzes (Buddhist priests), in particular the dignitary Hem Chieu, a teacher at the Pali school. Hem Chieu had been imprisoned for conspiracy by the French and on 20 July hundreds of monks marched through the streets of Phnom Penh in what could be described as the first collective demonstration of young Khmer nationalism.[9] Some of the strictly political groups sought the support of Tokyo. As the war progressed, the idea of replacing French authority was given increasingly serious consideration. To accomplish this change, the occupation forces began bringing together the various factions sympathetic to them. In the South, unification took place under the aegis of Cuong De's party, Phuc Quoc;[10] in the North, the factions united under the banner of the League for Vietnam, Dai Viet. The security service went on the offensive and reacted with a series of arrests. The Japanese hindered the repression on several occasions by transporting their protégés abroad. In Saigon, Ngo Dinh Diem was placed under protection from general headquarters.

The French now had a freer hand to combat communist agitation. In 1940, Party activists twice engaged in armed combat against the colonial power. The rebels, who included communists, held out for several months in the Langson region, attacking French posts and killing mandarins. The People's Army historians founded the first military section of the Indo-Chinese Communist Party in Bac Son. In November, Cochin-China was the setting for an uprising which differed greatly from the previous one. This one had been planned by local communist leaders. The defeat of France and its difficulties in Tongking had incited the action, and an opportunity was provided by the war against Thailand. Siamese harrassment forced the French authorities to despatch new forces to the west; rebellion among the soldiers of Annam was anticipated. Uprisings were to erupt in Saigon as well as in the provinces. Alerted by its informers, the security service was able to take precautions and the instigators were arrested. The measures adopted by the colonial authority and poor communications between the various committees of the Communist Party meant that the movement, which had started on the night of 22/23 November, was significantly curtailed. Saigon and Cholon stood firm. The insurrection only reached alarming proportions in the south of the Delta where leading figures were killed, administrative centres and communications equipment attacked. In Cochin-China, as in the Langson region, calm returned at the end of December.[11] Repression was severe. Believing they would serve as examples and taking no account of the call for moderation from Vichy, Decoux authorised death sentences to be passed at courts-martial.[12] Only at the very end of his proconsulate was the Admiral once more forced to deal with communist-led guerilla activities, once again in the areas near the Chinese border.

While the maintenance of order was important, the internal policy of the governor-general was certainly not meant to be reduced to this kind of repression. Rarely had the colonial administration been so enterprising, making more work for itself in many ways. With the prime objective of counteracting the cunning of Japanese propaganda, Decoux had been forced to innovate. He willingly paid homage to the local patriotic groups, provided the latter recognised the guardianship of France. "One of the essential aspects of my policy was, wherever possible, to show as much respect as possible towards the protected sovereigns and to do everything to enhance their reputations" (Decoux). Bao Dai was the first to benefit, although the two kingdoms to the west were not left out. The monarchs were honoured,[13] the nation's past exalted.[14] Patriotic groups were formed. In Cambodia the young were called upon to join the Yuvan movement, led by Sihanouk.[15] The Lao movement was founded at this time, its central theme being the great Lao homeland which "would one day bring together under the French flag all the temporarily separated children of this vast family". However, it was in the parties of the ancient Annamese empire that the Admiral's policy towards the natives proved to be the most audacious. The hitherto suspect term "Vietnam" was used by the governor-general. The country's great historic events were celebrated, education improved[16] and study of the national language was encouraged. Backed by Decoux, the Tri-Tan literary group was formed to study the past, adopting the slogan "To learn what is new we must look at the old." While the leading figures were resuming power in the villages, treatment of the mandarins was being re-assessed.

Support for traditional Vietnam was the result of political analysis as well as the personal option of the Admiral. Posts in the administration became increasingly open to local people[17] and the principle of "An equal position for equal rank, equal treatment for an equal position" adopted. A federal council was established with a consultative role, in which the Indo-Chinese were clearly in the majority.[18] The westernized minority also had a place in the system. "To give them a common ideal, to instil in them a spirit of discipline and cooperation, to make them young men who are useful to their country and empire", Captain Ducoroy[19] enrolled young people in associations which practised sport and uniformed parades, and in which homage was paid jointly to the French and Vietnamese flags. Another example of the coming together of the two nations was the celebration of the Trung sisters (two heroines who had protested against the invasion of China) on St Joan of Arc's Day. In the 1942 *concours général* (the final competitive examination set for the brightest students at the end of their schooling), candidates were asked to comment on the statement: "Young people, you have two nations to love and defend: France and Indo-China." Although simple, this sentence typified the policy of the Admiral: Vietnamese patriotism was on a par with Indo-Chinese solidarity under the aegis of the Empire.

The glorified French homeland was henceforward inaccessible. The break between Indo-China and France dictated certain decisions. The relief of officers was no longer guaranteed, since they were now trained in the Federation. The student élite could no longer study in Europe because institutions of higher learning had been established locally, and so on. Above all, the economy had to be adapted to respond to the new situation. On 15 October 1940 customs and excise autonomy was granted to the colony by law. But Indo-China's external trade continued to deteriorate. The severing of relations with France and the Anglo-Saxon world was only partially compensated for by the country's inclusion in Japan's "co-prosperity sphere". Consequently, Indo-China entered a phase of virtual self-sufficiency from which its cottage industries benefited enormously. As in many countries at that time, the economy was both closed and controlled. The administration assumed responsibility for supervising, distributing and selling essential goods. New industries had to be set up to satisfy basic needs.[20] Commitments to Japan meant that rice production had to be increased, while industrial cultivation was promoted to compensate for the lack of imports. Attempts were made to replace fuels and lubricants with substitutes. The economy had "not suffocated"; the piastre was not falling as some Cassandras had predicted. But the wear and tear on machinery, Japanese taxation and the American bombings made the situation very difficult. In Indo-China as elsewhere, world conflict brought about ruin, poverty and inflation.[21]

Like so many other servicemen at the time, Decoux, a naval man, was brought into the government. As proconsul, he admired Lyautey who had also served the Republic without approving of its principles. The ideology of the "national revolution" had to suit the governor-general. Here, as in other colonies, the colonial practice of the "French State" received the support of virtually the entire European population, flanked by the "legion of combatants". Right to the end, Pétain had a real cult following. Official speeches eulogised him, his portraits hung everywhere. Pétain represented faraway France, past glory, unity to be preserved. Furthermore, the Pétain cult seemed to suit the people of Indo-China perfectly. Did not the Marshal, by his life, his age, his messages, embody a kind of Confucian ideal? Praise for the leader of the "French State" was standard practice in the Ducoroy youth associations. These movements often transferred, lock, stock and barrel, to the Viet Minh side. The celebration of Ho Chin Minh was to replace that of Pétain.[22]

The "national revolution" exalted authority, responsibility and hierarchy—all notions in keeping with European attitudes in Indo-

China, particularly those of the Admiral. An ostentatious proconsul, Decoux loved and knew how to exercise his authority. To use a well-respected phrase among these people at the time, he was a leader. More esteemed than liked, he won the respect of his entourage which consisted of naval officers and senior officials. Gautier, the secretary general, and Boisanger, the diplomatic adviser, were his chief civilian collaborators. Like many servicemen, the Admiral mistrusted the Popular Front, condemning the relative liberalism it had introduced into the colonies. He thus devoted himself disinterestedly to the purge imposed by Vichy, disbanding the elected assemblies and replacing them with appointed councils, heavily censoring the press, and so on. The tradition of discipline, the prestige of the Marshal, the irritation of seeing Gaullist propaganda denouncing his policies and attempting to corrupt his officers, the fear that the Free French would jeopardise his task by an ill-considered policy, all this drove Decoux to denounce "dissidence". In the face of the natives and the Japanese, the French must stand firm behind Pétain. Gaullism meant risk, division and probably a kind of Popular Front in another guise. Local "dissidents" were severely dealt with. Pierre Boulle told how a member of the war council sentenced him to forced labour for going to Indo-China as de Gaulle's agent. Soon after the Japanese had entered the war and he had just been appointed High Commissioner in the Pacific, the Admiral prepared for action against New Caledonia which was dominated by "that sad group of misguided people known as Gaullists".[23] Developments in the world conflict were, however, to bring Decoux and de Gaulle into contact.

DE GAULLE'S INDO-CHINA

For many months, there were virtually no opportunities for de Gaulle to take action in Indo-China. The General's first appeals coincided with Japan's first ultimata. The pressure of the latter obviously made it impossible for the colony to lend support to the Free French. Important though it was, Catroux's adherence only engaged the person of the ex-governor-general. In reply to the letter sent to him by Cazaux, a senior Federation official, de Gaulle had to point out that any action was unrealistic at that time. However, after Pearl Harbor, the French National Committee declared war on Japan and called for Indo-China's resistance. The first decision seems ridiculous, the second dangerous. For de Gaulle it meant setting a date.

In the struggle against Tokyo, the Free French offered the Allies help from New Caledonia, under the command of Admiral Argenlieu. But on the continent, resources were sparse. Information was all that could be supplied. Networks were painstakingly established from India and China where the MMF (French Military Mission) was formed in January 1942. In July 1943, Langlade[24] arrived in Calcutta to run an Indo-Chinese intelligence service under British control. At the end of 1943, the arrangements of the French Committee of National Liberation (CFLN) vis-à-vis the Federation were specified. It was decided to form an expeditionary corps, a task given to General Blaizot. In a memo dated 18 September the Allies were informed of Algiers' decision to take part in the colony's liberation. The declaration of 8 December was a clear indication of the CFLN's desire to reinstate France fully in Indo-China. Promises of minor reforms were made. The natives were to be given access to jobs in the administration, and granted "customs and taxation autonomy". The creation of the Inter-ministerial Pacific Committee, which happened at this time, demonstrated Algiers' interest in the Far East.

It was then that Decoux sent an emissary to the CFLN. In despatching the banking manager François, the Admiral's intention was not to switch allegiance, but simply to inform and advise a power whose influence was growing and which might one day be the recognised government of France. François met General Giraud but de Gaulle refused to see him. Algiers was placing its bets on Mordant, the "génésuper". Decoux's allegiance to Pétain ruled him out, so it was quite natural to think that the oldest and most senior soldier would be the best person to organise the Indo-Chinese resistance. After all, here was a man who had covered for some of his subordinates when he had learned that they had been passing information to the Allies. In February, 1944 the Pacific Committee wrote a letter to Mordant, signed by de Gaulle. The message finally arrived in April. The Federation was to place itself under the control of the CFLN. France was to use force to liberate Indo-China; that was the condition for the full re-instatement of its sovereignty. This meant that the action of the internal resistance movement became a decisive factor. Mordant was to study the terms and put forward his proposals to the Committee. On 30 June, the General, who had reached retirement age, handed over command to his deputy, Aymé. Some days later, Langlade, who had been parachuted into North Tongking, arrived in Hanoi where he met both men. Since the new "génésuper" showed little enthusiasm for leading the resistance, there was no other solution than to confirm Mordant in this role (the official appointment took place on 23 August). The emissary from Algiers had also been instructed to contact Decoux. Since the Admiral was not in Hanoi at the time, Mordant used the poor state of communications to dissuade Langlade from meeting him. Decoux had to wait until 27 October for General Aymé to reveal the truth to him.

In the meantime, the collapse of the Vichy régime created a new situation. It was with this eventuality in mind that the governor-general had suggested to the Laval government that he be granted full powers "in the event of a breakdown in communication with the parent state". A law which went unpublished in the Official Gazette had been passed to this end. Thus, as Paris was being liberated and Mordant delegated as a general and leader of the resistance, Decoux had the law put into force hoping that by doing so the Japanese would consider the status quo in Indo-China unaltered. At the beginning of September, the Provisional Government of the French Republic (GPRF) was established in Paris. The Admiral had no option but to place himself under the authority of the new power. However, he feared the latter would embark on ill-timed initiatives. On 31 August, he sent a message recommending the continuation of the cautious policies he had been implementing for several years: "To ensure that French sovereignty in Indo-China and French interests in the Far East remain intact by the end of the conflict, it would seem both necessary and sufficient for the new French government to advise the Allies against any military attack on Indo-China and to refrain from any diplomatic and military initiatives likely to cause Japan to mistrust France".[25] Receiving no reply, the Admiral sent another message a few days later.

At the time, two contradictory policies were aimed at maintaining—and completely re-establishing—French sovereignty in Indo-China. Decoux represented the "wait and see" option, which could be summarized as follows. The conflict was to end in a few months with the defeat of the Axis powers. The map of the war in the Pacific showed that by overflying Indo-China, the Americans would soon be able to threaten the Japanese archipelago itself. In view of this, Indo-China could and should stay out of the fight. If the Japanese were not defied they would maintain the status quo and when they capitulated the colonial system would be intact. Any ill-considered activities could result in Tokyo liquidating the French presence which would be difficult to reinstate later.

The Admiral's warnings met with the barest response, since de Gaulle held a completely different view. In Asia, as in Europe, France's future position was to be determined by the role it played in the struggle against the Axis. It was only by fighting that France would remain a Far Eastern power. This stance was not evident to the Allies, and certainly not to its supreme commander. De Gaulle could hardly be unaware of

Roosevelt's opposition to a French presence in Indo-China. Although unclear in detail, the President's idea was to grant independence after a period of international trusteeship, and he had little difficulty getting this view accepted by Stalin and Chiang Kai-shek at the Teheran and Cairo Conferences. Only Britain, in the name of solidarity among colonial powers, expressed reservations.[26] The future of the Pacific was discussed at the Hot Springs Conference held in early 1945 and attended by France, and the question of trusteeship for the peninsula was still on the agenda.

Decoux was surprised and irritated when he learned of Mordant's appointment and immediately informed Paris that he would resign if full powers were not given to him. Langlade was once more parachuted into Indo-China and this time made contact with the Admiral who was given the order to stay in place and act as a "smokescreen". To help Mordant carry out his duties without arousing suspicion, Decoux was to make him inspector-general and to attach him to the Federation's government by appointing him vice-president of the specially instituted Council of Indo-China. In fact, for a few months the country would be living under a diarchy. Decoux, resigned but anxious and bitter, continued in an official capacity to manage the colony although Mordant, the only person in direct contact with Paris, considered himself the real governor. "Nimbus"—the code name given to him as a result of his physical appearance—led a kind of guerilla movement against the governor-general, on whom he was happy to take his revenge. The General lacked the qualities of his ambitions. His "notorious mediocrity" (an expression of Gautier's) had actually driven Langlade to put at his side a kind of double, Colonel Robert. The resultant chaos and duality of power inevitably caused some confusion in the French camp at a time when the resistance movement was organising itself.

At the end of the war there were many people, servicemen and civilians alike, who longed to take action against the occupation forces. The fever was at the same pitch as it had been during the old "wait and see" period. British parachute drops and other indiscreet activities alerted the Japanese. In January 1945, about forty Japanese ships were sunk in the open sea off the peninsula: there is no doubt that this action by the United States Air Force was the result of information passed via Indo-Chinese networks.

In the same month, Paris approved the plans drawn up by Mordant. Two scenarios were envisaged, an allied landing or a Japanese attack. In the event of the latter, the French forces would be grouped in the mountain areas (chiefly the highlands of Tongking and the Annam-Laos hinterland), from whence they could engage in guerilla activities. Adopting this plan would mean the redeployment of forces and much construction work. Such initiatives would only serve to confirm Japanese apprehensions.

Should the native people be involved in the struggle? De Gaulle's letter to Mordant showed that he was in favour of it. In September 1944 Pleven, then Minister for the Colonies, asked the head of the Indo-Chinese resistance to send a representative to France from among the local élite. This was not possible. In February 1945, Paul Mus was parachuted into Indo-China. Mus, a specialist on Vietnam, was instructed to contact the most established of the indigenous groups. There were several examples of Vietnamese who associated themselves with the French anti-Japanese resistance. However, whether out of hostility or scepticism, the French of Indo-China kept virtually all the natives out of the struggle. The resistance movement had been the property of a few hundred Europeans lost among the millions of Indo-Chinese. In this sense, their methods, copied from those used in France, proved inadequate.

INDO-CHINA WITHOUT THE FRENCH

There were several occasions after 1940 when the colonial authorities had feared a Japanese strike. However, in 1944 Decoux prided himself on having maintained French sovereignty and saved the country from war. Indo-China was thus the only remaining part of the Empire still under the control of the Vichy government. The Normandy landings and the subsequent fall of Pétain's régime created a new situation. The provisional government of the French Republic (GPRF), installed in Paris, was at war with Japan. Needless to say, the parody of a government set up by the Germans in Sigmaringen ("provisional seat of the French State") did not count. The Japanese authorities soon learned of the relations between Hanoi and Paris, and knew that the French administration in the peninsula was now responding to a new authority, which would obviously compromise the Japanese position. From this time on, those who favoured the elimination of France, arguing that the colonial officials and servicemen were now controlled by an enemy government, became more vociferous.

The local command (in Saigon) agreed with the Minister for Foreign Affairs that there should be a rapid strike which should end in independence for the three Indo-Chinese states—Vietnam, Laos and Cambodia. However, the Tokyo generals expressed caution. Their objection was not so much to the opportunity for conducting the operation but to the political solution involved. What they had in mind was military occupation and nothing more. The outcome of the Battle of the Philippines was to be the deciding factor.[27] While the fighting was still in progress, the high command had had no wish to engage in a test of strength in Indo-China, but with the loss of the archipelago, the main constituents of the problem changed. Indo-China was now a vital base for communications between Japan and the southern positions they still held— Malaya, Burma and Indonesia. Furthermore, an American landing was anticipated at any moment. The continued presence of an unreliable partner on the peninsula could not be tolerated by Tokyo, firstly because it might offer assistance to the landing troops and secondly because it would probably pass information to the Allies enabling them to cut the lines of communication.[28] On 1 February 1945, a few hours before the fall of Manila, the Supreme Conference on the Progress of the War decided to organize an attack on the colonial power within the next few weeks.

All that remained to be decided was Indo-China's new status. The diplomats were all in favour of independence. Only thus would Japan be able to hold the country once the French administration had gone. It would be essential to strengthen the hackneyed concept of liberation by the Empire of Greater Eastern Asia. Finally Russia, which had signed an alliance with France in December 1944, had to be taken into account. From enquiries made in Moscow, it was ascertained that the treaty did not refer to Indo-China, but if Japan wanted to avoid giving the Soviet Union a pretext for abandoning its neutrality, it would be better to be seen as the liberators rather than aggressors of this colonized people. These arguments finally convinced headquarters and at the end of February, support was given to the ideas of the Ministry for Foreign Affairs.

In the winter of 1944-5 the Japanese troops were reinforced. There was nothing unusual about that, given the progress of the war. In fact, immediately before the attack, relations between the colonial administration and the army of occupation presented no particular problems. Only two apparently minor questions caused friction; the amount of the foreign currency allowances[29] and the fate of allied aviators who had fallen into French hands and whom the latter refused to release. These two questions were scheduled to be dealt with in Saigon during one of Decoux's regular trips to the south. On 9 March, as arranged, the meeting between the governor-general and the Japanese Ambassador took place in the capital of Cochin-China. Initially everything went as planned and an agreement on the delivery of rice was initialled. The Ambassador then requested that the meeting be extended in private discussions. At 7.00 pm he put his ultimatum to Decoux. In accordance with the agreements on joint defence, and because of the risk of an American landing, the French forces must place themselves under the command of the Japanese. A reply must be received by 9.00 pm. Decoux, true to character, tried to salvage the situation. He rejected the Japanese demands but left the door open for possible negotiations.

But the time for compromise was over. Even before the deadline had passed, the imperial forces were attacking French troops in Saigon and throughout Indo-China. The Admiral and his entourage were arrested. Decoux bitterly abandoned his proconsulate convinced that the careless activities of the resistance were responsible for undermining a policy which had been painstakingly conducted and which could have been maintained until the Japanese capitulated.

On the evening of 9 March, the colonial army was fighting under adverse conditions. In fact, given the reinforcements they had just received, the Japanese were superior in numbers[30] and in weaponry. Against this modern operational force, the French had nothing but mediocre and outdated equipment (it consisted mainly of weather-damaged, 1940 weaponry). Lacking a commander, this army, which was further weighed down by the burden of its duties, was very dispersed. Its senior officers, few of whom had been replaced since 1940, lived a garrison life with their wives and children, which gave them no taste for adventure. The native troops could not be fully relied upon. Finally, in view of the overlap of the units, surprise was a determining factor in the Japanese success. Indo-Chinese informers had provided clear warnings that an attack was imminent. But whereas the security service was worried, the authorities remained sceptical; they had been given so many false alarms....

The citadel in Hanoi held out for several hours, but Generals Mordant and Aymé were finally forced to surrender. In Langson, where Colonel Robert had been drawn into an ambush, those who were strong enough held out until the evening of 10 March. The Japanese, who were free with their decapitations, massacred the survivors, among them Lemonnier.[31] At each garrison there was a different story. However, the colonial forces resisted as hard as they could, though in confusion due to the loss of radio communication and the arrest and death of their leaders. The Indo-Chinese army did not allow itself to be neutralized as the armistice army had been in November 1942. Yet its inferiority, and the effect of the surprise attack, had brought about defeat, its disjointed battles amounting to nothing more than fights of honour.

A few weak forces escaped the strike of 9 March. In the south of the peninsula some troops made for the jungle but were unable to survive. In Laos, the Japanese presence was slight. Groups who had taken refuge in the bush where they were supported by the local people were to be helped by Calcutta and would return to Luang Prabang after the Japanese capitulation. But most of the action took place in Tongking. Suspecting danger, General Sabattier had transferred his command post out of Hanoi just before the attack.[32] While in transit he had alerted his subordinate, General Alessandri. The two men led the resistance of about 6,000 men. In their retreat, the French hoped for assistance from the United States Air Force operating from its Chinese bases. General Chennault, commander of the 14th US Air Force, was in favour of such an operation but a pessimistic Roosevelt was against it despite the constant harangues from Paris.[33] This situation exacerbated the contentious relations between the two countries. For a time, Sabattier and Alessandri had believed that the Japanese would be content with the Indo-Chinese plains, the useful Indo-China, allowing the French to establish themselves in the Highlands until Tokyo capitulated. These were, in fact, the orders from Paris as relayed to Sabattier by Langlade during a meeting (also attended by Passy representing the DGER[34]) in the Dien Bien Phu Basin. In late March Sabattier, who had been granted all civil and military powers as part of his title of delegate-general, installed himself in this "capital" of the Thai country, leaving Alessandri in command so that he could concentrate on his political task.

However, the Japanese were determined to rid the country of the entire French presence and gave the fugitives no respite. The idea of setting up a retreat in the Highlands was abandoned and withdrawal to Yunnan became the only possible course of action.[35] The last French columns crossed the Chinese border during May, the last stage in their 1,000-kilometre retreat through mountains and jungle. Not only had they had to contend with the difficult conditions in terms of weather and terrain, the desertion of dozens of Annamite riflemen and incessant attacks from an implacable adversary, they had also experienced occasional hostility from the local people. The sufferings of the Tonkingese anabasis were followed by insults from the Chinese who were no more keen to see their so-called allies return to Indo-China than were the Americans.

Bao Dai was returning from one of his regular hunting parties on the evening of 9 March when his car was stopped by Japanese soldiers. The Emperor was informed of the attack, and learned that he was to be kept on the throne. On 11 March, on the orders of "supreme councillor"

Yokayama, the sovereign cancelled the treaties with France and declared the country to be independent. Cambodia followed suit on 13 March and Laos on 8 April[36]—the kings, and even the prime ministers, retaining office. Just as they had not judged it necessary to dethrone Bao Dai and replace him with their own protégé, Cuong De, the Japanese decided against making Diem the head of government, although his personality and relationships seemed particularly well suited to the post. In the end, it was a more unobtrusive personality who was appointed prime minister, a primary school inspector, Tran Trong Kim. He had to be brought back from Bangkok where the Japanese had sent him to protect him from the French repression. By 17 April, the members of the government were made known. They included doctors, lawyers, a teacher, an engineer. In short, this small team was a reflection of its leader. The ministers were not well-known politicians, but highly intelligent French-educated members of the bourgoisie (nearly all of them had studied in France), who were dedicated to Vietnamese nationalism whatever else they stood for. The cabinet contained a Minister for Foreign Affairs (Chuong, a lawyer who was both the strongest personality and most pro-Japanese member of the team), but no Minister for Defence since there was no wish to enter into open conflict with the Allies.

Although it had no great powers, resources or hopes, the new government took its job seriously. It worked particularly hard to see that the independence obtained was not a mere fiction. Consequently, since the Japanese, having made use of the French administrative structures, directly controlled Cochin-China, Hué repeatedly brought up the subject of the restoration of the province, in the name of the reunification of the country. The occupation forces were forced to agree on 14 August— after Nagasaki. At first, the new status of Indo-China was greeted by popular demonstrations and the Kim government took some credit. Broadly based on a rejection of colonialism, its propaganda received undisputed backing, such as that of the pro-Japanese groups (for example, the Dai Viet) who supported it. The political activities of these organizations did not prevent the new power from quickly losing its popularity. Difficult living conditions played a significant role. Public services, once run by the now-banished French, were deteriorating.[37] Inflation was rocketing and famine was spreading through the northern countries. "Wretched, appallingly thin people, lying on the pavement in front of the house, moan and die unnoticed by passers-by. There are no facilities to give any assistance and several days go by before the bodies are carried off by coolies whose first task is to strip them of their ragged clothing. Typhoid and cholera are rampant in the town." Thus read the notes made by Governor Gautier, who had been interned in Hanoi. Communications between Cochin-China and Tongking had virtually been cut off as a result of the American bombings. Multiple damage to the Trans-Indo-China railway meant it was no longer possible to transport rice from south to north. A government which had to meet the taxation demands of the Japanese under these difficult conditions could only bring itself into disrepute. Besides, as the Japanese now only controlled the major routes and conurbations, the authority of their protégés was correspondingly reduced. These weaknesses, inadequacies and compromises gave those nationalists, in particular the communists, who had refused to play the Japanese game their justification. Overwhelmed by its problems and its impotence and sensing that Japan would collapse after Hiroshima, the Kim government notified the Emperor of its resignation on 8 August. From this time on, there was talk of the Viet Minh, organised by the Communist Party of Indo-China, taking power.

The beginning of 1941 was a difficult time for an organization sorely tried by the recent repression. From his hideout in the mountains close to the Chinese border, Nguyen Ai Quoc, who had just returned to the country after a thirty-year absence, summoned the Party leaders. Thus, in May of that year, in the Pac Bo grotto beside the hill christened Karl Marx for the occasion, the Viet Minh was founded—"a broadly based national grouping not only of workers, peasants, the lower classes and the national bourgeoisie, but also of patriotic landowners". This creation was reminiscent, *mutatis mutandis*, of the united front which had linked the Kuomintang and the Chinese Communist Party since 1937.[38] Within a few weeks, German aggression against Russia was to cause the Comintern to applaud the creation of any national front. The prime aim of the Viet Nam Doc Lap Dong Minh, soon shortened to "Viet Minh", i.e. the League for the Independence of Vietnam, was to beat the "fascist Japanese" and their "French accomplices" so that an independent republic of Vietnam could be formed. A programme of reforms was proposed, which were thorough without being revolutionary, ranging from the distribution of land to the abolition of the mandarin system. In short, a kind of CNR charter.

The vigilance of the colonial system meant that nearly all the leaders were forced to live in South China where they were dependent on the good will of the Chongqing government. Relations were fairly complex. There was Chiang, the communists who were only theoretically under his control, the provincial potentates who were conducting their own brand of politics, and other Vietnamese nationalist groups with their various schemes. In all this Asiatic confusion, however, there was one

constant factor: Chiang wanted to unite and control the various Vietnamese factions.[39] In the short term, this would mean putting up an effective fight against the Japanese and, once they had been defeated,
turning this country newly liberated from colonial rule into a satellite.

At first, relations between the Viet Minh Front and the Chinese authorities were fairly difficult, and Nguyen Ai Quoc was gaoled for several months. Matters eventually improved. The other Annamite groups
were exasperating in that there was perpetual rivalry among their members, and disappointing in that they lacked influence in Indo-China.
The Chinese authorities consequently favoured the Viet Minh since it
was able to provide information. It was at this time that Nguyen Ai Quoc
took the name of Ho Chi Minh, in order to spread confusion and so as
not to alarm the most anti-communist of Chongqing's leaders. In March
1944, Chiang considered it was time to form a provisional Vietnamese
government and a congress of all the movements was convened in Liou
Cheou. Agreement was reached on the main patriotic ideals, such as opposition to Japan, elimination of the French presence and independence. The composition of the government was harder to determine. In
the cabinet which was eventually formed all the groups were represented under the leadership of a respectable old man with little personality. It had minimal Viet Minh presence in the shape of a single
minister—Ho Chi Minh. Chinese pressure meant that the Front had to
be satisfied with a very inferior position compared with its strength in the
field.

At this time, the Viet Minh was well organized in Indo-China. It was
arranged in tight cells, divided up in two ways, geographically and by
category. The Viet Minh had formed "committees for national safety" of
women, students, workers and so on. This system, which had been practised by other national fronts, allowed for adaptation to suit the genuine
needs of each group. The movement had flexibility and diversity at the
base, but rigidity and continuity at the top under the direction of Ho Chi
Minh. Once the Viet Minh had been formed, guerilla zones had to be set
up. Underground forces were organised along the Chinese border, in
those mountains traditionally used as a refuge by all kinds of outlaws.
Using propaganda and intimidation, the Front took control of several
villages in the area, and were able to dominate the local minorities
(Thos, Meos, etc.) The colonial administration was worried by these activities and in late 1943 the patrols were increased, forcing the guerilla
leaders to retreat to the most inaccessible regions. One year later, the
whole campaign had to begin from scratch. But then the Japanese *coup* of
9 March 1945 intervened just as the colonial government was preparing

to strike again.

The disappearance, within hours, of the colonial authority was manna from heaven to the Viet Minh organisers who wasted no time in turning it to their advantage. They took firm control of the Viet Bac (North Tongking) which had for a long time been the main revolutionary base of the country. They denounced leading figures known to be collaborators or profiteers, they stirred up and took control in the provinces. In the towns, they established cells within most of the official organisations. Contacts were established at all levels, including inside the government. On the Chinese border, the allied forces, who had received no further instructions from their French counterparts, had little option but to count on the Viet Minh networks. The American OSS[40] supplied arms and even men. The Front attacked a few isolated Japanese posts and organised passive resistance activities against the occupation forces. It had to be shown that they were helping the war effort on the side of the Allies. But the Japanese forces remained formidable. They could not be dealt blows that were too severe, or they might be provoked into launching large-scale operations against the guerillas. Ho Chi Minh had advised caution to those keen to begin the revolution after 9 March. He advised them to wait until "the time was right". The few revolutionary troops there were must remain intact so that they would be able to take control following Japan's capitulation—which was judged to be inevitable and imminent—and to oppose the reinstatement of the colonial system.

The Viet Minh had got into the habit of making a distinction between the bad and good French, between the "fascists" (Pétain, Decoux) and the "democrats" (the Gaullists and the members of the resistance). However, the Algiers declaration of December 1943, confirmed by later documents, showed that the new French power wished to maintain the colonial system in Indo-China, even if this meant a few reforms. The prospect of future struggles did not deter the Front from entering into relations with the representatives of the GPRF. Sainteny, Director of Mission 5, the information centre set up in Kunming by the DGER, was contacted by members of the Viet Minh. Through the OSS, he had received a particular document concerning the future of Indo-China,[41] a moderate message which called for independence only in the long term (within a maximum period of ten years). Provision was made for a meeting between Ho Chi Minh and Sainteny, but bad weather prevented it from taking place.[42] A French officer was nevertheless sent to the Communist Party from the Viet Minh. These contacts, established by an organisation which saw itself as the embodiment of the Vietnamese resistance opposed to Japan, did not rule out France as an adversary, an adversary which would have to be overcome quickly. After the Japanese collapse, a revolutionary authority would have to be established before the scheduled return of the colonial power.

After Hiroshima, Ho Chi Minh felt strong enough to take on the "provisional government" set up the previous year under the auspices of China. While Giap's 5,000 men adopted the title of Vietnamese Liberation Army, a Vietnam Liberation Committee was formed which was completely dominated by the communists. "Forward under the Viet Minh flag." On 14 August, immediately following Tokyo's long expected capitulation, a general rebellion broke out. There was a feeling of uneasy excitement in Hanoi (according to Party historians, this was a period of pre-revolution). On 19 August, after the imperial representative had been eliminated, the capital fell into the hands of the Front. This scenario was to be repeated in most of the cities. After a short period of confusion, the local authorities gave in to the revolutionary committees. The Japanese, defeated but still with an armed force in place, put up no opposition. The activists of Greater East Asia willingly hindered the return of the colonial powers, who were, in theory, victorious.[43]

In Hué, Kim confirmed that his first objective was to preserve the independence granted in March which the Japanese confirmed under pressure on 17 August[44] through the devolution of power to the three newly-constituted governments. To preserve this right, he launched an appeal for national unity and formed a weak committee for patriotic reunification. For his part, Bao Dai held talks with the five major victors to try and stop the return of colonial order.[45] For a time he thought of replacing the Kim cabinet with a revolutionary team. Having been emperor under the French and then the Japanese, why not stay emperor under the Viet Minh? Too compromised to be able to maintain his position, he was finally obliged to concede to the "revolutionary republican government" and abdicated.

In the South, the nationalist groups of the right predominated, as did the various militias created and armed by the Japanese. To establish control, the Viet Minh played upon feelings of nationalist solidarity. If the country's independence was to be preserved, the forces which had collaborated with the Japanese must not be allowed to dominate. It was essential that the Viet Minh, which was on the side of the victors, be allowed to act and even won over. On 25 August, an impressive unified demonstration took place in Saigon under the banner of the Front, while a Nambo[46] Revolutionary Committee was formed with a communist majority.

At the end of August, the Viet Minh flag was flying on the Chinese border and the Camau peninsula. This meant that the prudent neutrality of the Japanese and the insignificant reaction of the other Vietnamese forces had resulted in the revolution experiencing no difficulty between 14 and 25 August. This did not mean there was no violence. The Front liquidated several adversaries, in a broad range, covering Trotskyists, such as Ta Thu Thau, leading figures who had integrated into the French system, such as Tui Quang Chieu (founder of the Constitutional Party) and Pham Quynh. Colonists were attacked and some were killed.[47] On 2 September, at the very moment the Japanese were officially signing the capitulation on the aircraft carrier *Missouri*, the independent republic of Vietnam was declared. The text of the declaration was a surprise.[48] It began with a quotation from the American Declaration of Independence of 1776 and spoke of neither the USSR nor of social revolution. The USSR was a long way off and US anti-colonialism was counted on to recognize the new power, which in any case had the sympathy of Major Patti's OSS. The document went on to denounce the old colonial power in the strongest terms, in a manner reminiscent of the young Nguyen Ai Quoc's accusations in *Le Paria*. Naturally, Ho Chi Minh presided over the newly-formed cabinet, his principal collaborators being ministers.[49] Bao Dai, who had become citizen Vinh Thuy, was appointed supreme councillor to the government. Confronted with the foreigner, unity must come first.

"The August revolution was the first victory for Marxism/Leninism in a colonial and semi-feudal country" declared Giap.[50] While this was true, in the prevailing confusion most Vietnamese people did not realise that the government was now in the hands of the Communist Party and, as pointed out by Giap, "very few realised that uncle Ho and Nguyen Ai Quoc were one and the same". Within a few months, the colonial system and the old monarchy had been swept away. The "mandate from heaven" had been handed to the Viet Minh. The handing over of the great state seal to the government representatives by Bao Dai confirmed the legitimacy of the new power. "Our Annamites have changed", the Bishop of Saigon, Mgr Cassaigne, is reported to have said. Most of the French did not understand that their displacement following the Japanese attack of 9 March was considered to be an irreversible fact by many Vietnamese. The previously accepted imperial order had collapsed within the space of a few hours and now, six months later, it was was a thing of the past. The triumph of Marxism/Leninism for the ideologists of contemporary Vietnam, the transfer of the "mandate from heaven" from one authority to another in the best Confucian tradition, and the August revolution initially seemed to confirm the national *de facto* situation. In Algeria, there had been an uprising in North Constantine on 8 May following Germany's capitulation, and the Vietnam Republic had declared its independence on 2 September at the time of the Japanese surrender. The revolutionaries of both countries had shown, each in their own way, that the success of the allies had been based on the principle of the people's rights to self-determination, a principle stated in the Atlantic Pact and restated and clarified in the United Nations (UNO) Charter. On the day that world conflict ended, France found itself faced with the outbursts of Algerian and Vietnamese nationalism, against which would it was to engage in military conflict for over fifteen years. Could there be a better way to emphasise that decolonization was a direct consequence of World War II?

3

A Premonition

From the outset, Ho Chi Minh's government had to contend with British and Chinese troops. In fact, the Americans and British had secured from the Potsdam conference the right to settle, once and for all, to which theatre of operations Indo-China belonged.[1] On 23 July 1945, it was decided that the North was in the hands of the sector which had fallen to the Chinese. The South was under the British sphere of influence. The sixteenth parallel was to be the boundary between the zones, and consequently the boundary between the two armies responsible for disarming the Japanese. The armies had been in the country since September. Chinese troops from Luhan entered Tongking on 9 July bringing with them their Vietnamese protégés (men from the VNQDD and the Dong Minh Hoi). General Siao Wen, who advised and inspected the groups, was unpleasantly surprised to find the Viet Minh controlling the country. However he did not despair of turning the situation to his advantage again. Meanwhile, a new disaster added to the misfortunes of the people of Tongking. Troops from Luhan were exploiting a country which was already suffering famine.

While awaiting re-embarkation, the 100,000 Japanese had been busy. In the north, a local warlord's hordes were pillaging and intriguing on his behalf; in the south, the Indians of the British army were in combat. The revolutionary Vietnamese forces were everywhere; it was never certain whether they were simply representing the PCI or if a vast alliance of different groups united by nationalist aspirations was taking shape. In addition, there were American OSS operatives, governments who did not speak the same language as their representatives in the field—not to mention the special circumstances in Cambodia and Laos. This was the confused picture in September 1945 as the French were preparing to return to "their" Indo-China.

In the aftermath of the Japanese show of strength, Paris had indicated its readiness to re-establish its sovereignty over the peninsula. De Gaulle had been planning since 1940 to restore France's independence in its entirety. Germany's defeat was about to end in the liberation of mainland France: all that remained now to achieve the goal he had set himself was to liberate Indo-China. The restoration of national honour would culminate in Saigon and Hanoi.[2] In March 1945, de Gaulle made several pronouncements on the Indo-China issue. He denounced the "pretensions and wiles" used by Japan to conceal its "tyranny", and praised the heroism of the soldiers whose scattered and desperate engagements he mentioned as if they were part of a great battle. He congratulated himself on the loyalty of the native peoples. These myths were unanimously acclaimed by press and politicians alike. As for the public, it had other preoccupations: the ending of the war in Europe; the imminent return of the two million Frenchmen held in Germany; the events of the purge; and above all the difficulties of everyday life in a country facing ruin, poverty and inflation. The public was hardly interested in exotic colonial problems, an indifference which did not change in the following months.

On 24 March, the GPRF announced the status it was reserving for Indo-China.[3] The declaration broke new ground compared to the declaration of December 1943. Individual rights were clearly stated. The statement of intent of the 1946 constitution had to represent the spirit of the times.[4] The term "French Union" appeared officially for the first time, replacing "Empire". The Union no longer recognized natives or subjects, only citizens enjoying the liberties of the republican tradition. Indo-China became a federation. A type of Franco-Indo-Chinese co-sovereignty was established (along the lines of the Franco-Annamese co-operation recently strongly recommended by the Cochin-Chinese reformists) under the authority of a governor-general who would head the federal government. The text of the declaration would have seemed bold in the interwar period. Now that the Japanese had granted the three countries their independence, albeit fictitiously, the declaration seemed timid even to the most moderate nationalists. Oblivious to the reality of Vietnam, it remained faithful to the idea of dividing the area into "five countries". As for power-sharing, it was clear that the key areas of power remained under French control, in the person of the governor-general. Moreover, it was vague on many points, such as the inclusion of the Federation in the French Union. Its establishment was the prerogative of the Constituent Assembly, for whose election no date had yet been decided.[5] In fact, the 24 March declaration was based on the Brazzaville Conference, to which it even referred in its statement of intent.[6] It was generous compared to colonial tradition, but was soon overtaken by the ongoing process of decolonization which followed a war that had weakened the European countries, sapped their strength and turned two countries, both champions of anti-colonialism, into superpowers.

Like all colonial policy of the time, the declaration was a compromise between the need to restore order and the spirit of reform of the Liberation. It did, however, satisfy most commentators. "In general, these promises are encouraging", commented *L'Humanité*. *Le Monde* analysed the government's declaration and concluded: "The increasingly liberal evolution of our institutions must mean that France will make the magnificent opportunities of a community, comprising elements with such a diversity of races, civilizations and economical resources, grow as a harmonious whole." However, the initial reaction of the interested parties, 30,000 "Annamese", living in France, augured badly. Dominated by a few dozen intellectuals won over to the idea of independence,[7] the General Assembly of the Indo-Chinese in Paris forcefully denounced the new status. The conflict between the Vietnamese élite of the parent state and the public powers had begun. "The Indo-Chinese no longer believe in promises", was *Combat*'s headline of 11 July, explaining that colonial history justified this defiance.

Of course, policy towards Indo-China depended on the attitude of the French president. Yet even before the Japanese show of strength (on 28 February 1945), the Indo-China Committee had been created to help him in his task. Under the chairmanship of de Gaulle, it included the relevant ministers, the chief of staff, the head of the special services and Laurentie, the director of political affairs at the Ministry for the Colonies. The committee's work was prepared by an office run by Langlade. In fact, Langlade and Laurentie were the main inspiration for France's Indo-Chinese policy. Laurentie was a colonial administrator, secretary-general of the general government of the AEF between 1940 and 1943, and organizer of the Brazzaville conference. He was also the author of the two declarations on Indo-China.[8]

For de Gaulle and his colleagues, the re-establishment of French sovereignty in the peninsula meant participating in the fight against Japan. The formation of an Expeditionary Force was planned at the end of 1943. In September 1944, after the liberation of most of the French mainland, the GPRF had envisaged the creation of a Far East Army of 60,000 men. This FEFEO was to be under the command of General Blaizot.[9] In October, Blaizot reached Ceylon and settled in Kandy to direct the French military mission with Mountbatten, head of the SEAC. For several months, all that Blaizot had at his disposal was a chief of staff and the sonorous title of "Commander-Designate" of the FEFEO. The Wehrmacht was not collapsing, despite repeated defeats on all fronts. The meagre French forces had to be deployed on the final assault against the Reich, while the equipment and transportation of the new divisions depended on the Americans. In January 1945, Washington rejected France's requests regarding the hypothetical FEFEO on technical grounds.

But after May 1945, Germany's surrender made it possible to plan the transfer of troops to Asia. On 26 May, the Indo-China Committee decided to create a Far East expeditionary force consisting of two divisions. The war map showed that the Americans were now occupying Okinawa. Paris therefore proposed to put the troops under MacArthur's command, because he was directing operations in the Pacific. In July, Washington made its response known: the principle of an expeditionary force participating in the operations against Japan was acceptable... from the beginning of 1946. Thus, on the eve of the Japanese surrender, France had only moderate forces in the Far East. On the Chinese front, at the discretion of General Wedemeyer, Alessandri was commanding 5,000 survivors of the Indo-China Army. In India, Blaizot commanded less than a thousand men. To these could also be added the troops which Leclerc was mobilizing for the expeditionary force in mainland France and in the Empire, as envisaged under the 26 May decision.[10]

10 August: following the dropping of the atomic bombs on Hiroshima and Nagasaki, Japan offered an armistice. Taken aback by an event which they had not imagined to be so imminent, the French hurried to re-establish themselves in the peninsula as soon as possible. On 15 August, de Gaulle removed Sabattier and appointed Admiral d'Argenlieu as high commissioner for Indo-China, his "first mission being to restore French sovereignty in the Indo-China Union". Leclerc as supreme commander of the forces was his subordinate. Thus, because Langlade and Laurentie retained their posts, the four principal instigators of French policy on Indo-China were Gaullists from the outset. In order to be a Gaullist, there is no absolute requirement to agree with another Gaullist. Direct, dynamic, very popular in the army, Leclerc resented the shared responsibilities which placed him under the command of the haughty and secretive Admiral.

On 22 August, Leclerc arrived in Kandy, from whence he had to organize the transfer of the first troops to Indo-China. On the same day, Pierre Messmer parachuted into Tongking and Jean Cédile into Cochin-China. They were responsible for representing the GPRF before the arrival of the high commissioner. One was taken prisoner by the

Viet Minh while his radio operator was killed. The other was arrested by the Japanese. On reaching India, Leclerc learned from Mountbatten that the British were going to occupy the south of Indo-China and the Chinese the north. He asked de Gaulle, who was visiting the United States, to try to make Truman change his mind. It was a wasted effort: the Americans did not want to upset Chiang Kai-Shek.

The discussions in Washington were nevertheless far from negative. "In any case, as far as Indo-China is concerned, my government does not oppose the return of the authority of France and its army to the country", de Gaulle in his memoirs quotes the President of the United States as saying. The American position had evolved over several months. By the date of the Yalta conference (February 1945), it had been decided to retain the system of international trusteeship for the former mandates of the SDN, the colonies of the enemy countries, and the territories which would be voluntarily placed under this regime. Roosevelt remained hostile to the restoration of the colonial order in Indo-China and was finally induced to express his position under combined pressure from London and Paris: of course, Indo-China had to be granted complete independence soon but, provided that she formally accepted this final goal, France could exercise temporary trusteeship. This new direction was clearly confirmed by Truman, as he was more inclined than his predecessor to reconciliation with Paris.[11] This does not mean that if Roosevelt had lived a return of the former colonial power would have been unthinkable.[12] Yet it remains a fact that the change in presidency facilitated France's return.

In reality, however, American co-operation was by no means achieved. As soon as the news arrived of the Japanese surrender, Sainteny in Kunming received the order to "prepare as quickly as possible". He decided to go to Hanoi as soon as he could, but the ill-will of the local authorities and particularly of Major Patti, chief of the OSS for the north of Indo-China, was obvious. When, on 22 August, he finally reached the capital of Tongking,[13] he realized that there had been a revolution. This revolution did not frighten Patti. The major was well placed to participate in the demonstrations organized by the new power which he thereby seemed to be guaranteeing. He even helped draft the Declaration of Independence. Denying Sainteny any role other than a humanitarian one, he put the Hanoi authorities on guard against colonialism and advised them to trust the United States.[14]

On the Chinese side, there was the same ill feeling, and the same contradictions. Officially, Chongqing was not opposed to a French return to the peninsula. Soong, Chiang's Minister of Foreign Affairs, maintained this when de Gaulle met him in Washington in August, and then in Paris on 21 September. But the local leaders were creating additional difficulties. The members of the military mission who, on the advice of Sainteny, were trying to infiltrate Tongking, were prevented by force of arms when necessary. In spite of the friendly words addressed to him, Alessandri could not enter Indo-China with his 5,000 men, even accompanied by Kuomintang troops. The French also protested when the forces from Luhan struck at North Laos where there were no Japanese to disarm (the meagre forces stationed there had taken refuge in Thailand). The occupation was all the more disconcerting as the colonial power was in a strong position to re-establish itself in the country as a result of the action of the armed bands which had fled into the jungle after 9 March.[15] In Laos, as in the north of Vietnam, the Chinese soldiers persistently obstructed their supposed allies. Thanks to them, a large proportion of the arms recovered from the Japanese were sold to the Viet Minh. So, in these decisive days the various opposition forces, their local Japanese allies and the American and Chinese authorities combined to prevent the return of the colonial power into the southern part of Indo-China.

In the south, the situation was just as confused. However, the British were, of course, helping the French efforts. London did not consider France to be a rival, as it did in the Middle East. The two colonial powers collaborated freely. From 6 September, the units of the Indian division gradually arrived, seconded by the British command from the troops sent to Burma. General Gracey, who was in command, was all for collaborating with Cédile, in particular, to ensure the maintenance of order—a task which the Allied agreements had temporarily entrusted to the Japanese army, and which it had managed in its own way to achieve. After parachuting in, the GPRF representative had been authorized by the Japanese to take Saigon. He sized up the situation. Through the mediation of the Marxist cultural circle, he established contact with the leaders of the Viet Minh (one of whom was Giau). He discussed the text of 24 March, and his interlocutors insisted on independence as a condition. However, in the anarchical climate of Cochin-China, with the struggles between factions, the settling of scores, the nationalists[16] outbidding each other, the pillaging and the anti-French violence, the PCI seemed to Cédile to be a reasonable force with whom he could negotiate. From 20 September, Gracey, worried by the spread of instability, but confident after the arrival of new Indian troops, assumed the task of re-establishing order in Saigon.[17] To this end, he suspended newspapers in the vernacular, imposed a curfew, and ordered Viet-

namese groups to hand in their guns. At Cédile's instigation, he re-
armed the French prisoners.[18] He ordered them to close off Saigon's
main public buildings on the night of 23 September and then set a police
operation in motion, which he deemed necessary. The operation was interpreted as the first step towards the re-establishment of French
sovereignty, but was deemed to be an act of war by the executive committee of Nambo, which was forced under cover. It would thus be
reasonable to date the Indo-Chinese conflict to 23 September 1945.[19]

The events of the night of 23 September aroused the anger of some
ordinary white settlers who avenged themselves indiscriminately on the
Annamese for the recent affrays. The incidents forced Gracey to disarm
the French troops. On 25 September, fanatical gangs attacked one of
the European districts. Nearly 400 people were kidnapped or killed "in
horrible conditions, which at times surpassed the imagination" (Devillers). The Heyraud massacre—publicly rumoured to be the work of the
Viet Minh—would deeply scar the French settlers. Because of its savag-
ery and the impression it made on their minds, the episode is compara-
ble to the Philippeville killings of 20 August 1955. Gracey decided to re-
establish order, and he mobilized all the regular units available. He
criticized the Japanese, who still had the most troops, because they did
nothing, and ordered them to take a part in the police operations. He re-
armed the French ex-prisoners. He set the Indians against the groups of
insurgents.[20] He was impatient to be finished with these repressive tasks
which were outside the remit of his initial mission. Gracey was relieved
to welcome Leclerc and the first part of the expeditionary force in October.

This event was enthusiastically welcomed by the Europeans in
Saigon. Imprisoned or confined to their quarters by the Japanese, sometimes harrassed by them, they had lived in terror since the start of the revolution. For them, the arrival of French troops in Cochin-China was
true liberation.

At home in France, the press belatedly informed the public in vague
terms[21] that the Viet Minh had seized power. News of events in Indo-
China was absent-mindedly followed by poorly informed opinion. What
with the news of the Laval trial, the preparations for the next elections,
and the typical preoccupations of government, public opinion had
difficultly in acquainting itself with the throng of unknown names (Vietnam, Viet Minh, Ho Chi Minh, Tran Traong Kim) which it often confused. Even knowledgeable observers did not quite grasp what was happening. Colonel Bernard, a specialist on the issue, wondered in *Combat*
of 15 September "if there is a Marxist party in Indo-China". To make

the situation known and explain the government's policy, Laurentie organized a press conference on 13 September at which he gave a progressive interpretation of the declaration of 24 March. In spite of the Viet Minh revolution, the declaration was still the basis of French policy. When he learned of recent events, Leclerc asked the GPRF (in his report on 25 September) to "state our position with regard to the different countries in the Indo-Chinese Union", if needs be with a statement "extending the 24 March declaration". Paris said no. New concessions would have "all the appearance of a step backwards and would complicate the situation". De Gaulle therefore stuck to the policy which had already been defined for several months, even if the details had altered to some extent. The message that the head of government addressed to the people of the peninsula on 19 August—the day the Viet Minh took power in Hanoi—begins with these words: "The enemy is vanquished. Tomorrow Indo-China will be free." Suffice it to say that the liberation of the country would only be accomplished by the return of France.... However, de Gaulle deleted the phrase "from the five countries" from the original text. ("The motherland addresses the expression of its joy to its children from the five countries of the Indo-Chinese Union.") In similar vein, d'Argenlieu was given the title of high commissioner and not governor-general. The instructions issued to the Admiral on 16 August—and repeated in a letter to Leclerc—make de Gaulle's position at that time clear. A great distrust of the Allies (even the British, the Levant affair being imminent) is expressed together with the idea that "nothing will be agreed with the locals so long as we do not have power".[22] "Do not give, and do not allow anyone else to give, any undertaking with regards to the Viet Minh. You can make certain contacts if they are discreet and involve no intermediary, whether British, Chinese or American", de Gaulle told d'Argenlieu. France had collapsed in 1940 and its army had immediately been defeated by the Japanese. France had lost face. The image of a conquered country had to be dispelled. It had to make a show of strength. When France had demonstrated its power, a lasting political solution could be planned.

To this effect, de Gaulle nurtured a "secret plan". He would assist Prince Vinh San reclaim the throne of Annam. Deposed in 1916 for conspiracy and forced into exile, the ex-Emperor had enlisted in the Free French forces. He was a Vietnamese nationalist and a Gaullist. This augured well that "something new and reasonable" would be done in Indo-China, as elsewhere. But, for the time being, the military question took precedence.

FROM SAIGON TO HANOI: REINSTATEMENT

It was not until 5 October that Leclerc finally managed to land in Saigon. He had made the most of his enforced stay at Kandy to make preparations for the expeditionary force. Mountbatten helped him as much as he could by providing him with the necessary colonial equipment. However, they then faced the problem of transportation. London was giving priority to repatriating the British troops. As for the French Air Minister, Tillon, he was uncooperative.

"It seems to me that General Leclerc should go to Saigon without delay and establish himself there. The effectiveness of troops temporarily at his disposal is of secondary importance to the necessity of his being there", de Gaulle wrote to d'Argenlieu on 29 September. In fact, when the high commissioner *ad interim* arrived, he found a meagre French Indo-Chinese military presence. There were 1,400 ex-prisoners from the 11th RIC, reinforced by two companies which had landed in September with the British. These few hundred men were the most active against the revolutionary forces. Exhausted by their recent confrontations[23] they were holding on to a town without water and electricity, abandoned on Giau's orders by a section of the Vietnamese population and blockaded by the partisans. The initial fighting directed by Leclerc therefore took place in the immediate vicinity of Saigon with British backing. However, during the month of October units of the 2nd DB (Massu Group) disembarked bringing large supplies of weapons with them. Consequently, from 25 October, there were large-scale military operations aimed at liberating the capital of Cochin-China. A series of assaults which lasted for two months opened essential supply routes and secured the occupation of the urban centres. The Executive Committee, now reduced to its communist nucleus, ordered a scorched earth policy. The towns and cities won back by Massu's men were largely destroyed. Here and there, the corpses of pro-French or eminent citizens were found, often mutilated. After the devastation of Germany, the soldiers of the 2nd DB were now seeing the face of war in Asia.

"The people were expecting liberators, but it was the police who came." (*Combat*, 14 October.) In France, this policy of the use of force provoked criticism from some of the left-wing press. *L'Humanité* set the tone: "For how long will the interests of the Banque d'Indochine and trusts take precedence over democracy and France's interests in the Far East?" (30 October).[24] In September, the French Communist Party modified its stance on Indo-China. The declaration of 24 March was then described as "a regrettable step backwards in relation to that of the

President on 25 October 1944". It was not the first time that the opponents of the Gaullists' colonial policy had quoted de Gaulle in opposing a government decision. If a quote from de Gaulle openly opposed to colonisation was required, they could refer to the press conference of 25 October 1944: "French policy consists of leading each of these peoples along a line of development which will allow them to administer themselves and at a later stage to govern themselves". "Prince of ambiguity", was how one of the negotiators at Evian later described de Gaulle. Certain people were already criticising his ambiguities, because the future French Union was at stake. "When France regains Indo-China, she solemnly declares herself ready to carry out the undertakings that she has assumed for the good of all", promised the message to Indo-China of 19 August. Yes, but which undertakings? wondered *Combat*. Those of the 24 March declaration or those of the press conference of 25 October 1944?

"The threat of the restoration of colonial domination in its previous form is unacceptable to the people of Indo-China and is facing growing resistance. The sympathies of the progressive forces of the entire world are unanimously on the side of the masses who aspire to liberty and have the right to be free", proclaimed the Soviet magazine *Novoe Vremeni* (New Times) in November 1945. Nor was the armed return of the French appreciated to any greater degree by the American newspapers. British opinion was mostly interested in Gracey's actions. The participation of British troops in the peace-keeping operations in early autumn was criticised by the Labour majority. Opponents of Gracey's policies particularly feared the reaction of Indians whose fellow-countrymen were engaged in the repression of a national movement. In the Commons, Ernest Bevin had to defend Gracey, who "had to deal severely with pillaging and the continuous attacks of the armed Annamese gangs directed against civilians and French property and put an end to the conflict between these groups and the French forces under his command."

In January 1946, Gracey managed to transfer his powers to the French. Re-embarkation began and was completed in March. The small sector in which the Indian division was concentrated was then hemmed in by the expeditionary force looking for Viet Minh elements which had found refuge there. As for the Japanese, they did not leave until May-June 1946. Since their surrender they had continued to play a highly ambivalent role. They were required by the Allied Command to assist in the operations led by the British and the French. But they allowed the revolution to continue to exist even if they did not encourage it. Their agents had kept in touch with the nationalists, recently reputed to be pro-Japanese, and with the militia which they had armed and trained. They left arms and deserters for the Viet Minh in which their former auxiliaries were active.

In early 1946, when the British were beginning to pull out, the French were practically masters of Indo-China south of the sixteenth parallel. In the sector handed over to the British army by the Potsdam agreements, the revolutionary forces whose units had now disbanded were left with only one bastion at the Pointe de Camau to which the executive committee had fled and which would be occupied in February.

The war changed course. Thorough searches replaced large-scale operations. "It is a difficult and unrewarding task in a land of water and mud, paddy-fields and orchards of areca palms and fruit trees, segmented by complicated networks of canals, rivers, arroyos and ditches, dotted with villages, hamlets and isolated houses, many of which are accessible only by water. The rebels were in their element. Benefiting from the voluntary or forced complicity of the population, they could change from peaceful peasants into guerillas and vice versa with the greatest of ease. They moved through the maze of waterways quickly and silently on tiny sampans. They knew the secrets of the delayed tides of the most remote arroyos" (R. Dronne). The missions were difficult and required many men. They were provided by the 9th DIC[25] of General Valluy who had arrived in late 1945, then by the 3rd DIC under General Nyo[26] which disembarked in February 1946. The French constructed forts, armed partisans, and led laborious mopping-up operations. The Viet Minh fomented instability, instilling fear through threats of execution into those collaborating with the colonial authority. Just as the administrators and leading citizens of the old order were re-establishing themselves in the ravaged country, guerilla warfare was also becoming widespread.

On 1 October, Decoux left Indo-China, having vainly attempted to convince Cédile to allow him continue in office until his successor arrived. On his arrival in Paris, L'Humanité demanded that he be shot on the spot. It was not a time for subtlety. Like the Admiral, the army officers and the civil servants liberated from the Japanese camps were surprised at the bitterness of the purge. They thought they had served their country well, even heroically, during those difficult years. Now they were treated as suspicious persons, as collaborators. There was no doubt that these "New French", the "French of the class of '45", were a peculiar lot.[27]

One admiral succeeded another. On 31 October, the high commissioner arrived in Saigon from Chandernagor. He did not think it fitting to meet his predecessor. As a naval officer during World War I, d'Argenlieu had left the forces after the fighting was over to join the priesthood. In 1939, the friar Louis de la Trinité had been recalled to serve as captain of a corvette. He had been imprisoned and had escaped. In 1940, he reached London. At the time, sailors were hardly rallying to the Free French flag. So, de Gaulle made d'Argenlieu an admiral and entrusted him with important missions such as that of high commissioner of New Caledonia. He was fifty-six years old, thin, of average height with a bony face. This was the man installing himself in the Norodom Palace, the seat of government and symbol of colonial pomp and splendour. "The will of the GPRF is to start afresh but in an orderly and reasoned manner", the Admiral wrote to Leclerc, copying de Gaulle. His instructions of 15 September had explained the new status of Indo-China to his subordinates: each one of the five countries would enjoy autonomy; France would, however, exercise its powers on a federal level.

On 1 November d'Argenlieu published the first issue of the *Journal officiel* of Indo-China. In an attempt to wipe the slate clean, it announced the creation of the state of Indo-China by setting up a federal government. The team was not without talent (Bloch-Lainé was in Finance), but in the circumstances it did not include one Indo-Chinese member, contrary to what had been proposed in the reference document, the 24 March declaration. As far as "something new" was concerned, it was a curious beginning. As far as the "local governments" were concerned Cambodia posed fewest problems. On his arrival in Saigon, Leclerc had sent some men to Phnom Penh to re-establish French sovereignty there. The operation took place peacefully. The head of the government, Son Ngoc Thanh,[28] was arrested and exiled. Saigon did not hold Sihanouk responsible for his recent mistakes. The sovereign, having an understanding of the new alignment of forces, renounced the short-lived independence of his kingdom. He had to accept the working agreement of January 1946, placing the Khmer state within the Federation. In Cochin-China, political life was beginning again. The Democratic Party was re-formed under the leadership of the president, Doctor Tinh. He had formerly been a leading politician in the south, and had been harrassed during the revolutionary period, of which he had terrible memories. This patrician continued to dominate the Saigon scene. Under the auspices of the administration, a Cochin-Chinese party, led by Cuong, was also established, but its links with the Sûreté were notorious. Basically, these two groups formed the consultative council of Cochin-China in

February 1946, which, in addition to giving advice, had to draw up a constitution.

On 14 December, de Gaulle had received Vinh San. The prince stated his ideas in *Combat* (a united Vietnam within the Indo-Chinese Federation which in the medium term would be granted the status of an independent state). He was soon expecting to be replaced on the throne of Hué by the head of government, who was to make a triumphal journey through the peninsula. In Saigon, Doctor Tan launched a newspaper to prepare the public for the restoration. On 26 December an airplane accident put an end to Vinh San's hypothetical solution.[29] When de Gaulle left power a month later—to the detriment of his loyal d'Argenlieu—he had not completed the liberation of all the French sovereign territories as he had intended. The whole of northern Indo-China had been omitted from the plan. In that area, the return of the former colonial power depended both on the occupying Chinese and on what the authorities in Saigon called the GRA (Revolutionary Annamese Government).

Marxist-Leninists held key positions but theoretically shared power with other revolutionary forces. Reforms were fast and furious. The government was crippled by internal problems and from external threats. It found it difficult to get the local soviets to listen to it. The beginnings of the GRA are reminiscent of those of its Bolshevik big brother. From September, the pro-Japanese groups were outlawed, their leaders arrested; popular committees were created to replace leading citizens and mandarins. The election of a constituent assembly was provided for and was to be elected by universal suffrage (male and female). The principle of equality of all the ethnic groups was proclaimed. The old taxation system was abolished. An eight-hour day was introduced, together with a minimum wage and the right to strike, whilst agrarian reform reduced farm rents and debts, shared out common land and confiscated the properties of "colonialists and traitors" in favour of the poor peasants. A literacy campaign[30] was launched which mobilized millions of voluntary instructors, its aim being to teach reading skills within one year to all Vietnamese over the age of eight. The Vietnamese language was promoted at all levels. Decisions combined propaganda, statements of principle and affirmations of accomplished facts.

However, the first task of a government is to feed its population. The poor maintenance of dikes during the previous months had resulted in flooding and the destruction of a large part of the rice crop. Since the Vietnamese were cut off from the South, they could not count on Cochin-Chinese surpluses. The famine which had already claimed hundreds of thousands of victims threatened to become worse. The authorities therefore immediately launched a vast "campaign for mutual help and solidarity". Propaganda called on people to save the smallest scrap of food "following the example of President Ho Chi Minh". The government increased the number of days for fasting. While waiting for the next crop, the cultivation of short-cycle plants (sweet potatoes, marrows, etc.) was encouraged even in public parks. And finally, the population was mobilized to repair the dikes.

As with many revolutions, the Vietnamese revolution faced financial problems. The system of "colonialist taxes" had been abolished, and the coffers were empty. The authorities were turning everything into money. But neither calls for "patriotic payments" nor ingenious methods of finding resources sufficed. It was not long before civil servants were not paid. As for the disturbances, they continued despite the declaration of independence. Intellectuals, Christians and prominent citizens were the principal victims. The fact that many of their leaders (such as Nguyen Manh Ha, leader of the Catholic youth) were linked to the revolutionary cause was not enough to protect them from violence. Harassment had been officially condemned but it led to the creation of the first self-defence groups.

All these difficulties were amplified and complicated by the Chinese presence, nine divisions (as against a single British division in the South), or nearly 200,000 men. The Chinese had arrived in force. From the commander-in-chief to the private, everyone had set about pillaging the country. Plunder is part of military tradition and there was nothing more natural for the Chinese. Thanks to them, trafficking of all sorts and the black market flourished in a capital which began to look more and more like a Chinese city.[31] Customs duties which might have relieved the GRA's financial squeeze were reduced to insignificant levels as they allowed large quantities of goods through in their convoys.

The politicians continued to envisage the country becoming a satellite of China. On the map distributed to the new graduates of the military academy of Whampoa, China extended into Tongking. This great plan might have been founded on history, the presence of the Chinese communities in Indo-China, as well as on the willingness of the nationalists who had recently been welcomed to Yunnan and were thought to be under an obligation. General Siao Wen and the men of the Kuomintang were mostly counting on the VNQDD and the DMH to whom the Luhan army on its march towards Hanoi had given control of a number of regions from which the Viet Minh had been excluded. In the capital, the government had to take account of the paramilitary organizations of the different parties. The militia escalated the violence: kidnap, assassination, torture, and various acts of provocation. Outbidding each other in their anti-French fervour, the VNQDD and DMH demanded that the government be re-constituted in their favour. For their leaders, as for Siao Wen, it was actually a matter of reforming the Liou Cheou front. Accused of having broken the agreements in August, and called on to return to the "national union", Ho Chi Minh was acting astutely and evasively. In November, the PC decided to commit hara-kiri so as to be sure of what would happen. Of course, the Viet Minh would continue to be tightly controlled by the leaders of this zombie party.[32] The elections to the Constituent Assembly held in January 1946 (theoretically throughout Vietnam) saw the Front triumph. The elections, whose free nature may seem contestable in comparison with the practices of a liberal democracy,[33] nevertheless confirmed the legitimacy of the revolutionary power. The intellectual superiority of its leaders was appreciated for what it was by Siao Wen, who had been disappointed by his allies and drew up contingency plans: to set up cells among the Viet Minh.

After their show of strength, the Japanese had concentrated most of the Europeans of Tongking in the capital. The 25,000 French from Hanoi were therefore hostages of a kind, both to the GRA and to the Chinese. Sainteny—with a good track record, luck and resilience—was confirmed by d'Argenlieu as representative of France for North Vietnam, reassuring the French settlers with an official presence. His mission was barely tolerated and encountered the hostility of the nationalists as well as the affronts of the Yunnanese occupiers. The overriding aim of the delegate from the GPRF was to help his compatriots and prevent them being massacred, then to re-establish French authority without violence. Aware of the dangers of a solution through force, he attempted negotiation. He had to come to some agreement with the Chinese who had the numerical advantage and the status of a great power. Fighting them would result in serious losses and diplomatic complications. He had also to come to an understanding with the Viet Minh, the most dynamic force in the country. If the GRA was routed from Hanoi by the expeditionary force, it would organise guerilla warfare which would be even more awkward to subdue than that being waged in the South by the Nambo Committee. In any event, a military solution would expose the Europeans to the danger of a massacre.

Leclerc had evaluated the problems of a military solution during the latest of his operations. In late November in Saigon, he received Pierre Messmer who had escaped. "They are just waiting for us to return", people would volunteer in Cochin-Chinese colonial circles. The future prime minister of France, who had spent more than two months in the Viet Minh zone, confirmed the consolidation of revolutionary power in the countryside. The authoritative opinions of Messmer only reinforced the views of a liberal entourage dominated by reserve officers, Colonel Repiton-Preneuf and Commander Mus. Leclerc consequently supported Sainteny in his attempts to arrive at a compromise with Ho Chi Minh.[34]

In January 1946, Sino-French negotiations opened at Chongqing. On the French side negotiations were conducted by the ambassador, assisted by General Salan (who had now replaced Alessandri) and by the high commissioner's diplomatic advisor. The Chinese had many means of applying pressure so that the negotiations would end in their favour. In particular, they could, as they had already done, suspend the air link which had been restored in November between Saigon and Hanoi, or else place loyal troops in their midst to threaten the safety of the French.[35] A heavy price had to be paid to persuade the troops to leave. Officially, they were only there to disarm the Japanese on behalf of the colonial power. France abandoned the last remains of the unfair treaties (concessions, leased territories, privileges for the Yunnan railway), and granted China commercial advantages in Tongking[36] and a new status for its nationals. The relief of the troops at Luhan would be completed on 31 March. The practicalities would be determined by the military authorities.

Discussions with the Viet Minh had been in progress for a long time. From 28 September 1945, General Alessandri, accompanied by Pignon, had been having talks with Ho Chi Minh. Sainteny took over. He met the communist leader in secret. The negotiations were laborious, encountering the same problems again and again—problems which would continue for months—the issue of unity (unity of the three *ky*, as the GRA referred to it) and independence (*doc lap* in Vietnamese).[37] This last condition was of such importance that in Hanoi and Saigon, requests were made for the word "independence" to be accepted, but its meaning to be limited by phrases of the type "within the framework of the Indo-China Federation and the French Union".[38] Ho Chi Minh was finally forced to conclude an agreement, partly because of the situation at home, but mostly because of the alignment of the international powers. His government was not recognized by any capital. The USSR was remote and appeared indifferent. The time had not yet arrived for the politics of power blocs. Moscow was looking after its interests in France, where the Communist Party was firmly entrenched; its diplomacy made a show of supporting independence. As for China, all that it was interested in at that time was Chiang Kai-Shek's independence movement. Its manouevrings and ulterior motives were known.[39] As far as Mao was concerned, his bases were thousands of miles away. The United States had distanced itself from the revolutionary government and its complicity with France was developing. Of course, nothing was expected of Great Britain.

The realities of this situation caused an agreement to be concluded with France, a France led by men of the resistance, and in which the Communist Party shared power. The Chongqing negotiations precipitated matters. The revolutionary government risked being exposed by the collusion between the Chinese occupier and the former colonial power, whose counter-offensive was imminent. The Secretary of the SFIO federation in Hanoi, Caput, contributed to the removal of the last obstacles between the two parties. The agreement which Leclerc, high commissioner *ad interim*,[40] was pressuring Sainteny into accepting was imminent. Paris was notified of its contents. Before signing, however, Ho Chi Minh altered his team to form a national unity government, which Siao Wen and nationalist groups had been demanding for months.[41] These groups had always denounced any form of negotiation with France. But now as parties to the agreement they were compromised and their bids for power were thus prevented.

The treaty with the Chinese was ratified, and Ho Chi Minh was ready to follow. Leclerc gave orders for the fleet to set sail for the north. The tides forced the ships to disembark the de Valluy troops on 6 March. Yet on the eve of this event, nothing had yet been settled. The Kuomintang generals found more excuses for refusing to withdraw their forces, their last argument being that if the expeditionary force disembarked it would jeopardize the Chinese communities there because the revolutionary government had still not consented to the return of the French. The reluctance with which the officers of the occupation army acted was encouraged by the manoeuvres of the nationalist groups who were determined to retain the troops which were protecting them. The confrontation that Sainteny feared could still take place.

On the morning of 6 March, Leclerc began the disembarkation operation. The Chinese general commanding the garrison at Haiphong ordered his men to fire on the French ships. They returned fire after twenty minutes,[42] causing the explosion of the munitions and equipment piled up by officers from Luhan on the quays in readiness for their departure. After several hours of cannon-fire, a cease-fire was concluded at Haiphong, whilst in Hanoi the long-awaited agreement was signed by Sainteny and Ho Chi Minh. Once the inevitable last-minute difficulties, created by the Chinese and the Viet Minh, were resolved Leclerc managed to make his entry into the capital on 18 March, to the relief of Sainteny and the European colony which had been living in a state of anxiety for months. The general's statement that "Hanoi is the last stage of the Liberation" probably reflected the opinion of the "new French", but it was not a blow to Vietnamese nationalism.

"DOC LAP", THE THREE KYS

1. The French government recognizes the Republic of Vietnam as a free state with its own government, parliament, army and finances, forming a part of the Indo-China Federation and the French Union.

As far as the reunion of the three *ky*s is concerned, the French government undertakes to ratify the decisions taken by the population who shall be consulted in a referendum.

2. The government of Vietnam declares itself ready to welcome the French army amicably when, in accordance with the international agreements, it relieves the Chinese troops.

An agreement appended to this present preliminary accord will stipulate how the relief operations shall be effected.

3. The above stipulations shall become valid immediately. As soon as the exchange of signatures has occurred, each of the main contracting parties will take any measures necessary to cause the immediate cessation of hostilities, to maintain its troops in their respective positions and to create the favourable atmosphere necessary for the immediate opening of friendly and frank negotiations. These negotiations shall be chiefly concerned with:

a) Vietnam's diplomatic relations with foreign states;

b) the future status of Indo-China;

c) French cultural and economic interests in Vietnam.

Hanoi, Saigon or Paris may be chosen as venues for the Conference.

The concessions made by Ho Chi Minh are obvious.[43] Independence, though a condition for any agreement, was not achieved, any more than unity was. Because sovereignty was the issue, everything revolved around the interpretation of the word "free", on whose vagueness agreement was reached. What would be the nature of the Indo-China Federation? What would be the structure of the French Union which the deputies of the French parliament were in the process of creating while they were completing the draft constitutional plan? The degree of "freedom" granted to the Vietnamese state depended on the reply to these two questions. Moreover, the borders of the country had not been fixed, since Ho Chi Minh accepted that the case of Cochin-China be held in abeyance. Legally it was a question of a colony, not a protectorate, in the imperial tradition. In fact, France's authority was fully exercised there. The most immediate consequence and the most obvious concession of the treaty was that Leclerc's troops managed to reinstall themselves throughout the country and were liable to assist the establishment of the colonial status quo. However, Hanoi had obtained recognition by the revolutionary government; and it could be supposed that in the short term, unity (if the Cochin-Chinese voted yes in the proposed referendum) and independence would be achieved. It was stipulated in the military agreement appended to the treaty—this was the passage which worried Paris—that the "units responsible, in collaboration with the Vietnamese army, for ensuring the maintenance of order and the security of Vietnamese territory" would be gradually replaced by the national army, one-fifth of the complement to change annually. Consequently after five years the troops would be completely relieved.[44]

The international press welcomed the agreement. It embellished the theme. France had been in difficulties for several months in South East Asia, but had now managed to recover its position, and its agreement with an insurgent government was a lesson to all. The Dutch, facing similar problems in Indonesia, considered following suit.[45] Vietnamese nationalist opinion was disappointed. After the violent anti-French campaigns which had lasted to the bitter end, the return of the colonial order was not easy to accept. The fact that the DMH and VNQDD were to participate in the government, and that Khanh, one of the leaders of the VNQDD, was forced to co-sign the agreement did not protect Ho Chi Minh from attack and provocation. From 7 March onwards, the leaders of the Viet Minh had to explain themselves at a meeting. Giap, on this occasion, justified the convention because of the international situation, comparing it to the Treaty of Brest-Litovsk which allowed Lenin to save the Bolshevik revolution through temporary concessions to German imperialism. On the French side, officially, everyone expressed satisfaction beginning with Moulet, the Overseas Minister in the Gouin government. Thierry d'Argenlieu approved it in a communiqué:

> The agreement which has resolved a serious problem to the advantage of both contracting parties is an interesting document from three points of view:
>
> 1. On the international level, the agreement has proved that France remains faithful to the spirit of the United Nations Charter.
>
> 2. On the regional level, particularly the Asian region, this agree-

ment is the first example of a freely-debated accord between a colonial power and a South East Asian nation.

3. On the French level, the armed forces are assured of a friendly reception and we are pre-empting any reproach for opening hostilities which certain people might have been able to label as acts of conquest. We are fully safeguarding French economic and cultural interests now and for the future.

The high commissioner went to meet Ho Chi Minh on 24 March in Along Bay. This was an opportunity to display his power and his troops. France had lost face in the preceding period, and needed to show her muscle. In Saigon, however, there was resentment at what the Admiral was privately calling a new Munich. Concessions had been made to a tiny group of prison escapees. A communist power had been recognized; instead of the benevolent and competent authority of the colonial administration, the population would be subjected to the whims and expediency of fanatics; even Cochin-China, jewel of the Federation, would be delivered to them in the short term. These were the most common criticisms formulated by the colonials and administrators. As for Cédile, he claimed to see in the agreement a simple local contract between the Commissioner of the Republic for Tongking and North Annam and an established authority.[46] The rest of Indo-China was not involved. In any case, Cochin-China was an integral part of the national territory, since it was legally a colony.

On 9 March 1946 *Le Monde* commented: "The authorities are congratulating themselves on the results they have achieved. In any case, even if the agreement has been signed, it remains to be implemented. Much caution needs to be shown." In fact, discussion proved difficult from the outset. There was even a problem in choosing the city in which to host the conference provided for in the document of 6 March. Paris, suggested Ho Chi Minh; Dalat, replied d'Argenlieu. The Admiral did not want the Viet Minh to influence French opinion and wanted to prevent any state-to-state negotiation. In his view, discussion should be restricted to the framework of the Indo-Chinese federation, in accordance with the 24 March declaration. Eventually, it was decided upon Dalat, then Paris. The Dalat conference achieved no results, apart from showing the extent of differences. When the president of the Vietnamese government arrived in France in early June for the next meeting, everything still remained to be settled. Ho Chi Minh had been preceded in France by a friendship "mission" (led by Pham Van Dong) which was to prepare the ground. D'Argenlieu tried to counter its influence by sending a Cochin-Chinese delegation under Colonel Xuan.

In June 1946, the French political scene was restless. The first constitutional plan (and therefore the first organization of the French Union) had just been rejected in a referendum. A second constituent assembly had to be elected. A ministry was created under the direction of the leader of the MRP, Bidault. De Gaulle made his political comeback with the Bayeux speech.[47] While the new government was being established, Ho Chi Minh was kept waiting with a trip to the South-West of France. Bidault finally organized his team. On 22 June the Vietnamese president, accompanied by Sainteny who was chaperoning him, left Biarritz for the capital. The Viet Minh flag, a sickle on a star, was hoisted next to the Tricolour; there were sonorous speeches, official receptions. The former outlaw was received as a head of state. This veteran of the revolution, turned president in fatigue jacket, was an intriguing figure. Playing on this fascinating image, he imposed his image as a bearded, likeable, even good-natured, Annamese scholar.

The Fontainebleau conference opened on 6 July. The Vietnamese under Pham Van Dong confronted a French delegation which, under the chairmanship of Max André,[48] did not include any high-level politicians—only experts.[49] Ho Chi Minh did not participate in the negotiations, being busy with his public relations exercises. He was counting on his contacts[50] with the Socialists and Communists—although these two parties had narrowly lost their majority in the second constituent assembly—to help him realise his claims. Five questions were tabled for the conference: the integration of Vietnam into the French Union (which was to be defined by the new assembly), the integration of Vietnam into the Indo-China Federation, the unity of the three *ky*s, the solving of economic problems, and the treaty plan.

The Vietnamese and the French had completely different concepts of the French Union and the Indo-China Federation. For the Vietnamese, they could only be structures to ensure co-operation to which Vietnam would belong as a completely sovereign state. However, for the French, there was no question of granting external sovereignty. Diplomatic relations could only derive from the Union, which was the French Republic. Internal sovereignty was also out of the question, since the Indo-China Federation would have a genuine government at its disposal under the control of the high commissioner. Ho Chi Minh interpreted "a free state" as being an independent state which would nevertheless maintain close ties with Laos, Cambodia and France. This would be independence combined with co-operation agreements. For the other side, "free" meant enjoying a limited amount of autonomy. This was the solution which was being adopted in the kingdoms of the West, as well as in Cochin-China.

On 1 June, Cochin-China was, in effect, proclaimed a republic at the instigation of d'Argenlieu. "Free state" was defined in the same terms used in the March convention for Vietnam. Of course, the foundation declaration made the republic seem provisional, since it specified "subject to the result of the referendum provided for in the 6 March agreement". The Admiral's initiative did not contradict the letter of the treaty between Ho Chi Minh and Sainteny, only its spirit. In addition to illustrating what Paris meant by a "free state"—the relative freedom it granted the leaders of the republic in comparison to the French administration and the colonial officials—this creation clearly aimed at hindering reunification. Against revolutionary North Vietnam, the Admiral intended to oppose the "moderate" bloc of the Mekong countries (Laos, Cambodia, Cochin-China).[52] This initiative, which led some members of the GRA delegation to foresee the annulment of the Fontainebleau conference, was reinforced by the policy conducted by Saigon in the Annamese cordillera. The deployment of the expeditionary force in South Vietnamese territory and the arrival of a Commission of the Montagnards were interpreted by Hanoi as a move to detach the Vietnam region by applying the old colonial formula "divide and rule". The Fontainebleau conference faltered on the question of sovereignty. What would be the subject of the Cochin-China referendum? How would the elections be organized and on what date? For the delegation from Hanoi, the question of Nambo belonging to Vietnam was not discussed and the comparison was already being readily made with Alsace-Lorraine; the purpose of the vote could only be to determine its place in the state. Paris had to stop humouring the crowds. It had to give a date for the referendum on self-determination. This could not be brought about by the colonial administration; the representatives of the Vietnamese government needed to participate in the control of operations. To none of these points did the French plenipotentiaries provide a satisfactory reply. Furthermore, the colonial officials in Saigon made repeated demands to stand firm. The high commissioner recommended the interruption of the negotiations: no concessions should be made to this band of agitators.

Agreement seemed most problematical on the interpretation of *doc lap*, and even more so on the unity of the three *ky*s. On 1 August, Pham Van Dong suspended talks. The excuse was provided by a new initiative from d'Argenlieu. He had just assembled delegates from Cochin-China, Laos and Cambodia[53] in Dalat to organize the Indo-China Federation, as well as show that in no case could Ho Chi Minh be considered as the sole spokesman in negotiations with the French. In denouncing the intransigence of the Viet Minh, *Le Monde* adequately reflected the official point of view: "We wish that public opinion would finally awake from its ideological dreams; we should like the public to realise what problems lie behind the conciliatory speeches and the roses.[54] France desires to establish a sincere and cordial accord in the Indo-China Federation. How could it permit the imposition of a new oppressive order on populations that have suffered one conquest after another? Because that is the aim."[55]

Should the guidelines of the declaration of 24 March be adhered to? D'Argenlieu considered it to be well on the way to implementation, since to complete the structure all that needed settling was the problem of Annam and Tongking. Or was it necessary resolutely to break new ground and accept that Vietnam had to gain its unity and independence soon? The fact that communists were running the government in Hanoi did not encourage the French to choose this line of action. Would a new imperial structure permit rapid evolution towards decolonization or was it only a question of secretly maintaining the old order? The question was not only being asked as far as Indo-China was concerned, even if Indo-China had prompted it, but for the whole French Union.

Since the Liberation, the question of the Empire and its evolution had given rise to wide-ranging and confused debates which scarcely convinced those who were unfamiliar with these problems. In fact, the general opinion was that colonization was justified and should remain permanent.[56] The positions of the major parties were ambiguous. According to Stalin "the question of the right of nations is not an isolated and self-contained problem; it is a part of the general question of the proletarian revolution, subordinate to the whole and demanding examination from the point of view of the whole."[57] Based on this analysis, the Communist Party admitted the theoretical right of every nation to independence, but in practice recognised that for now independence would be dangerous for most of the local populations; the colonies were "absolutely incapable of self-sufficiency economically and consequently politically as independent nations", and would risk falling under the domination of others. It was therefore necessary not to take a lead in dismembering the Empire, but to "create the conditions for a free, trusting and brotherly union of the colonial people with the people of France" by radical reform (as Thorez recalled at the 1945 party congress, using the expression employed in 1937 at Arles).[58] Although they were critical of colonialism, the Socialists mistrusted any surge of nationalism. In their opinion, the future lay with free cooperation between peoples. The French Union was to be one of those bodies which worked for the emancipation of individuals[59] by linking the motherland with its ex-colonies. While not repudiating its history of annexation, the Socialists recommended a kind of "democratic federalism". The MRP resorted to the teachings of Catholic tradition. Colonialism was legitimate but temporary and it involved granting rights and assuming responsibilities. Full of magnanimous sentiments, the MRP were ready to prove their generosity to the local peoples, but the left's actions often worried them. The major parties held 80 per cent of the seats and dominated the two assemblies. Trounced in the post-Liberation elections, the radicals and moderates did not make much of an impression, but claimed to know enough about foreign affairs to oppose the innovations.[60] The GPRF had granted the colonial world about sixty deputies. Indo-China, however, was not represented even though the setting up of the French Union and the solution of the Vietnamese question were closely connected. "Without the Empire, France would only be a liberated country today. Thanks to the Empire, France is a conquering country", noted the Guyanese deputy Monnerville on 25 May 1945, in a speech to the consultative assembly. Thanks to the role they had played and their loyalty,[61] the colonies deserved to be part of metropolitan France, or so their deputies thought, emphasizing the change in the international climate.

The constitution rejected by the French on 5 May 1946 mentioned the Union in an occasional paragraph, of somewhat heterogeneous inspiration, but its generally progressive tone led the few natives eligible to vote in the referendum to approve it overwhelmingly. The second constituent assembly gave more time to the question than did the first. In the commission, the "native" deputies, supported by the Communists and the Socialists, approved the adoption of a quite a novel plan. France "shall abandon all unilateral sovereignty over the colonized peoples. It recognizes their freedom to self-government and to conduct their own affairs democratically." The Union was thus conceived as a federation. Each territory would chose its regime. Details of the organization of this federation would be regulated by an Assembly of the Union elected by universal suffrage.

This egalitarian federalism, to be specified by a federal constituent assembly in which the representatives of the ex-colonies would be in a majority, seemed revolutionary to the head of government. Bidault, often all too ready to interfere in the commission's work, had the text withdrawn. On 20 August, the assembly began public discussion of the plan for the constitution. At first, Section VIII—which grouped together the articles covering the French Union—was attacked by the right, led by the Radicals Bastid and Herriot. The latter, having passionately praised colonization, the masterpiece of the Third Republic, resented the "acephalous" and "anarchic" federalism of Section VIII. Herriot quoted the example of the "well-constituted federalism" of the USSR, and spoke in favour of the "federating body—France."[62] These criticisms led to the separation of the issue of the French Union from the rest of the plan and the return to the commission of the "generous but insufficiently considered text on which the vote as it had been presented would 'by constitutionalizing the possible secession', condemn to death what only yesterday was being called the French Empire", wrote *Le Monde* on 29 August. Interfering once again in the task of drafting a constitution, the government in the person of Moutet, the Overseas Minister, had a new draft adopted. It was not until 18 September that the assembly could discuss the definitive text which was adopted on 21 September.

France with its overseas peoples forms a Union founded on the equality of rights and duties irrespective of race or religion.

The French Union consists of nations and people who share or co-ordinate their resources and their efforts to develop their respective civilizations, to improve their well-being and to ensure their security.

Faithful to its traditional mission, France intends to lead the peoples for which it has accepted responsibility to freedom of self-administration, and to the freedom to conduct their own affairs democratically; utterly denouncing colonization based on arbitrary power, it guarantees equal access to all men to public services and the individual or collective exercise of the rights and liberties proclaimed above.

The principles had been laid down before the end of the constitutional statement of intent. The traditional vocabulary had disappeared (no more mention of natives, empire, colonies) and the inspiration was eminently progressive. Yet even now a need arose for ambiguity. Was the proclaimed equality between individuals or the equality between peoples? Was there not a contradiction between the first two paragraphs which seemed to recognize the disappearance of the colonial status quo, and the last which justified French domination?.

Art. 60. The French Union consists, on the one hand, of the French Republic which includes mainland France, the overseas departments and territories, and on the other the territories and associated states.

Art. 61. The position of the associated states in the French Union arises for each state from the act which defines its relationship with France.

ART. 62. The members of the French Union combine all their resources to guarantee the defence of the whole of the Union. The government of the Republic assumes the co-ordination of these resources and the administration of the appropriate policy to prepare and ensure this defence.

ART. 63. The central bodies of the French Union are the presidency of the French Union whose permanent interests it represents.

ART. 64. Under the chairmanship of the president of the Union, the high council of the French Union is composed of a delegation of the French government and representation which each of the associated states may agree with the president of the Union. Its function is to assist the government in the general conduct of the Union.

ART. 71. The assembly of the French Union is familiar with programmes and proposals which are submitted to it for consideration [...].

So, the French government had "the general management of the Union",[63] the high council not being a decision-making but merely a consultative body. As for the assembly of the Union, it was only the shadow of the large legislative body desired by some. Relegated, in fact, to the statement of intent of this composite text, progressive principles grew more and more vague as the realities dawned. Many nationalist leaders referred to Houphouët-Boigny's statement at the 19 September meeting: "On one side, the generous principles which unfortunately do not have the force of law. On the other, the formulation through a constitutional text of an accomplished fact." In any case, it was clear that as an associated state, Vietnam—of which moreover, there had been little mention in the constitutional debate—could not enjoy independence in a French Union conceived in this way. Article 62, which had been added at Herriot's instigation, was opposed to it. As Lord Salisbury once said, "The shield protecting the empire must be held in a single hand."

The Vietnamese delegation left Paris before the assembly adopted the articles of the constitution relating to the French Union. However, Ho Chi Minh extended his stay and at the last moment he signed a partial agreement with Moutet covering what they had already discussed at length. Through this working agreement of 14 September 1946, "the two governments believe the time has come to mark a new step in the development of relations between France and Vietnam, expecting circumstances to be right for the conclusion of a complete and definitive agreement." The negotiations would resume as soon as possible, at the latest in January 1947. France—and the French Union—would then have a constitution and the Fourth Republic would finally be in place. In the meantime, the Vietnamese government agreed to put an end to the "acts of hostility and violence in Cochin-China" and recognized the principle of monetary and customs union in Indo-China.[64] The creation of mixed commissions was arranged for the problems which remained unresolved. After making these concessions, Ho Chi Minh left France. On 20 October, after more talks with Admiral d'Argenlieu in the China Sea, he disembarked in Haiphong and resumed contact with a country in which the situation had rapidly changed during his absence.

In the Nambo, Giau had been dismissed, and guerilla warfare had been resumed by Nguyen Binh, nicknamed "the one-eyed". This former member of the VNQDD revealed himself to be an excellent organizer. By 30 October, when the fighting ceased because the working agreement came into force, the Viet Minh held a large part of the Cochin-Chinese countryside, from which eminent citizens and civil servants had fled. In the towns, movements and newspapers sharply criticised the Thinh government's policy. If "unionism" had not been accepted, "separatism" would not have much success either. Anyway, the circumstances called for prudence. Ho Chi Minh had just been received in Paris as a true head of state, so why be compromised in a dubious act when unification would doubtless happen soon under the control of the people in Hanoi? Thinh had been reduced by the French to a subordinate power, attacked for his weakness by the colonial hardliners grouped into the UDOFI.[65] He was hardly backed by the population, and felt that the attempt was bound to fail. Exhausted and bitter, he committed suicide on 9 November.

On that same day, the national assembly meeting in the Tongkingese capital proclaimed the constitution of Vietnam. It was a highly democratic constitution (but hypothetical in view of the circumstances) but did not mention the Indo-China Federation nor the French Union and combined Cochin-China with the national territories. Only 242 deputies participated in the meeting. The departure of the Chinese allowed Giap to conduct a far-reaching purge. The Luhan forces, in fact, had finally left the country during the summer, though not without increasing the number of incidents right up to the last moment. Having run out of excuses to stay, they were all too ready at times during their retreat to make their way home, as if overwhelmed by regret. Giap's troops replaced the Luhan forces shortly afterwards, establishing Viet Minh power in the zones recently controlled by the DMG or the VNQDD. In Hanoi, looting and arrests continued until October. Thus, when the assembly met again in November the Viet Minh opposition had disappeared, at least officially. Most of its leaders had managed to reach China. Some had managed to gain backing where they were. The new Ho Chi Minh government now consisted only of men faithful to the president. The Kuomintang's protégés had not put an end to their provocations, and were still making nationalist promises. Refusing to participate in the Fontainebleau conference, they let it be understood that the negotiators were traitors, because they had reached a compromise with colonialism. The French did not therefore oppose the purge, and may even have contributed to it in their benevolent neutrality.

Rid of the Chinese, the Viet Minh only needed to fear the colonizer's presence. There were boycotts of imported goods, intimidation, action by the only trade union.[68] Pressure was exerted to force the French to abandon their interests, while ever more frequent incidents set the two armies against each other.[69] Convinced of a stalemate in the negotiations, Giap was actively preparing to resume the fighting. The economic and financial policy of the revolutionary government was directed to this end. People had to get used to poverty and national self-sufficiency; they had to sacrifice the state's scanty resources to buy as many arms as they could. Giap assembled an army of 50,000 men, highly trained ideologically, and advised, if needed, by Japanese deserters. These regular, well-trained units were doubled in size by the addition of the self-defence militia (the *tu vê*). Because a protracted war was expected, bases were organised in the highlands and provisions stockpiled. Hanoi reverberated every day to sirens summoning militiamen, soldiers and workers to physical training and military exercises. The population was mobilized for different reasons almost on a daily basis. The young people were particularly receptive to this conditioning.[70]

The French and Vietnamese had been arguing over the question of customs since early autumn. The former wanted the working agreement which gave them control of the Federation; they wanted to collect duties immediately, because for the time being the high commission ruled Indo-China. This interpretation was forcefully contested by Hanoi. Whilst the delegations quibbled over the constitution of the mixed commissions provided for in the 14 September agreement, incidents were becoming more widespread. On 20 November, a detachment was making its way to the cemetery when it was attacked at Langson, and a French boat towing a contraband launch that the military police had just seized was fired on in Haiphong. Barricades were set up, lone soldiers were killed in towns, the shooting was becoming more widespread. General Morlière, commander of the Tongking troops, managed to obtain a ceasefire on the 21st. His desire to prevent confrontation at any price was shared neither by his subordinate, Colonel Dèbes, who administered the Haiphong sector, nor by his superior, General Valluy, who had replaced Leclerc in July and was acting as interim high commissioner in the absence of the Admiral, who was once again in Paris. Valluy pleaded for a policy of firmness towards the Viet Minh. On 22 November, the commander-in-chief sent this order to Morlière and Dèbes: "The time has come to give a hard lesson to those who have treacherously attacked us. You must make yourselves absolute masters of Haiphong by all the means at your disposal and force the command of the Vietnamese army to repent." The following day, after launching an ultimatum, the French moved in to attack. The air force and navy took part in the assault. On the 28th Dèbes was in total control of the town.

The same day, the Bidault government resigned. The institutions of the Fourth Republic were becoming established. In spite of the opposition of de Gaulle, the French voted *yes* in the referendum of 13 October. On 10 November, they voted for the national assembly. The composition of the new chamber was similar to that of the two constituent assemblies. It was dominated by three parties. This time, the Communists with 183 seats outstripped the MRP (167 seats) and the Socialists (105 seats). The Communist success made the constitution of the new ministry difficult. The demands of the "first party of France" were unacceptable for the MRP which led its campaign with the theme "Bidault without Thorez". Blum was then called in as the traditional recourse to the old and wise in difficult times, hoping they can rise above the confusion. The Socialist leader resolved to set up an all-party ministry in which the immutable Marius Moutet was responsible for colonial policy. It was agreed that this would be only a transitional government responsible for leading the country for some weeks until the institutions of the new regime were in place. Blum was sworn in on 12 December. On the previous day, he had stated in the *Populaire* that Vietnam's independence should be recognized.[73]

Could the change of ministry permit the settlement of the Haiphong affair and the resumption of negotiations on the question of sovereignty and unity? On 15 December, Ho Chi Minh sent a message to this end to the new president of the Council, which was taken as a sign of good will amongst other things. On 6 December, Hanoi had launched an appeal on the radio to the French assembly. On 11 December, the head of the

Vietnamese government gave an interview to *Paris-Saigon* in which he stated: "We want to avoid this war at any cost. We are passionate for our independence within the French Union." From 2 December onwards, discussions took place almost daily with Sainteny, who after having left his post in June for personal reasons, had finally agreed to return for his peace of mind.

While Ho Chi Minh appeared conciliatory, Giap was increasing his military preparations. Trenches were dug in the roads of Hanoi, barricades were set up, walls between houses were smashed to facilitate street fighting. French people were kidnapped or murdered. Others would try and avenge them. Giap was convinced that confrontation was inevitable and that in spite of the changes made by the war, French colonialism could not give way on the essential issue. He believed in using force to put an end to the manoeuvrings and feeble machinations of the high commission. He feared that after Haiphong,[74] the expeditionary force would attempt to strike in Hanoi, and re-attempting the operation of 23 September in Saigon would try to take control of the town and even of the Vietnamese government. He decided to move into action quickly while his forces had a numerical advantage.

On 19 December, appeasement seemed to prevail. In the morning, Ho Chi Minh sent a friendly note to Sainteny while it was suggested to General Morlière that he cancel the order confining the troops to barracks to defuse the atmosphere. In the afternoon, the French authorities learned through their agents that the Viet Minh were preparing to strike that night. The men on leave who had just left the town were hastily recalled. An attempt was even made to assemble as many European civilians as possible. At 8.00 pm, sabotage of the electrical power station plunged Hanoi into darkness. Trees were cut down and the level crossings were obstructed by wagons to hinder the passage of the French troops. Mines were placed at crossroads. Throughout the town, the *tu vé* attacked the positions of the expeditionary force and the houses of the colonists. The order from Giap was "arrest the invaders and save the nation". Dozens of civilians (whites and Eurasians) were killed or taken hostage.[75] Sainteny was wounded. But Giap did not manage to repeat the Japanese success of 9 March 1945. Morlière's troops resisted. On 20 December, they occupied the town centre where they had besieged the public buildings. Ho Chi Minh, who had sought refuge about six miles outside of Hanoi, made an appeal on 21 December for a struggle to the bitter end. Only after the end of hostilities did the message sent on 15 December by the Vietnamese president reach Blum. The message had been "retained" by Saigon. While the United States was granting the Philippines the independence which had been promised before the war and delayed by the Japanese, while Great Britain was relinquishing the Indian sub-continent, the Fourth Republic was establishing itself just as its first colonial war was beginning.

4

A Forgotten Colonial War

Each side blamed the other for the confrontation. The Vietnamese quoted the provocative behaviour of the colonialists and made much of the Haiphong affair.[1] The high commission maintained that the French had shown great patience and had tried against all the odds to come to a negotiated settlement. The French, they added, could have "licked" the revolutionary authorities. They didn't do so, even though the simultaneity of the attacks on 19 December showed clearly enough who had decided to resort to violence. The press in the French capital—which had no correspondent in Hanoi—eagerly repeated the statements coming out of Saigon, describing the horrors and defeat of this night of the long knives.

Did the spread of the fighting cause the prospect of a negotiated solution to disappear? After sending Minister Moutet and General Leclerc to ascertain the situation, Blum told the deputies on 23 December that "It is a question of taking up where we left off, in other words of establishing a free Vietnam within an Indo-Chinese Union freely associated with the French Union. But above all, peace, which will act as a necessary basis for the contracts to be performed, must be re-established." D'Argenlieu arrived in Saigon on the day the Prime Minister made his declaration. Having constantly advocated a firm approach during his stay in Paris, he arranged Moutet's visit in such a way as to ensure that the latter would return convinced that the Viet Minh leaders could no longer be considered worthy negotiators, and that their calls for the talks to be recommenced were mere propaganda. The position of the high commission was made very clear in an interview given to France-Soir on 2 January 1947: "It is no longer possible for us to deal with Ho Chi Minh. We will find other people in the country with whom we can deal, who will also no doubt be nationalists, but these people have disqualified themselves." Bao Dai already appeared to be a viable solution. The ex-Emperor, still officially an advisor to the revolutionary government, had been living in Hong Kong for several months.

In his report to the government, the Admiral suggested that Bao Dai be reinstated. Anticipating the events of 1947, he considered the Indo-Chinese affair to be part of the cold war. In February, d'Argenlieu suggested capturing the revolutionary government, whose whereabouts had been determined as the Hadong Caves, some ten kilometres from Hanoi. Paris rejected this proposal. A few days later, d'Argenlieu was replaced by Bollaert, who had been a prominent member of the French Resistance and who had the additional merit of not being an outspoken opponent of the regime.[2]

On 22 January 1947, the first government of the Fourth Republic took office. It consisted of nine SFIO members, five Communists and five MRP deputies; the tripartite system continued under the leadership of the Socialist Ramadier. In his inaugural speech, the new Prime Minister spoke of the "union of the three Annamitic countries" and mentioned the word "independence" but qualified it by adding "within the framework of the French Union and the Indo-Chinese Federation."[3] In fact, the government was strongly divided over the problem of Vietnam, as the Council of 5 March clearly showed, when a debate only led to a negative decision, that of relieving the Admiral of his post. The MRP was not insensitive to the theories put forward by d'Argenlieu, but the Communist Party called for the immediate resumption of talks with Ho Chi Minh. Addressing the assembly on 14 January, with all the authority of his years, Marcel Cachin considered that it was "not too late to resume discussions with Vietnam, based on the agreement of 6 March 1946". And the account in the *Journal officiel* recorded "strong opposition from the right and centre". Although hostile to voting for military credits, the Communists did not, however, wish to bring down the coalition government on this matter. Ramadier put the motion for a vote of no confidence, but the Communist deputies did vote, and Communist ministers gave the ministry their support (22 March).[4] Strange indeed were the sessions that took place during that March, at which Minister of Defence Billoux refused to participate in the tribute paid by the chamber to the troops on active service, and the revolutionaries resorted to the kind of tactics which had previously seemed the prerogative of the reactionary radicals. The SFIO, which devoted its National Council of the 19 and 20 March to discussing the French Union, using the theme of "No surrender or return to outdated colonialism", appeared hesitant. Vigorous anti-colonialist feelings were being expressed within the bodies closest to home (the National Council and the Congress) which were hardly echoed in practice by the Ministers responsible, such as Ramadier and Moutet. This discrepancy between militant phraseology and government action was to be a feature of much of the Fourth Republic. Concerning negotiations in Indo-China, on 20 March Lussy stated in the name of his faction to the assembly: "As far as we are concerned, we do not accept that a single name should be added or removed." To paper over the splits in the party, the SFIO recommended a full debate.

This was the policy that the new high commissioner outlined in his Hanoi speech on 15 May. "France will stay in Indo-China and Indo-China will remain at the heart of the French Union. That is the basis of our policy. Let the representatives of all its political parties come to us. I repeat, of all its parties, for we do not accept that any party has the monopoly in representing the Vietnamese people." Three authorities could act as participants in the dialogue: the Viet Minh, the Cochin-Chinese government now led by the Caodaist Lê Van Hoach, and the Front of the National Union of Vietnam, which had just been formed in Southern China from the nationalist splinter groups suppressed by Giap the year before. On 19 April, Ho Chi Minh, who had been blowing hot and cold since December, issued a new and solemn appeal for negotiations, putting Socialist ministers in a tight spot. The Saigon authorities balked at the idea of dealing with the perpetrators of the 19 December coup. They kept on repeating "We made Ho Chi Minh what he is." In their view, the French had recognized the Hanoi government in 1946, accorded it privileged status in the discussions, recognized its president as head of state, facilitated the liquidation of the anti-Viet Minh groups in Tongking—in others words they had legitimized and buttressed the power of a revolutionary party which wanted nothing more than their complete departure.[5] Everyone now knew where these policies had led and recriminations were absolutely useless.

Paul Mus, an advisor of Bollaert's, did not share this view. He was appointed by the high commission to make contact with the Vietnamese government. In the Viet Bac jungle he met with the Minister of Foreign Affairs, the Socialist Giam. Then, on 12 May, he met Ho Chi Minh to whom he set out the French plans for a ceasefire, plans drawn up by General Valluy and ratified by Ramadier. The Viet Minh were to refrain from any hostilities, to let the troops of the expeditionary force move around freely, hand over part of its military equipment and return hostages, prisoners and deserters. These conditions were rejected, since they were considered to be tantamount to surrender. Each party denounced the other for its lack of good faith. For Saigon, Ho Chi Minh's refusal was sufficient proof that his calls for negotiations were nothing more than propaganda. To the Viet Minh it seemed that the colonialists, by effectively demanding a capitulation, were entirely responsible for the continuation of the fighting.[6] Once the obstacle created by Ho Chi Minh had been removed, as the parliamentary jargon of the time put it, the Bao Dai solution could be implemented.

The circumstances were favourable, both at a national and international level. On 5 May, the tripartite arrangement broke down. The Communist Party ministers were ousted after differences of opinion over economic and social policies.[7]

A few days after Ramadier's decision, the other Western European governments shed their Communist ministers. In September, at a conference of European Communist parties held in Poland, the French delegates were reprimanded. It was explained to them that the world was divided into two opposing blocs. The meeting concluded with the formation of the Cominform. From then on, the French Communists readopted the tactic of "class warfare" and were again relegated to a political ghetto. In November, it dragged the Confédération générale du Travail (the French equivalent of the British TUC or the American AFL-CIO) into violent strike action which seemed to signal a desire for insurrection. France thus entered the torment of the cold war. It became the norm to think of problems, and in particular those in Indo-China, in terms of East-West confrontation.

With the Communists gone, the MRP and SFIO had to govern with the Radicals and a section of the moderates. The Socialists, who had hitherto been in the centre of the tripartite coalition, found themselves pushed to the left where they were at the heart of the third force. At the beginning of the war in Indo-China, they had played a crucial role in French colonial policy, since they held both the Premiership and the Ministry for French Overseas Territories. That autumn, they lost both posts to the MRP.

Thenceforward, the MRP played a major role from its central position in determining and conducting policy in Indo-China. Throughout the period that the Bao Dai solution was being formulated, the Popular Republican Coste-Floret was Minister for French Overseas Territories. This was the same Coste-Floret who, prior to holding this portfolio in the Schuman government (from November 1947 to July 1948), had already been involved in the Vietnamese problem, not in a conciliatory capacity towards the Viet Minh, but as Minister for War in the Ramadier cabinet.

Meanwhile in China, vain attempts at agreement and a final, short truce in June 1946 were followed by a resumption in the fighting between Mao and Chiang. In the United States, President Truman had just announced his policy of containment. The leaders of the Kuomintang and the American forces supporting them thus forced the Vietnamese nationalists who had taken refuge in China to break with the revolutionary government. There could be no question of a sacred union against colonialism, as had been advocated by some of these refugees since the outbreak of hostilities. The Front of the National Union of Vietnam, which had been formed only a month previously, "withdrew its support for the Ho Chi Minh government (which represented only the Communists)" at its congress in Canton in late March, placing itself under Bao Dai's authority. A campaign was mounted within the three *ky*s for the restoration of the monarchy. It had the support of certain Caodaists, representatives of the mandarinate and of the provisional administrative committees which the French had just established in Hué and Hanoi.

Bao Dai was sounded out, financed and sought after, but he adopted a very prudent line. At first, he may have feared that the overtures made towards him were no more than a means found by the French to bring the Viet Minh to conciliation talks. Had not a leader like Blum not proposed in *Le Populaire* on 6 August that negotiations be renewed?[8] Giap, considered by many to have been behind the 19 December coup, was pushed aside in a reshuffle of the revolutionary government on 19 July. Was this not a conciliatory gesture which might bring about a ceasefire?[9] In fact, some of his advisors, unwilling to give up hope of a negotiated settlement, urged the high commissioner to make a peace initiative. Bollaert decided to strike a blow for peace in a speech he was going to make on 15 August, the day on which India was to be granted independence. He would declare himself openly in favour of the sovereignty and unity of Vietnam, and would not hesitate to use the word "independence", although he would add "within the framework of the French Union", a phrase not challenged by Ho Chi Minh. In any case, it was intended by the weight of the comment to make the Viet Minh and international opinion realise—this being the eve of the United Nations general assembly—that France was ready for a real transfer of sovereignty. Bollaert's speech was to announce an end to the military operations so that the dynamics of peace could be set in motion. The cessation was to be unilateral and reversible, under an ingenious plan which linked the prolongation of the truce to the acceptance by the enemy of certain specific conditions. The French would thus suspend hostilities on 15 August, but the suspension was to be confirmed from 1 September onwards only if hostages had been freed by that date.[10]

The plan aroused strong opposition in political circles in Saigon (especially those whose sympathies lay with the MRP or the young RPF) and particularly in General Valluy. The Commander-in-Chief countered Bollaert's argument that it was a good time to negotiate since the Viet Minh were now in a weaker position with his own theory that the Viet Minh indeed being more vulnerable this was no time to give it any grounds for optimism. The two men were called to Paris and the government postponed the date of the speech. Then from one draft to another it was polished, cut and watered down so much so that the text finally read out in Hadong on 10 September, in which the word "independence" did not appear, said nothing really new. Paris seemed to abandon once and for all any idea of coming to an understanding with Ho Chi Minh. Bao Dai could abandon his reserve.[11]

In an address to the Vietnamese people on 18 September, Bao Dai denounced the dictatorship of the revolutionary government, to whom he still officially acted as advisor. He declared himself "ready to make contact with the French authorities", but only so as to obtain independence and unity. Once this had been achieved, he would use his "authority to arbitrate the conflict" between the Vietnamese. Presenting himself as a patriot and mediator who stood apart from the crowd, the ex-Emperor had not openly broken with the "Democratic Republic". The opportunities opened up remained vague. The first step had been made, but the developments the French right wing was counting on were still a long way off. For them, the Viet Minh's authority having been challenged, it was a question of finding a more understanding interlocutor. As many forces as possible had to be gathered around Bao Dai so as to isolate the nationalist movement and reduce Ho Chi Minh to the role of communist guerilla leader. Relying on the traditionalism of the masses, the ex-Emperor, to whom formal concessions could be made, would guarantee the bulk of French interests and would at last permit the existence of an associated state of Vietnam under the terms set by the constitution, safeguarding the structure of the French Union. With the colonial status quo on the one hand and a nationalist-communist revolution on the other, the Bao Dai solution appeared as a third option which nevertheless fitted into the framework of the incipient cold war. However the Emperor, considered a *bon viveur* who was easily manipulated, was to reveal himself a tough politician who did not want to return to power as a puppet of the high commission but as the leader of a united and sovereign state.

It was not until December 1947 that direct talks began between Bollaert and citizen Vinh Thuy, Paris having ruled out any possibility of talks with Ho Chi Minh.[12] The Along Bay meeting led to the signing of a dual document. It consisted of a short joint declaration in principle to satisfy Vietnamese nationalism, plus a lengthy protocol which withdrew item by item what had supposedly been offered as a whole and cast serious doubts over the theoretical recognition of independence. When the ex-Emperor returned to Hong Kong, his entourage strongly criticized the document. For several months, Bao Dai manoeuvred and dithered but, after a futile trip to France, he finally agreed to see the high commissioner again so as to make the December agreement official.

This time, General Xuan attended the second meeting at Along Bay. He had replaced Hoach at the head of the Cochin-Chinese government in 1947. Educated at the Ecole Polytechnique in Paris, Xuan had support amongst certain members of the left in the French capital. In between the revolution represented by Ho Chi Minh and the reaction symbolized by the ex-Emperor, was there not room for a third option? Could one not see Xuan, having eliminated both of them, creating a Vietnamese Republic whose association with the French Republic would be the easier since both states were based on the same fundamental principles? If Bao Dai was the candidate supported by Catholic circles and by the right, ranging from the MRP to the RPF, Xuan seemed to be supported by the Freemasons and the Socialist Party. From the time he assumed power, Xuan challenged Cochin-Chinese separatism.[13] He simultaneously posed as a mediator, making overtures towards members of the underground and towards Hong Kong. Early in 1948, he discussed the possibility with Bao Dai of creating a national Vietnamese government. Vinh Thuy, meanwhile, accepted this proposal, while increasing his semantic precautions. This would be, he stated on 26 March 1948, a matter of a "provisional" cabinet, intended only to "conclude with France a *modus vivendi* with limited effect", in case "the existing revolutionary government, as a result of unfavourable circumstances internationally", was not in a position to lead the negotiations. The high commissioner agreed to this formula and in April, Xuan moved towards the idea of a "central provisional government of Vietnam", consisting of ministers from the Cochin-Chinese cabinet as well as from the administrative committees in Hanoi and Hué.

    1. France formally recognizes the independence of Vietnam, which must now freely bring about its unification. For its part, Vietnam declares its membership of the French Union as a state associated with France. The independence of Vietnam has no restrictions other than those imposed upon it through its member-

ship of the French Union.

2. Vietnam undertakes to respect the rights and interests of French nationals, unconditionally to ensure respect for democratic principles and to call upon French advisors and experts to give priority to the task of organizing its internal affairs and economy.

3. As soon as a provisional government is formed, Vietnamese representatives, together with representatives of the French Republic, will enact the various specific, appropriate measures of a cultural, diplomatic, military, economic, financial and technical nature.

Produced in two copies, at Along Bay, on the fifth day of June nineteen hundred and forty-eight.

Although the declaration was published, the protocol, now officially renamed a "*modus vivendi* with limited effect", remained secret. Bao Dai was thus merely a "witness" to the agreement, for which the Xuan government accepted responsibility, evidence of the great caution he was again exhibiting concerning the extent of his involvement. He accepted the formation of a central government and the signature of the Along Bay documents. Yet he allowed Xuan to compromise himself, while he waited, before returning home to take over the leadership, for the French to give concrete proof of their recognition of the unity and independence of Vietnam, for Cochin-China to be truly integrated, for power to be transferred to the central government and for the text of the "*modus vivendi*" to be modified in a way that was favourable to Vietnamese sovereignty.

The agreement had barely been signed when Coste-Floret gave it his own restrictive interpretation. Speaking in the national assembly on 8 June 1948, he said:

I have mentioned on several occasions to the high commissioner of France the desire of the government of the Republic to maintain the unity of the Union in terms of diplomacy and defence. I informed him that the Vietnamese armed forces constituted police forces charged with the internal security of the country. Lastly, as for the status of Cochin-Cchina, it has been clearly stated that the documents which were to be signed at Along Bay would not imply the automatic recognition of the union of the three *ky*s by France, but that France would await the actions of the Xuan government before adopting a definite stance. The French government made no pronouncement at that time concerning the union of the three *ky*s. It will not oppose the unification of Vietnam, if this is the wish democratically expressed by the people. It insists that no change in the status of Cochin-China can occur without the consent of the sovereign parliament. The status of the three Vietnamese-speaking countries, established under the treaty signed with the Court of Annam, has therefore not changed.

Whereas some ministers such as Bidault were slamming on the brakes and certain Gaullists were threatening to sell the Empire off cheaply, in Indo-China itself those in favour of retaining the status of colony, including several leading Cochin-Chinese, denounced the abandonment of the colony—an "integral part of French territory"[14]— and colonial officials retained their powers. Furthermore, the Xuan government was exposed to quarrelling factions; discredited and lacking in authority, it appeared to be merely a continuation of d'Argenlieu's Cochin-Chinese manoeuvre, and other groups besides the Viet Minh referred to it as a "puppet" government.

It seemed that whenever there was one step forward, there would be another one step back. The prevaricating, bargaining, manoeuvring, and shuttling back and forth continued for another year before the Bao Dai solution materialized. In March 1949, an exchange of letters between Auriol, acting in his capacity of President of the French Union,[15] and the ex-Emperor settled in detail the terms under which Vietnamese independence would be established. In April, a Cochin-Chinese assembly, elected for the purpose by an electoral college of notables (of whom the French formed a large minority), voted for the integration of the colony.[16] Bao Dai could return to Indo-China and assume the leadership of the "state of Vietnam" which was proclaimed on 2 July 1949. Though affirmed and reaffirmed, its independence was accompanied by numerous restrictions, especially in matters of a military and diplomatic, but even of an economic, nature. The war and the state's position as a member of the French Union justified these limitations, as did membership of the Indo-Chinese Union. Indeed, the idea of an Indo-Chinese state was quickly abandoned. The agreements of 1949 foresaw a monetary and tariff union, under French control of course, between Cambodia, Laos and Vietnam, as well as the continuation of joint technical services. Although for two years the Emperor's return had been heralded and there had been the granting of an independence and unity without any substance to them, the actual arrival of Bao Dai and the constitution of the single state of Vietnam did not rouse much enthusiasm or passion, especially since he disappeared yet again. He was expected to arrive amid pomp and ceremony. Instead, he made a discreet arrival and then, refusing to take up residence in Saigon, for there could be no question of handing over to him the Norodom Palace which was the seat of the high commission, he withdrew to a distance, taking up residence in Dalat.[17] But this was of no importance. The Bao Dai solution had at last been carried out, even if this had meant granting the sovereign what Ho Chi Minh had been refused.

Both Bao Dai and Xuan, now vice-Premier of the new government, claimed to be mediators right until the end. On 1 May 1949, the General was still stating: "The possibility of Ho Chi Minh serving in a future government is not excluded *a priori*." During his Hanoi trip in July, the new head of state laid a wreath in honour of the Viet Minh fighters who died in December 1946. Such gestures, which greatly annoyed the French, were not to be repeated. The main thing was that from then on a new government, a new legitimate entity, a new nationalism, claiming it would achieve total independence through negotiations rather than violence, was in opposition to the members of the underground. In August 1949, the delegation of the Democratic Republic of Vietnam in Paris decided to close its doors. It was to have fallen to Pignon, now high commissioner, to implement the final stages of a solution which, as advisor to Admiral d'Argenlieu, he had been advocating since the beginning of the war, as he wrote in a note on 4 January 1947: "Our objective, which we have already clearly stated, is to transfer our dispute with the Viet Minh party into the Annamite interior, and to involve ourselves as little as possible in campaigns and reprisals which should be dealt with by opponents of that party within the country itself."[18]

The political situation seemed simpler and more clearly defined in the two monarchies to the west of Vietnam. In 1949, while they were installing Bao Dai on the throne, the French noted with satisfaction that the two monarchs whom they were "protecting", in Phnom Penh and in Luang Prabang, had apparently regained control of their respective countries. In Cambodia, the *modus vivendi* signed in January 1946 had defined the new status for the kingdom, on a principle of internal autonomy. This autonomy, however, was seriously restricted through membership of the Indo-Chinese Union, whose authority was ensured, for the time being at least, by the high commissioner. The *modus vivendi*, however, broke with certain past practices. For instance, French residents were replaced by Khmer officials (backed up by counsellors), and direct administration was being phased out. In a word, the supposed internal autonomy had more in common with a protectorate. As Bourguiba was to remark, when the French speak of a protectorate, they really mean direct administration—if they talk of internal autonomy, they mean protectorate, and what they call independence is nothing more than internal autonomy.

The real innovation in the kingdom was the upsurge of genuine political activity. Sihanouk and the French agreed to establish a representative regime. The transition from absolute monarchy to constitutional monarchy was theoretically to occur following consultation with the people. In September 1946, an assembly was elected by direct universal suffrage. The Democrats won 50 of the 67 seats. They had just called for a "return to France"; now they dominated the assembly. This grouping, which was linked with the left in the French capital, was intended to appear as the embodiment of modernity and Khmer patriotism. It was led by Prince Youthevong,[19] and immediately gained the support of a large section of the young people and administration of the country. It turned the chamber, in principle consultative, into a true constituent assembly. In May 1947, Cambodia acquired institutions partially modelled on those of the Fourth Republic. The king, who in theory was the source of all power, found himself placed, in practice, at the head of an assembly over which the Democrats once again ruled after their victory in the legislative elections of November 1947. Indeed, the Khmer chamber and the cabinet attached to it exercised little power. The blind hostility shown towards the French by the ruling political party caused them considerable anxiety, especially since certain leaders of the grouping were known to have links with the "Issarak" (free) Khmer groups that had come into existence since colonial government had been re-established.

In fact, behind the slogans, the political struggle barely masked the traditional opposition of the two branches of the royal family, the rivalries between princes and clans and their supporters. In the Democratic party itself, unity did not even outlive Youthevong, who died in July 1947. Thus, although the party enjoyed an absolute majority, the contest for lucrative posts, the attempts of the nationalist to outbid each other[20] and the battles between individuals and factions, all entailed ministerial instability. Sihanouk, who had been kept on the sidelines by the turbulent assembly, took advantage of the dissension at the heart of the majority party and dissolved the chamber on 18 September 1949. His government did not arrange for new elections, on the pretext of the instability prevalent in certain regions of the country. Once he had rid himself of any parliamentary opposition, and comforted by the allegiance of one of the most important Issarak leaders (Dap Chuon), Sihanouk was able to initiate discussions immediately with the high commissioner.

Since the concessions made to Bao Dai, the kingdom could not feel satisfied with the *modus vivendi* of 1946. In December 1948, a letter from Auriol to the monarch along the lines of the Along Bay accords had talked of "the independence of Cambodia within the framework of the French union". It was now a question of this concept becoming reality. The negotiations moved at a brisk pace, the Franco-Vietnamese accords serving as an example. In November 1949, the Franco-Khmer treaty was signed, abolishing the protectorate conventions and recognizing the independence of the kingdom in Article 1.

In Laos, the situation at the start had been complicated by the Chinese occupation. The occupation had deferred the return of the French and given Prime Minister Pethsarath the chance to proclaim the unity and independence of the country, and become Lao head of state (Pathet Lao). The francophile King Sisavang had been forced to abdicate in his favour. Two of Pethsarath's brothers,[21] Souvanna Phouma and Souphanouvong, who had engineered the "return to France" were members of this government of princes. The latter, who was known to have links with the Vietnamese, had taken over the Ministry of Defence and the command of the weak Lao Issara (Free Laos) forces. The signing of the Franco-Chinese accords in February 1946 had led to the armed return of the colonizer and the monarchy, and to the exile of the Pathet Lao government in Siam. A Franco-Laotian treaty, modelled on the Cambodian *modus vivendi*, was signed in August. Thenceforward, the King of Luang Prabang exerted his power over the whole country and even, like the Cambodian monarchy, regained the provinces lost in 1941. The beginnings of the new regime were not easy. While the influential families fought for power and its benefits in a country ruined by Chinese plundering, the new administration showed remarkable incompetence, and its arrogant domination aroused the hostility of the ethnic minorities. Bands of Lao Isara fighters were beginning to exacerbate an already unstable situation.

In July 1949, the country gained "independence within the framework of the French Union". The royal government and the French services used the treaty to make the Pathet Lao end its resistance. Souphanouvong, who by now almost qualified as a dissident, had for a long time been a source of anxiety to his colleagues, both ministers and princes, due to his close links with the Viet Minh. They wanted sovereignty and power, but not revolution, and furthermore they feared the hegemony of their powerful neighbour. The Bangkok government declared its own dissolution in October. Souvanna Phouma and the majority of ministers returned home, Souphanouvong being left to continue the struggle alone.[22] This event gave new hope to the supporters of the Bao Dai solution, but Vietnam was not Laos and the Viet Minh was not the Pathet Lao.

FIGHTING

France had been forced to grant semi-independence to Laos and Cambodia, so as to bring the situation in those countries in line with that of Vietnam, and not because armed resistance, which had never been a great threat, had forced them to do so. In 1949, Souphanouvong's forces were reduced to a few bands in the Annamite mountain range at points of contact with zones held by the Viet Minh. As for the Issarak Khmers, some were active along the border with Thailand, others at the edges of Cochin-China with the help of the troops of Nguyen Binh. Vast areas, and notably most farming land, were practically unaffected by the "rebellion". In 1949, the Indo-Chinese war was still essentially a Vietnamese war.

Giap's coup had placed the expeditionary corps in a critical situation. Yet all the military positions held fast, except the small Vinh garrison, which was forced to surrender. The fighting was particularly fierce in Hanoi, where the recapture of the town was led by General Morlière, whose conduct prior to 19 December had been criticized, before he was relieved of his command.[23] Having quickly recaptured the European quarter, French troops, provided with fresh supplies by what amounted to an air shuttle service from Haiphong, encountered stubborn resistance in the narrow, winding streets of the native quarter. Subjected to a blockade, the sector was not completely "cleaned up" until 17 February, after the last *tu vé* had fled by river. Two months of fighting had left a town in ruins, abandoned by most of the inhabitants. The women, children and old people had been evacuated by agreement during the fighting. The imperial capital, in which a French battalion had withstood a seven-week siege, was also littered with debris, and the palace ransacked. Thanks to its military superiority, within three months the expeditionary force had liberated its garrisons, occupied the main towns and taken control of the major roads used by its convoys of armoured vehicles. The French held their Vietnam, the Vietnam they had helped to create, with its modern cities and wide roads. But, in Annam and Tongking, this French Vietnam had been partially destroyed. The Viet Minh had blocked the roads, razed any multi-story buildings to the ground and totally annihilated various small colonial towns such as Hadong and Hoa Binh. While the revolutionary authorities, protected by the regular army which had not participated in the fighting in Hanoi, were reaching the jungles of the Viet Bac, the country was reverting to the rice fields and straw huts of the past. In Cochin-China, where the guerilla forces had increased in strength since December 1946, the expeditionary force had some control over this Vietnam of villages, but almost nowhere else. This would be the highest stake in the battle to come. For the time being, the Viet Minh had vanished into the jungle. Ho Chi Minh was demanding a ceasefire and Minister of War Coste-Floret was able to announce in May, on his return from a tour of inspection: "There are no longer any problems of a military nature in Indo-China."

Valluy had run the relief operations energetically that winter and was determined to "strike at the heart", in other words to attack the Viet Minh sanctuary itself.[24] He needed reinforcements, favourable weather conditions and the go-ahead from Paris in order to carry out this ambitious plan. In December, at the time of Giap's coup, the troops were being changed over and so the expeditionary force only numbered 85,000 men. Fresh troops gradually kept arriving until September 1947, increasing the total to 115,000. Part of the intended reinforcements had been diverted to Madagascar, where another colonial war had started in March. The government was being very economical with its army, due to a difficult period of reconstruction in the country,[25] so it decided to reduce the number of troops to 90,000 by the start of the following year. Under these conditions, Valluy had at his disposal neither the numbers nor the time he had desired. Plans were modified so that the campaign was to be reduced from six to three months. It was almost the dry season and the Bao Dai solution was taking shape when Paris gave its consent.

In October, Valluy was able to undertake Operation "Léa". Its aim was to strike at the Viet Minh territory, 8,000 sq km of difficult and mountainous terrain covered with tropical forest. The command assembled all available troops and equipment, and engaged 12,000 men in the assault under the orders of General Salan. A pincer movement was planned. One column transported by a flotilla would travel up the Red River and the Claire River, another would set off from Langson, occupy Cao Bang and then march inland towards the South. The two groups would meet near Bac Kan, in the very heart of Viet Minh territory. The enemy would be on its guard, in view of the extensive resources deployed, but the parachutists' landing was still intended to come as a surprise.

The operation was completed at the end of the year. The army regretted that Paris should have restricted the resources deployed, and deplored the fact that it had had insufficient manpower to allow it to hold firmly onto zones in which it had established itself. By 17 November, Salan was stating in his report: "Territory held by the Viet Minh has now almost ceased to exist. It has been fragmented and its most important areas have been wiped out." Indeed, the troops engaged had covered the highlands in all directions, proving that the revolutionaries were not safe anywhere and that a French company could now outclass any Viet Minh unit. Hostages had been set free, arms and documents had been recovered, and the "Voice of Vietnam", the Viet Bac radio, had been destroyed. New positions had been taken up in Cao Bang, Bac Kan, and other border towns from which it was hoped the Chinese frontier could be held more effectively, the ethnic minorities rallied in support and the enemy forces disrupted. But Ho Chi Minh's government had avoided capture, although very narrowly.[26] As for the enemy battle corps, it had disappeared. The Viet Minh, in other words, had been severely tested, but had not been forced to capitulate by a model campaign. There were to be many subsequent operations of importance, but their objectives would be more limited. The fact that operation Léa had not been an unqualified success meant that hope had been abandoned of ending the war in one go, with a grand finale.

For months, the government of the Democratic Republic of Vietnam had been preparing for a long war and had decided to deploy its forces strategically so as to disperse its opponents' efforts. It was now even more determined to use time to its advantage, wearing down its stronger opponent until it finally got the better of it. Former (and future) Secretary-General of the Communist Party, and President of the Association for the Propagation of Marxism, Truong Chinh had outlined the theory behind this revolutionary war in his 1947 pamphlet entitled *Our victory is certain*. He identified three stages. First, the struggle was essentially defensive and consisted of guerilla warfare. In the second or balance stage, a war of strategic moves took place in addition to guerilla warfare. Lastly, during the third stage, the battle corps which had been built up progressively would become powerful enough to progress to a general counter-offensive. The Viet Minh, however, had not devised this strategy by itself. A few lessons could be drawn on this occasion from the long struggle waged by the intellectuals against colonization. The French Resistance had also provided some useful precedents. In 1946, at the time of the Fontainebleau conference, Vietnamese military leaders had made contact with former FTP leaders, from whom they received a wealth of information on the techniques of guerilla warfare. But the main body of their knowledge came from the Chinese communists, with whom their links, which had been rather vague, had become closer in 1946. Trained in Mao's school, Giap measured up to his master.

The mountainous terrain covered in tropical forests provided an ideal setting for this type of combat. The population, which consisted of ethnic minorities, did not however automatically support the nationalist struggle of the Vietnamese. Benefiting from experiences at the end of World War II, the Viet Minh adapted itself to these minorities. Ho Chi Minh watched his fighters very closely, ensuring that customs and taboos should be respected. The jungle being "neutral",[27] both in human and geographical terms—the Vietnamese were no more acclimatized to it than were the men of the expeditionary force—both French and "Viets" had to conquer it. In the plains, use could be made of the local population, but at first glance, the terrain did not seem to lend itself to organized guerilla warfare. Access to certain areas was indeed very difficult. The Plain of Reeds, a vast swampy area 5,000 kilometres square to the south of Saigon, at the very heart of French defences in Cochin-China, was similarly daunting. With no roads, the plain served as a refuge for the guerillas, as well as a base for their operations. It sheltered arms deposits and workshops and for a long time kept Nguyen Binh's "capital" well hidden. Of the thousands of villages, how many could be easily controlled by the French? The majority could not even be reached by road. In the Red River Delta, it was necessary more often than not to follow dikes on foot so as to reach a village. In his *Lessons From the War in Indo-China*, Salan wrote: "The speed at which the men advanced was reduced to that of a foot soldier trudging through mud, and the scale of manoeuvres could be summed up by the following strange equation: one village—one battalion—half a day." A Vietnamese village, protected by a fearsome bamboo palisade and set out haphazardly within this enclosure, defended itself very efficiently, as the nineteenth-century conquerors had discovered. "A Viet very cleverly digs his hideouts under a bank and links them to a waterhole by means of a U-bend tunnel which prevents them from being flooded. A length of bamboo sticks out through the roof of the hideouts and allows him to breathe".[28] This example shows the ingenuity of the Viet Minh guerillas and the problems facing the expeditionary force when it had to make a thorough search of an area. Traps set by the Viet Minh made the search all the more difficult.[29] The multiplicity of these small hideouts was a reflection of the type of war being waged. It was a fight without impedimenta, unrestricted by heavy logistics, and it had the support of the people.

"To avoid the enemy when he is strong, to attack him when he is weak, to disperse and regroup, to fight so as to wear down resistance or annihilate him, depending on the circumstances, to attack the enemy everywhere so that he will find himself constantly submerged by a tide of hostile, heavily-armed men, and thus undermine his morale and wear

out his strength." Such was Giap's description of guerilla warfare in
The People's War, the People's Army. He continued, "In addition to small
groups whose mission is to harass the enemy, it is necessary to bring together, under the appropriate conditions, a greater number of men who
will annihilate the enemy by means of operational superiority at a given
location. Just as an accumulation of gusts of wind constitutes a gale, so
the accumulation of victories in minor confrontations gradually wears
down the active enemy forces, while steadily increasing our own potential. The annihilation of the enemy's active forces must be the principal
aim of combat, and we must never exhaust our own forces when defending or occupying a territory." The technique of guerilla warfare
"also has great significance in revolutionary terms—it allows the masses
to launch minor insurrections and to seize power at grassroots level".[30]
But guerilla warfare was not an end in itself. In May 1949, Giap summoned the principal military leaders to explain to them how they must
move away from "guerillaism" and on to the next stage. By October, the
first offensive of any significance had been launched.[31] It was named
"Lê Loi", after the fifteenth-century king of that name who used an underground army to reconquer his kingdom from the invader.

The military structures of the Viet Minh were already well established. They were based on a compound structure, in both their general
and detailed organization. Three men formed a basic cell, three cells
formed a group and so on. The forces were divided into regular troops,
regional forces and people's militia. The aim of the regular troops was
"to move over a vast area with the objective of annihilating the enemy's
active forces, that of the regional troops was to operate within their region and to coordinate, together with the regular troops, the activities of
partisans and guerillas. The objective of the partisans and guerillas was
to defend their village, to participate in production and to join forces
with regular troops and regional units in both preparing for and leading
the fighting."[32] In addition to its flexibility, the system had the merit of
ensuring dual selection of the principal forces (*chu luc*). The militia elite
graduated to the regional troops, whose elite then passed into the regular troops.[33] The "people's army", the revolutionary army, could therefore draw on the vast reservoir of local militias, which were for all in-
tents and purposes the paramilitary organization of the rural masses.

Vietnamese soldiers, drawn from a peasant population used to living
on very little and working hard, were tough fighters. Sober and lightly-
equipped, they could march for days in the jungle and hide for hours in
a rice field or in the forests. Whereas the expeditionary force depended
on the scarce roads and aerodromes, the PVA (Popular Vietnamese

which possessed almost no vehicles and moved about on foot, could go anywhere. However, any large-scale manoeuvre entailed long delays in its organization, since an advance of some twenty kilometres would take a whole day and the mobilization of a large number of coolies had to be taken into account. Carrying munitions, kit and food supplies ("rice sausage" for a week and salt), the soldiers marched mainly by night, and crossed the rivers during the hours of darkness. By day they advanced camouflaged with foliage. They would capture as many weapons as possible from the French, this being one of the main aims of the attacks on army posts, but the French often retrieved them during their own operations. The Vietnamese therefore had to set up workshops to produce and repair weapons, which meant making purchases in China and Thailand.[34] The sale of opium from the highlands, as well as revenue from the revolutionary tax paid in regions held by the enemy, served to finance these purchases. The insurgents compensated for their lack of weapons by using traditional traps, which had the various advantages of demoralizing the enemy, causing it considerable losses—for infections spread quickly in this climate—and finally, of possibly playing a tactical role, because scouts feared falling into them and so resorted to using roads and paths, which in turn made them easier to ambush. This illustrates well how the war in Indo-China combined both ancient and modern tactics.

In *Problems of War and Strategy*, Mao wrote: "We work on the principle that the Party controls the rifles. We do not accept that the rifles should control the Party." Politics took precedence over military considerations at every level. The officers underwent frequent periods of ideological training. The general level of the soldiers' education was raised before taking their political education any further. A "democratic army", the Vietnamese army devoted many meetings to discussions in which every soldier had to be able to express himself on any subject. Each soldier had to make confessions in countless sessions of self-criticism, which were sometimes broadcast over the radio. At the end of an important engagement, they would have a meeting to analyze the sequence of events in detail and to draw lessons from it. According to Chou En-Lai "the soul of the army is its political commissar". It was this commissar who ensured, at every level of the hierarchy, that the correct line defined by the Front was being followed. His universal control was exercised through a series of interlinking networks. His role was perhaps most important amongst the junior officers, some of whom had distinguished themselves in battle but were not necessarily ideologically sound. Thanks to its commissars, the Front could avoid the twin pitfalls of "militarism", conceiving the battle and relations within the army in purely military terms, and of "dispersionism", too strong a taste for individual initiative. It also had to combat the defeatism of those in whom long periods of combat had given rise to doubt about the successful outcome of the war, as well as subjectivism, arrogant optimism which refused to take into account the true situation of the forces. It further had to ensure that the troops behaved properly towards the population, respecting Item 9 of the oath sworn by every soldier, "In your contacts with the people, follow these three principles: respect the people, help the people and defend the people so as to gain its confidence and its affection and to create a good understanding between the people and the army." As an "army of the people", the Viet Minh had to enjoy their full support and thus wage a "people's war".

Mobilized, trained and indoctrinated, the whole population had to participate in the struggle for liberation, the prime aim of the revolutionary authorities being to make it into a "vast ocean" which would eventually submerge the "colonialists" and the "puppet politicians". Any doubtful elements, which sometimes included an entire village, were liquidated, a fact which often prevented information from falling into the hands of the French, who were themselves under the constant surveillance of numerous Viet Minh agents.[35] Punishments were staged to serve as intimidation. The propaganda endlessly repeated the same slogans. Praising the heroism of the fighters, it ran hate campaigns against the French, without much regard for the truth. From 1945 onwards, there were many instances of exaggerated statistics and improbable stories spread by this brainwashing campaign. For example, among the atrocities allegedly committed by the expeditionary force, a platoon of sixty men were supposed to have raped 700 women in one afternoon.[36] Among the exploits of the Viet Minh fighters, it was claimed that a diver sank the *Richelieu* using nothing but a chisel!

The training of the population was all the more thorough, since it was based on a double hierarchy. Associations had always played an important part in Vietnamese life, the inhabitants forming themselves in Gourou's words into "area associations, and associations and societies of intellectuals, military mandarins, old people, fighters, singers, musicians, shopkeepers, cock-fighting spectators, songbird breeders, and pupils of the same teacher". The Viet Minh made use of this tradition. Grouped into a network of societies and fraternities, the population was additionally subjected to a structure based on territorial divisions. "This system of parallel hierarchies has been compared to a set of accounts checked by two accountants—no 'irregularity' could escape them."[37]

The Viet Minh's hold was strong even in areas which, in theory, were under French control. The popular, political and military committee of a village, for example, did not exist permanently on village territory. It was a fluid and mobile entity when the circumstances required, and it came together again when the danger was past. But wherever it was, it continued to play its role.[38] Compelled by force or acting from personal conviction, nearly all Vietnamese living in an "occupied zone" payed the revolutionary tax. It was collected by hand-picked financial cadres, whose scrupulous honesty contrasted with the more customary corruption.

Until March 1948, Vietnam was divided into fourteen zones or *khus*. After that date, it was divided into six interzones or *lien khus*, vast areas whose boundaries were drawn along political, economic and military lines and each enjoying a high degree of autonomy. Cochin-China constituted one interzone, Annam two, Tongking three, including the Viet Bac, from whence Ho Chi Minh's government continued to direct the fight, and where it had installed its central administration, developed a crafts-based industry and was in the process of creating a system of higher education. In each interzone, the Viet Minh maintained traditional territorial divisions such as the province or *huyen*, the district or *phu* and the village or *xa*. Documents dating from 1945–6 outlined the election at each of these levels of a deliberative assembly by direct universal suffrage. Each assembly was to choose its own executive, or *uy ban hanh chinh*. War had increased the degree of centralization. The assemblies were suspended, the committees were taken in hand and transformed into resistance and administration committees (*uy ban khang chien/hanh chinh* or UBKC/HC). Their designation was followed by an indication of their administrative level. Elected or not, the UBKC/HC *xas* were placed under the strict control of senior committees, and the reams of paper which circulated within this pyramidal system effectively supplied the French Deuxième Bureau (the French equivalent of MI-6 or the CIA) with much political information. In addition to its UBKC/HC and its association sections, Salan noted that "the village had an information section. The system of popular education included at least one representative per village and one per hamlet. The security force had a main cell in the village and an 'enquiry cell' in the hamlet.... There was a 'communications cell' in each locality. Finally, the village included a social service committee." Naturally, when it came down to details the rules of operation of such an active and complex organization varied according to the zone, whether Republican, French or disputed territory.

Each *lien khu* did indeed include "liberated" sectors and "controlled" sectors, separated by a vaguely-drawn and ever-changing boundary. Since 1945, the revolutionary authorities had controlled a large section of the country. The principal campaigns in the Red River Delta and the Viet Bac, the north and south of Annam, the Plain of Reeds and the Pointe de Camau constituted the basic territory held by the Democratic Republic of Vietnam. The national currency, the dong, was introduced. Reforms were pursued along the same lines as those of 1945–6. Since Vietnam remained at a stage of "national democratic popular revolution", the building of socialism was not on the agenda. No progress had been made on the vital issue of land reform, and the death penalty was decreed in cases of attacks on small landlords. "The landowning class had not been clearly defined as the object of the revolution", complained General Giap in *People's War, People's Army*. He also states that "the scale of the anti-feudalist task of the first few years of popular power had been underestimated." When addressing the agrarian problem, rather than advocating brutal innovations, the Viet Minh seemed to want to right recent wrongs and return to a traditional agrarian community system. Even the term used to describe socialization, "Xa Hoi Hoa", was charged with traditional connotations, imbued with familiar imagery. Ho Chi Minh continued to present himself not as a communist leader, but as the leader of a vast national front whose main purpose was the struggle against colonialism.

The total war taking place on their own territory which involved the whole Vietnamese people in a struggle to gain power through revolution, was, in French eyes,[39] a rather shameful affair waged in a remote part of the world. It occupied only a few lines in the appointment notices, using carefully-balanced, stock phrases. In his speech of 22 November 1947, Robert Schuman did not even mention the word "Indo-China". The press slipped in a paragraph from time to time about the ins and outs of the Bao Dai affair or some newsworthy military event. The saga, with its interminable negotiations and vague intelligence of engagements in places nobody had ever heard of did not interest public opinion. The territory was remote and unknown,[40] there was no European community of any importance, no conscripts were involved, there were no great battles, the governments were very reticent—all this contributed towards making it a forgotten war. In November 1948, when the French were asked to list their country's problems, they placed Indo-China at the bottom of their list. Indifference or ignorance were obvious in every survey carried out between 1945 and 1954: between 20 per cent and 30 per cent of people had no opinion at all on the matter. The conflict only concerned small minorities, in particular the professional army, in which all the officers had, in theory, to do a stint in Indo-China.[41] There were never more than 100,000 French serving in Indo-China during the war, of which around a third were civilians. The further down the military hierarchy one went, the fewer French there were. They dominated the higher ranks, but over the years they became more of a minority among the troops, a fact which caused complaints from the commanding officers. On 1 January 1950, when the French army numbered 700,000 men,[42] the expeditionary force consisted of 68,000 Europeans (including legionnaires), 54,000 Africans (Moroccans, Algerians, Senegalese) and 45,000 Indo-Chinese (not including auxiliaries). A hierarchy was established among the units of this motley army. The parachutists, mobilized in difficult not to say desperate cases, considered themselves the elite, and cultivated a form of Nietzscheanism.

Leclerc, Valluy, Salan, Blaizot, Carpentier.... If there was a high "turnover" among the officers, the same went for the high command. At the end of 1949, Carpentier and Alessandri were directing the war. The commander-in-chief accepted the post at the instigation of Juin, his boss. Pessimistic as to the progress of the conflict and more interested in the situation in Africa, Carpentier got on badly with his subordinate. Alessandri, with many years of service in Indo-China behind him, had expected to succeed Blaizot, but he was merely reassigned to other duties on Blaizot's departure within the framework of a reorganization of the command. Under Blaizot, he had directed the land-based forces. This function was subsequently carried out by the general-in-chief. Alessandri, who was given command of Tongking, found the administrative supervision of Saigon hard to bear. Even without taking individual sensibilities into account, the French generals faced a constant dilemma. Should they concentrate their forces where they were already in a strong position and, proceeding one step at a time, complete the pacification process (this being the approach favoured in 1948 by General de Latour who commanded the south), or should they concentrate on Tongking, where the fighting was at its worst? In the latter case another choice had to be made—whether to "strike at the heart" by leading ambitious operations in the highlands, the option favoured by Blaizot, or to go instead for the strategically-useful Tongking, the Red River Delta at the historical and demographic heart of the country, systematic control of which would lead to the stifling of the rebellion.

Alessandri made a case for this course of action. The debate became more complicated still when political considerations involving the Bao Dai solution interfered with military necessity. Bollaert and Pignon also played their part in the indecisiveness of French policy. More generally, the generals of the expeditionary corps always had to decide between two options—either to concentrate their forces at the risk of abandoning a large part of the country to "Viet" control, or to disperse their strength so as to hold as much terrain as possible, with the danger of exposing themselves to the attacks of their adversaries.

While the geography of the war changed continually, the French never lost their hold over the main cities and principal roads once they had regained control of them in the winter of 1946–7. But the sabotage and Viet Minh attacks made the movement of troops very difficult. On 1 March 1948, a civilian convoy heading under escort from Saigon to Dalat was ambushed on reaching the Mois plateaus. Eighty-two men were killed (one of them being Colonel de Sairigné) and dozens of hostages were taken. The matter was serious enough to merit a few lines in the French press.

There were several attacks on the cities which attracted public attention,[43] but the French were securely established there and the population continued to increase with the arrival of new refugees. This was how the urban area of Saigon-Cholon, which numbered barely 300,000 inhabitants on the eve of World War II and had been semi-deserted at the beginning of autumn 1945, gradually increased to a population of 2 million by 1954. The war created a great deal of activity and prosperity in Saigon from which the leaders of the corrupt regime were quick to benefit. High society frequented the Rue Catinata and the *Cercle sportif*, while the hoi-polloi amused itself in the biggest dive in the Far East, *le Grand Monde*. The hordes of prostitutes, from the sophisticated creatures of the Rainbow to the girls of Buffalo Park—a huge military brothel—provided the warriors with pleasurable relaxation. Barely twenty kilometres from this westernized metropolis began the Plain of Reeds. Just twenty kilometres separated the capitalist Babylon, into which millions of people poured as a result of the war, and the Viet Minh Sparta. It was a wonderful contrast for moralists and a good example of the nature of a conflict in which towns were besieged during campaigns. The bustle of Saigon and its artificial prosperity should not have deluded anyone. French interests had started to pull out in 1948; yet only the year before that, a plan of reconstruction, modernization and development was to have brought in considerable investment. The plantations were over-exploited, a few firms ceased trading, and the biggest of them began to spread the risks geographically, the Banque d'Indochine setting the example. New enterprises were nearly always set up in other parts of the French Union.[44]

INCREASE IN ASSETS OF COLONIAL COMPANIES
(IN MILLIONS OF 1938 FRANCS)

	1945	'46	'47	'48	'49	'50	'51	'52	'53
Indo-China	321	263	182	127	132	141	98	91	90
Black Africa (including Madagascar)	127	154	146	137	197	205	158	223	229

After J. Marseille, in a paper entitled "The events leading up to French decolonization", 1984.

Indo-China was seen as a special case and not as the beginning of the disintegration of the Empire. It was considered to be a specifically Vietnamese problem rather than a more generalised problem of decolonization. Hanoi rather than artificially bustling Saigon truly reflected the situation, for while commercial activity in the capital of Tongking gradually resumed, a proportion of French business interests had departed and commerce was now in the hands of the Chinese and the Indians.

There had been no fighting in the towns for several years. Garrison life there was almost as quiet as in Lons-le-Saulnier or Bar-le-Duc. The fighting took place in the rice fields and in the jungle. At the end of 1949, the French could have been under the impression that they controlled the whole of useful Vietnam. The richest and most populous plains gradually passed into their hands. Alessandri was completing the occupation of the Red River Delta, where his soldiers were generally received as intruders in the villages which had lived under Viet Minh authority since 1945. But where underground organizations had not been destroyed, French administration of a region was only superficial. More often than not, the country was under the control of the expeditionary force by day, and under the revolutionary forces by night. Nor could anything stop the constant exchanges between pacified regions, the "controlled regions" of the Viet Minh, and regions of operations, or "liberated regions". Men, rice and industrial products indispensable to the underground passed from one to the other.[45] The "Viets" jeopardized the secure hold of the French in their regions, while the French made incursions into Viet Minh territory, preventing it from becoming part of the *kys*. According to Giap, "the armed forces of the two sides were enmeshed like hair in a comb".

The men of the expeditionary force had difficulty in coming to grips with a war without fronts, where the enemy, everywhere and nowhere at the same time, disappeared into the surrounding countryside, into the population, and seemingly into the ground. How could they tell from the inscrutable faces of the *nha qué*, the peasants, if they were enemies or not? How were they to behave towards a population which they suspected of being in one way or another in league with the enemy? Through the use of terror, the Viet Minh pushed its soldiers into brutal, often blind acts of retaliation. "If, by misfortune, one of us is captured alive, a terrifying end awaits us with tortures from another age. The other day, for example, one of my comrades was found two hundred metres from the post where I was. His head had been cut off, his skull crushed, his eyes gouged out and everything else that could be done to a man", wrote a correspondent in *Témoignage Chrétien* (Christian Testimony)[46] to explain, and deplore, the reprisals. If the logic of the revolutionary authorities was clear to the villagers, the attitude of the French troops was disconcerting, inasmuch as each group in the motley army behaved in a completely different way. Their violence often seemed as incomprehensible as their kindnesses. At the approach of troops, villagers often chose to hide, fearing pillage, or even rape, arson and executions.[47] Distrust and mutual incomprehension were the rule between the men of the expeditionary force and the peasants.

As for the French officers who knew their history, they tried to draw lessons from the war of conquest, to follow the examples of Gallieni and Lyautey, and for example, to follow the "oil stain" principle.[48] These were no longer dispersed fighting rebels, of which a centralized authority of superior resources could easily dispose. The enemy could only harass the expeditionary force without striking it any decisive blows. But the actions of the expeditionary force, whether ambitious, spectacular operations or small multiple missions combined with routine pacification, were often unsuccessful. In the case of the former, the preparations for operating the heavy artillery immediately alerted the enemy. There could be no element of surprise and however much equipment or however many troops were deployed, the area was rarely brought under total French control. In any operation, it was always difficult to choose between speed, which prevented the thorough "cleansing" of the area, and systematic "combing", which gave the insurgents time to disappear. The difference in strength between the two sides at the time made any defeat inconceivable and the affair invariably concluded with a dispatch such as the following:

> We have it from military sources that operations have been in progress for several days on the Plain of Reeds to the north of Cai Bé. Heavy losses have been inflicted on the supporters of Ho Chi Minh's government, who left 200 dead and abandoned a considerable amount of equipment in the field. A training centre for officers was also destroyed. On the French side, a few losses have been notified—*AFP*.[49]

A few "Viets" killed, some arms and equipment recovered, a favourable communiqué—it was easy for any military leader to undertake without much risk grand but ineffectual operations.

Most of the French forces, known as "territorial" forces, were split into small units which were responsible for holding the country. The war, with its profusion of military installations, left its mark on the Cochin-Chinese landscape in particular. General de Latour had towers, nearly always of bamboo, built every kilometre along the roads. These constructions, surrounded by barbed wire, were guarded by partisans who would draw up the access ladder at night and huddle into the small room at the top, protected by rudimentary weapons. The role of these partisans was to watch the road and, if necessary, alert the neighbouring outpost. The French military presence thus left its mark on the entire territory of the peninsula. The outposts differed in size, location and materials, but all had a surrounding wall, a corner blockhouse armed with machine guns, a watchtower and a French flag flying from the flagstaff. A young officer or non-commissioned officer commanded a few Europeans or Africans or more frequently some Vietnamese (snipers or auxiliaries) the defenders of such small, jerry-built forts. To quote Bodard: "The straw huts of the concubines, old women providing food, bartenders, guides, interpreters, boys and beps[50] sprang up like mushrooms all around it." Patrols left the small fort to go in search of the "Viets" and their arms' caches, to reassure the population and win them over to the French side. Actions of a purely military nature were backed up by a whole range of social activity. Schools and markets had to be opened, the *nha qué* had to be taken care of and administered. If all went well, self-defence units would be formed. French order was established. A post which did not exert any influence over the surrounding area was of little use. It created supply problems for the command, while doing nothing to hinder the passage of bands of rebels.

The task of pacification was indeed a thankless one, as it had to be constantly embarked upon all over again. The patrols found little, hardly reassured the population and could fall into a trap or ambush at any moment. The winning over of villages to the French side was easily reversible. On one day, one might encounter the head of a notable or *viet gian*[51] with his stomach slit open—unmistakeable signs of the Viet Minh's presence. "There were times when we were so discouraged that we felt like giving up completely. Posts were constantly being attacked, roads were always being blocked, convoys always had to have an escort, attempts were made on the lives of isolated soldiers, there was gunfire in all directions every night, and to cap it all, France was completely indifferent to the situation", complained one sergeant in a letter.[52] From time to time, an announcement would be made that an outpost had fallen into enemy hands. In view of the disparity of weapons between the two sides, this rarely happened. But amidst the monotony of garrison life, of days filled with routine tasks, the constant surveillance of the cunning, ever-resourceful Viet Minh could be strongly sensed. The thought that they might have been betrayed, that they might be murdered in their sleep, or that the fort might be overrun by *nhac*[53] preyed constantly on the mind of many outpost commanders. Night attacks in which dozens of Viets would hurl themselves at their adversaries without a thought for their own safety were typical incidents in this war.

There was something medieval about the conflict, the countryside spiked with towers and outposts with dungeons, a war consisting of thousands of small wars each conducted in distant isolation from the bureaucracy of Saigon, in which every civil or military warlord—French or Vietnamese—would take on auxiliaries whom he paid as best he could. Life came cheap in Indo-China. The army operated on the basis of personal allegiance to officers with strong personalities. The war shattered Indo-China into principalities, especially in Cochin-China where there was a proliferation of the expeditionary force's bamboo towers.

The Cochin-Chinese sects had participated in the revolution of August 1945, but the Viet Minh system proved itself too restrictive for them and the French forces therefore gradually won them over to their side. The return of "Pope" Pham Cong Tac in August 1946 had precipitated the break between the Caodaists and Nguyen Binh. The movement participated in the creation of the Cochin-Chinese Republic (with Doctor Hoach) and upheld the restoration of Bao Dai. The political entity which embodied the movement, the Viet Nam Phuc Quoc Hoi, had representatives in the government which Bao Dai formed in 1949. With its own party, militias, and its theocratic principality around Tay Ninh, the sect was a force to be reckoned with. But it did not play fair, which meant that the French had considerable difficulty in following its manoeuvres. General Chanson, who had been in charge of the forces in South Vietnam since 1949, paid for this duplicity with his life. On 31 July 1951, he was killed in a kamikaze attack organized by a Caodaist "dissident".[54]

The Hoa Hao broke their uneasy alliance with the Viet Minh[55] in April 1947, after the "mad bonze" had been lured into a trap and liquidated by order of Nguyen Binh. The principal military leader of the sect, Nam Lua, was an illiterate former bus driver whose wife, a former ticket collector, had formed a corps of fearsome amazons. The French made this colourful character Commander-in-Chief of the Hoa Hao army, gave him the rank of general and a decoration (before he awarded himself a second one). He was allowed to reap the benefits of their patronage and become very rich. The allegiance of Nam Lua did not, however, entail the allegiance of the whole sect. The agents of the Deuxième Bureau had to deal with the complex rivalries of these petty warlords. Some liquidated their rivals, using the arms and military advisors they had received from the French, and then went off to fight on their own account. Making a record number of recantations, one of them, Ba Cut, signed an oath of allegiance five times. Protecting the Hoa Hao and making them allies had some effect locally in the Cantho region, but there were no wider political consequences. The Dan Xa Party, who represented them, was never much more than a loose collection of small groups.

Originally members of the Viet Minh Front, the Binh Xuyen were also persuaded to change sides in 1948. The organization would best be termed a gang rather than a sect. It included adventurers and outlaws taking refuge in the Rung Sat, the swampy region to the south of Saigon. Its leader, Bai Vien, had escaped from the island prison of Poulo Condore. The Binh Xuyen, almost completely wiped out by Nguyen Binh, found their salvation in submission. Bai Vien, who was also given the rank of general, made a sort of pact with the colonial authorities in which he guaranteed the security of metropolitan Saigon in return for financial advantages. The Binh Xuyen dealt in opium, prostitution, and so on and they soon ousted the Chinese and took control of *le Grand Monde*. The Deuxième Bureau therefore judged it opportune to ensure the salvation of these minorities, to arm them and to grant them their own small preserves. Handling all these sects was hardly an easy task. The changing line of the Caodaists, whose "Pope" wanted to impose his religion on the whole of Cochin-China, the sudden about-turns of the Hoa Hao leaders, the greed of the Binh Xuyen mafia, all had to be faced. Indeed, these diverse principalities did not submit to the Viet Minh, but were still curious allies and doubtful sources of support for Bao Dai.

Winning him the support of all the Catholics in Vietnam was another matter. Most Catholic leaders had, in fact, approved of the revolution of 1945. On 23 September of that year, on the very day on which the French re-occupied the public buildings in Saigon, the four native bishops had made an appeal to the Pope for Rome to support the new independent government. Even in 1948, when Monsignor Cassaigne in Saigon had sent a telegram of congratulations to General Xuan on the occasion of the constitution of the central government, Father Nguyen Ba Luat, one of the most influential members of the Cochin-Chinese clergy, made it known that he had sent a message to Ho Chi Minh reaffirming his support. Following the example of the ex-Emperor, the Bishop of Phat Diem was the official counsellor of the revolutionary government for several years. Phat Diem, as the French knew, was of great significance to the Catholics of Indo-China. Situated to the south of the Red River Delta, it was the most important bishopric in the country. The first native bishop had been appointed there (as a suffragan), and it was the first area to have been handed over entirely to the local clergy. According to Graham Greene, it was led by "a very austere man with the face of a sad, meditating monkey", Monsignor Lê Huu Thu. Monsignor Thu officiated in more than 500 parishes over which only the Vatican flag flew. He collected taxes and had his own militia, and ran the administration and the courts as he pleased.

The French leaders urged the Pope to put pressure on the Indo-Chinese Catholic community. It became the custom for French statesmen to stop off in Rome on their trips between Paris and Saigon. As far as Pope Pius XII was concerned, when it came to anti-communism one merely had to ask. *La Croix* of 1 June 1948 reproduced the following communiqué from the Catholic news agency Fides:

> Gradually, the excesses have shown that the communists, in Vietnam as elsewhere, do not work for the good of the country, but above all for the victory of one party, an anti-religious party, with which, sooner or later, conflict is inevitable. Already, there have been some murders of priests and Christians, various confiscations of Church property, and a tendency to portray Christians as enemies of the homeland, as an omen of systematic persecution.[56]

Rome was trying to trump Ho Chi Minh by playing the Bao Dai card. In any case, it was in the nature of things that Rome would support a policy which in Paris was that of the MRP. Certain Catholic circles placed great faith in the crown prince. Bao Long had been brought up in the faith by a Christian mother, and some saw him as the Clovis of Vietnam.

Back in Vietnam, meanwhile, relations gradually deteriorated between Monsignor Lê Huu Thu and the revolutionary government. In September 1949, the expeditionary force, which since July had gradually been conquering the whole Delta, launched a combined operation which military humour had codenamed "anthracite". The occupation of Phat Diem and the important neighbouring bishopric of Bui Chu had begun. The two prelates, who were becoming nervous of the stronger and stronger pressure from the Viet Minh on their principalities, were not opposed to a simulation of combat. On 1 July, a decree from the Holy Office condemned "atheistic communism" and forbade any Catholic participation in organizations of that persuasion. The Vietnamese bishops took up the theme, especially in their pastoral letter compiled at their convention of September 1951. At the very moment that the Bao Dai solution was being implemented, Catholicism appeared to be an anti-Viet Minh force. Yet what had applied to the sects also applied to the Church: this rallying did not imply a frank and total loyalty to the French cause. Monsignor Lê Huu Thu was to continue to pursue an individualistic and tortuous policy of his own.

Phat Diem and Bui Chu were two great Catholic strongholds, but Vietnam had other little theocracies which rallied to the Vatican standard and were protected by their own militias. The principality which Colonel Leroy had carved out for himself in the Bentré region of Cochin-China also seemed to claim to be Christian. His armed forces called themselves "mobile units for the defense of Christianity". When in 1947 this Eurasian officer had begun, with the support of Saigon, to lead the hunt for Viet Minh bands, he had recruited his men from among the Catholics whose villages he pacified. The label remained, but the fiefdom had now extended to include 500,000 souls of every religious persuasion in the region. In the preface to *The Quiet American*, Graham Greene recalls "this little medieval state founded and governed by a young half-breed, Colonel Leroy, who read Tocqueville, kept dancing-girls and attacked the communists in his district with the suddenness and cruelty of a tiger." Leroy was no theocrat, but one of those charismatic personalities thrown up by war; this enlightened sociofeudal warlord led his anti-guerilla attacks in Asiatic style, with the same brutality and efficiency that the Viet Minh themselves used.[57]

In the mountains, the principalities on which the expeditionary force relied to wage their struggle were more traditionalist. In the western Tongkingese highlands, where Thai feudalism was dominant, the French presence relied on those colourful barons who ruled in the Chinese style from their *yamen*s, and especially upon Deo Van Long, leader of the White Thais[58] and ruler of Laichau, son of the head of the black standard-bearers of whom history has left a frightening portrait. This despot had facilitated the French return in 1946, and the French had accordingly placed him at the head of the Thai Federation created by them in 1948.[59] Potentates of every colour had thus been used in the jungle region in which the army established outposts. The army supplied them with provisions and ancient, barely airworthy, planes. Everywhere the French played upon the traditional local wariness of everything Vietnamese. The conflict between the French and the Viet Minh spanned centuries, civilizations and armaments, and extended to all the ethnic minorities and all the mountain tribes. It crossed the ancient rivalries between clans and races. In the Meo territory, it even became an opium war.

It was in this jungle that the expeditionary force suffered its worst setback in 1949, along the *Route Coloniale* No. 4. RC 4 ran for 116 kilometres from Langson to Cao Bang, in the heart of Viet Minh territory. The last part of the highway, from That Khê to Cao Bang, covered particularly difficult terrain. This fifty-kilometre stretch through tropical forest and narrow gorges, up steep hills and down sheer cliffs, was particularly hard to defend. The provisioning of Cao Bang became an onerous task for the expeditionary force. A line of outposts had been marked out but the jungle could not be controlled, and it was from here that the Viet Minh would emerge to set up their ever more murderous ambushes against convoys which were ever more heavily armed.

This revival of guerilla action along the frontier coincided with the movements of Chinese communist bands. In March 1949, guerillas captured an outpost on the outskirts of That Khê, while the Chinese captured the town of Monkay for several hours. The cooperation which had existed for some months between Mao's clandestine fighters and those of Ho Chi Minh caused the French command to sketch out a collaboration with the local Chinese Nationalist leaders. However, the Kuomintang armies were crushed in the course of 1949 and China was declared a People's Republic on 1 October. The debris of the Nationalist forces, hotly pursued by those of Lin Biao, finally reached the Indo-Chinese frontier after a series of disastrous defeats. The French had been put on their guard by the new power. They decided to bar the passage of the defeated forces, so as not to risk a possible invasion by the victors. Chiang's generals had to submit to Saigon's conditions and their 30,000 men were disarmed and interned.[60] The French frontier garrisons extricated themselves from this dreaded operation without much difficulty. Among the bedraggled soldiers who crossed the Tongkingese frontier in December 1949 there were a few Vietnamese, including Vu Hong Khanh, cosignatory of the Sainteny-Ho Chi Minh agreements, who vainly tried to force his way through with a small band.

In that same month, one decolonization was achieved. The Dutch granted independence to Indonesia. The colony had been run before the war by an omnipotent, paternalist administration. There then followed the Japanese invasion and the consequent disappearance of the white power. In August 1945 there was a revolution and finally independence, proclaimed at the very moment of the Japanese capitulation. This left a vacuum, despite the expected, armed return of the colonizer with a plan which it considered to be liberal. There was hesitation by the departing power between the use of force and negotiation, and an attempt to integrate the revolutionary state into a federation which would itself be a member of a multi-continental union actually run from the mother country.[61] This plan failed and caused a colonial war. All these events were very reminiscent of the situation in Indo-China. The Netherlands was ultimately defeated and international pressure, especially from the United Nations[62] and the United States, were largely responsible for this defeat. Even if on this subject France was not the object of similar entreaties, its leaders could not ignore the world climate and that particular example of it. President Auriol, speaking in the assembly, warned General Aumeran, one of the defenders of the colonial tradition: "One must take account of the wind blowing through Asia. One must take account of evolution, however disagreeable this may be for us. One must try to restrain this movement wisely. On the other hand, there is the United Nations and you can see what is happening in Indonesia."[63] In 1949, the Americans even threatened to withdraw Marshall Aid from the Dutch, causing their allies to make decisive concessions. This was because the government of the Indonesian Republic had liquidated a communist dissident movement in September 1948, thus proving their *bona fides* in Washington's eyes. This episode was not without interest for the anti-Viet Minh nationalists. First there were the Philippines, India, Pakistan, Ceylon and Burma, now there was Indonesia. The decolonization of South-East Asia was proceeding apace, and the United States might help in bringing about the same situation in a Vietnam loyal to Bao Dai.

In December 1949, Vietnamese independence seemed to be emerging into the limelight. France signed a string of agreements and transferred its sovereignty in theory and a whole series of powers in practice to the Saigon government. The Bao Dai solution, however tardily and laboriously instituted, took effect at the moment when Mao's victory presented the Viet Minh with vast new possibilities. A few French experts expressed the view that French policy had lost its way, and that the new regional status quo meant that agreement ought to be reached with Ho Chi Minh. However, by denying him any legitimacy, and placing a new Vietnamese power in opposition to him, any move towards such vital negotiation had been blocked.

Hitherto, the Viet Minh had been conducting a battle in the paddy-fields and jungles with few means at its disposal. It was an isolated guerilla war, following the example of other guerillas in that Asia of monsoons in which no country was at peace. The Huks[64] were fighting the Phillippines government with the support of the Americans, the Indonesians were confronting the Dutch, and so on. There had definitely been a thrust by communist armies since 1948. While Mao was clearly gaining the advantage in the Chinese civil war, the British were being confronted by the Malaysian guerillas,[65] and the new Burmese republic was facing a communist insurrection. The Cominform profited from the Indian Communist Party congress held in February in Calcutta to urge the South-East Asian communists to engage in this type of struggle. New theatres of war had opened up without the nature of the struggle led by the Viet Minh being altered. Yet ever since Lin Biao's troops had reached the Tongkingese border in December 1949, the Democratic Republic of Vietnam had relied on its "great Chinese hinterland"—in effect, on all the Soviet bloc.

In 1949, Mao had won; the USSR had acquired the atom bomb, and it had achieved the construction of its East European bulwark with the creation of the German Democratic Republic. Marxist-Leninism seemed to bestride an apparently homogenous world from the Viet Bac to the Elbe, a world whose Mecca was Moscow. Giap accused the "imperialists of hysterically opposing the offensive of world revolution" and claimed that "With the triumph of the Chinese revolution and the foundation of the People's Republic of China, the forces of world revolution, whose central nucleus is the socialist camp, has surpassed the victories of counter-revolution and imperialism".[66] Thenceforward, the intellectuals of those countries within the Chinese sphere of influence considered China, because it was "beneath heaven", as the Empire of the Centre, the land of civilization. Other nations living at the four corners of the earth were considered to be barbarians because they did not benefit from China's celestial outpourings. Since 1949, China had covered a much wider territory. Why not consider the compact mass of this vast communist bloc as the new civilizing system?

5

Front Line in the Cold War

THE "DIRTY WAR"

December 1949 was also the time that the public first heard of the so-called "affair of the generals". In May of that year, General Revers, who had just worked out the Atlantic pact with the Allies, had been sent on a mission to Indo-China by the Minister of Defence, Ramadier, who was worried about the development of the conflict. The commander-in-chief of the army, former leader of the ORA,[1] seemed particularly qualified to understand the kind of war which was being waged in the Far East. Revers travelled across the country, met many people, and compiled a voluminous report from his conclusions after these few weeks. The document was uncomplacent and sceptical of the Bao Dai solution. It was also pessimistic about a military solution. It recommended a series of practical measures. The Vietnamese armed forces needed to be expanded; vulnerable positions, such as Cao Bang, had to be evacuated (so that the French lines became shorter and Tongking, which was useful, could be held better); the civilian and military powers needed to be concentrated under one authority. The report was exhaustive and critical. It was the reference document for General Mast, the "prestigious and authoritative military chief" whom Revers called upon to succeed both Pignon and Blaizot. A former resident-general in Tunisia and currently director of the Institute for Higher National Defence Studies, Mast's name had been circulating for several months and he had already been mentioned as a successor to Bollaert at the beginning of the previous year.

Beginning in August, extracts of the report were broadcast by the Viet Minh radio. Then on 18 September, an argument broke out on a bus platform between a former member of the expeditionary force and two Vietnamese. The three men were taken to the police station, and a copy of part of the document was discovered in the briefcase of a man called Do Dai. An inquiry implicated Hoang Van Co, a member of the delegation of Baodaist Vietnam and an important distributor of funds (particularly to General Mast). He said that he had received it from a certain Peyré, a man involved in various shady dealings, an SDECE agent and a crook. It appeared that this man was a close friend of General Mast and used the General to probe political circles where he took advantage of his contacts both for his own purposes and those of Mast.

Both Revers and Mast, two supposedly left-wing military chiefs, were now in a position which embarrassed Ramadier. He had prompted a mission in the hope of changing Indo-Chinese policy to the detriment of the MRP. Ramadier and his party comrade, Jules Moch, then in the Ministry of the Interior, agreed with Prime Minister Queuille to suppress the scandal. Peyré was freed and discreetly embarked for Brazil with his family. But while this was going on, the Queuille cabinet was being succeeded by the Bidault cabinet. The new Minister of Defence, René Pleven, dismissed Revers and replaced him with General Blanc in December. From then on, the press, beginning with the American magazine, *Time*, seized on the affair which until then only the limited circulation *Bulletin Dehème* had mentioned.

On 17 January 1950, Bidault informed the national assembly. It immediately set up a commission of inquiry of twelve members. The Communist Kriegel-Valrimont was a member; he regularly leaked the investigations.[2] The affair of the generals was in the headlines for the whole of 1950. To top it all, the press devoted passage upon passage to the Indo-China war, but only to mention obscure plots, dubious people, stories about cheques, secret ambitions and the secret services, and even secret societies. Influenced by the exaggerations of headline-seeking newspapers, public opinion was submerged in these stories of high politics and low deeds, of petty schemes and great secrets, of Xuanist politicians and Baodaist agents, all of whom were at times capable of exploiting their Viet Minh acquaintances for their wheeling and dealing. The public could only be worried by these revelations which threw a harsh light on the relationships between military chiefs and political circles, on the struggles inside the Third Force, on the rivalries between special services, and on the corruption which had increased in the shadow of the war. The story had a bit of everything. Even the head of state had been brought into question. After all, *Carrefour* and certain communist bodies let it be understood that the "Paul" in the Peyré papers was Auriol's son. The opponents of the regime which had besmirched itself in this way were heartily enjoying themselves.

Moving from one event to another, the mini-series threw an interesting light on the corridors of power, but became lost in connected issues.

This confused, intrigued, and finally exhausted public interest. In the end, no one understood what the crux of the matter was, namely, that the excessively political Generals Mast and Revers had paid with their careers. It was as if, with the help of the secret services—the DST and the BTL[3] against the SDECE—the Minister of French Possessions overseas, Coste-Floret, had wanted to discredit the chief of staff of the army whose report had criticized the then current policy. "Without speaking of the consequences to my personal authority, a new blow, and the most serious to date, had been inflicted on the 'Bao Dai experiment', whose beginnings were surrounded by ambiguity and scepticism", Pignon wrote to Coste-Floret on 15 June 1949. The affair, which had raised doubts about some of the key leaders of the Socialist Party, thus actually ended in confirming the old choice, cutting short any socialist efforts to initiate a different Indo-Chinese policy.

One scandal may conceal another. During the affair of the generals, the black market in piastres was raised by Kriegel-Valrimont and Revers. The General even submitted a memorandum on this subject in which he revealed the mechanism and named names. The value of the Indo-Chinese currency had been fixed in December 1945 when the franc was devalued. A piastre was then worth seventeen francs. On the Far East markets, the rate of exchange for the piastre varied during these years between seven and nineteen francs. To benefit from the official rate of exchange, it was necessary to obtain authorization to transfer the money to mainland France. In certain cases, this happened automatically, but depended on the goodwill of the Exchange Office in Saigon. The overvaluation of the piastre made payments and salaries to the French serving in Indo-China worthwhile. It allowed certain Vietnamese to be rewarded (Bao Dai and his entourage benefited from significant transfers), and it favoured all sorts of lucrative ventures conducted by all manner of people. The large firms, principally the banks (Banque de l'Indochine, Chartered Bank, Franco-Chinoise, Financière, BNCI) and the world of import-export, dominated by the powerful and respected company Denis Frères, made large profits. The transactions depended on a series of documents. The professional black marketeers—Corsican and Chinese secret societies played a part—had to obtain transfers to the mainland at the official rate, then repatriate the sums involved by converting the francs into gold or dollars which were clandestinely introduced into Indo-China where they were exchanged for piastres. These transactions yielded profit margins of more than 100 per cent. Even the Viet Minh profited from the piastre at seventeen francs, as General Revers complained in his memoirs.[4] But in 1950, this new affair did not matter. It was not until early 1953 that a newspaper campaign was conducted on the subject of the black market in piastres.[5] Parliamentarians took over, like the Gaullist Dronne who suggested decreasing the civil budget of the associated states by way of protest. Finally, the piastre was devalued and a commission of inquiry was set up in July 1953. It was thought appropriate to bury the report. Eliminating the black market and the war went hand in hand.

These scandals were hugely exploited by the Communists. In 1950, the French Communist Party's action against the Indo-Chinese conflict reached its peak. The affair of the generals and the other related scandals had reached a point where they fed Party propaganda. The Party itself discovered that here was an excellent opportunity for settling scores with its greatest enemies. Revers, Ramadier and Moch had led the repression in 1947–8. Ramadier was represented by the cartoonist Mitelberg with other "carrion-eaters", as the cartoon was entitled, hovering over corpses. Moch was particularly hated and narrowly escaped a Supreme Court hearing which is what Kriegel-Valrimont had in mind for him. At other times, the Party found it a pleasure to compromise lesser personalities such as Bouzanquet,[6] one of the people responsible for the 1947 split in the trades union federation. The Communists continually repeated that the war in Indo-China was a dirty war and that it was natural that it should dirty those waging it. The purity of the Communists, "the clean party", was contrasted with the regime's own decay.

"The forces of reaction are accusing the Communists of wanting to abandon Indo-China, though nothing could be further from the truth", wrote *France nouvelle* on 5 April 1947. From the start, the Communists led the struggle against the war, claiming that negotiations with Ho Chi Minh would result in the preservation of the ties between the French and Vietnamese peoples in a different form. Leaflets were handed out in factories demanding the cessation of hostilities, and for troops no longer to be sent. Leaflets were distributed near barracks; direct action was waged against conscripts in the Communist districts. The same arguments were tirelessly developed against the "dirty war"—the phrase, taken from Beuve-Méry, was used from January 1948.[7] The conflict was futile and murderous, compromising Franco-Vietnamese relationships. It went against the 1946 constitution.[8] Indo-China swallowed billions of francs and raised doubts about France's economic balance and social progress. It was a ridiculous waste for a country still in ruins and penury. As evidence to back up the protest the Party gave details. An item of weaponry cost the same as a socially-useful piece of equipment; so many days of war equalled so many francs in wage claims for the working class.

If required, diagrams could be drawn to make the point even more obvious. The Party thus linked its fight to stop the war with the daily social struggle. In fact the Communist argument, here as elsewhere, also claimed that the Third Force served the interests of the capitalists (they quoted, for example, Edmond Giscard d'Estaing), the big banks (particularly the Banque de l'Indochine) and played the old trick of claiming that all of these interests were serving an American master. On 22 December 1947, *L'Humanité*'s headline was: "Washington is dictating French policy in Vietnam." So the French and Vietnamese peoples had the same enemies, their struggles were the same. "The interest of the French public is that the people of Vietnam beat the French imperialists, the French colonialists and, of course, their masters, the American imperialists", Marty declared.[9] The Communists had to embellish the stories and adapt them to the circumstances right until the last moment.

In 1949, the Communist press launched a campaign against the peace-keeping methods. In fact, this theme was not absolutely new. Since December 1945, the Party newspapers had been condemning the "atrocities" committed by the expeditionary force from time to time.[10] Hitherto, these had been quoted as exceptional cases, such as the scandals of Germans or militiamen scandalously involved with the army.[11] "Let's open the file on crimes committed in Vietnam", was the headline in *Action* of 30 June 1949. Eyewitness accounts of Indo-China veterans—varying in degrees of accuracy—told of pillaging, executions of civilians and hostages, massive reprisals[12] and different types of torture. All of these atrocities were denounced. On several occasions, the Minister of Defence instigated prosecutions for "defamatory remarks about the French army". During the debate of 19 October 1950, René Pleven told the assembly that so far, sixty-one official complaints had been made. The government's argument was that if crimes had been committed, they had been committed by the Viet Minh (the press gave particularly gory details of the events of 19 December 1946), rarely by the soldiers of the expeditionary force who in this case were punished;[13] and some humane officer from the command was quoted.[14]

In May 1949, the Communists launched the slogan: "No more men, no more money for the war in Indo-China." Campaigns for collecting signatures were organized, together with demonstrations which were often not announced officially. The dockers, over whom the CGT had a monopoly, were called to action. Refusals to load military equipment for the Far East became more frequent towards the end of the year. In December the National Association of Indo-Chinese Repatriated People and Families of Victims was created. It was supposed to provide evidence and counteract the "fascist propaganda". In the same month, Jeannette Vermeersch arrived to celebrate Mao's victory by attending the International Congress of Women in Peking where she met and embraced the delegate from the Democratic Republic of Vietnam. "We should now pass on to concrete struggle, in mass, against the manufacture, transportation and maintenance of military equipment", wrote Frachon in *L'Humanité* on 13 December. This command was acted upon in the following weeks. The Communist Party had become more active in the preceding months, and now threw itself wholeheartedly into the fight against the "dirty war" between December 1949 and January 1950. It was now clear that the conflict in Vietnam "was developing as a part of the struggle between the two camps"[15] as Marty stated in *France nouvelle* on 17 December.

The "dirty war" was denounced in all the speeches made by leaders of the Communist Party and CGT, and in particular during the 12th Congress, during which long debates were devoted to the defence of peace in Indo-China and elsewhere—it was the time of the Stockholm Appeal. Every day, *L'Humanité* quoted an initiative by the militants against French involvement in Vietnam. The dockers were especially honoured, as their action forced the military authorities to load the arms themselves which were destined for the expeditionary force.[16] Armaments trains were halted; convoys had to be escorted by the gendarmerie. Certain equipment was evidently defective.[17] These actions caused the law of 8 March 1950 to be passed, whereby "acts of sabotage of army equipment, those hindering the movement of military materiel, those involved in operations to demoralise the army" were punished with penal servitude. The deputy Citerne called the law "Hitlerian"—this was not a period of Communist understatement—but the bill was adopted in a stormy atmosphere. There were bitter speeches and insults,[18] rows preventing ministers from making themselves heard, obstructionist tactics, affrays, and the *gardes républicains* had to be called in. The two debates devoted to Indo-China held in early 1950 (this and the one in January, at which the agreements made in the previous year with the associated states were discussed) were amongst the most violent and the bitterest in French parliamentary history.

The repression allowed the Party to praise its heroes. It conducted a campaign on behalf of Raymonde Dien who spent nine months in prison because she had prevented a train of military equipment from leaving Saint-Pierre-des-Corps in February 1950, but especially on behalf of Henri Martin. As a young resistance fighter, he had, like many others, been in the Indo-China army. On returning to France, he had been

posted to a base in Toulon where he was involved in anti-military propaganda, as he was in contact with the Communist leadership. He was arrested in March 1950 for distributing leaflets, but convicted in Toulon
in October for the sabotage of a ship. Acknowledging his militant actions, but disputing the charge of sabotage, he was sentenced to five
years' hard labour by the military tribunal. The judgment was thrown
out on procedural grounds, but was confirmed by a new trial in Brest.
Prompted by Marty, the Communists very soon decided to make Henri
Martin's case a focus for discontent. Because of his background (he had
been a resistance fighter at sixteen), his personality and his build, the
young man had everything a real hero needed for public opinion to be
moved by his misfortunes. The militants wrote "Free Henri Martin" in
the most inaccessible places. Petitions were started. Government officials, intellectuals and organizations were harried. Roads were renamed. Songs were composed and cartoons drawn to glorify him.
Picasso painted his portrait. For two years, the play *Drame à Toulon* was
staged almost everywhere in France. This was a fine example of agit-
prop: the show was followed by speeches, debates, collections and petitions. Finally in August 1953, Auriol took advantage of a number of
presidential pardons to free Henri Martin who then became a prominent figure on Communist Party platforms.

In the first months of 1950 the Communist Party attacked the Indo-
China war and one of its leaders travelled to Vietnam. Figuères, a
member of the Central Committee and general secretary of the UJRF
(Union of Republican Youth in France) crossed the Viet Bac and met
leaders of the Democratic Republic of Vietnam, in particular Ho Chi
Minh whom he interviewed for *L'Humanité*. On his return 200,000
copies of his account, *Returning from Free Vietnam*, were distributed
(whilst the author disappeared into semi-hiding because a warrant had
been issued for his arrest). This enthusiastic description was followed by
others, such as that of Chesneux in *Action* in September 1950, and that
of the journalist Courtade in his novel *The Black River*. Figuères's stay
also resulted in two French Party activists being sent as representatives
to the Democratic Republic of Vietnam at the request of the Vietnamese. They would chiefly advise the Viet Minh on the question of
prisoners and propaganda to be developed with the expeditionary force
in mind.

At the Liberation in 1945, more than 2,000 French officers were
card-carrying Communists, including three generals (Tubert, Petit,
Malleret-Joinville). The chief of staff, distrustful of them, became hostile when the three-party system broke down. The Party leadership then

asked its activists not to leave the army, which meant agreeing to fight in Indo-China where they were advised to "work for the masses". In fact, some preferred to resign, others were put out to grass (like Rol-Tanguy and Beaufils who ended up being confined with other Communist officers in the Versailles barracks). Although the Party propaganda did succeed in affecting the conscripts, the expeditionary force itself was unaffected. The senior officers in Indo-China were isolated and adopted different attitudes. Some of them were committed to the war and were no different from other French servicemen. Others were happy to do as little as possible or to be used in sabotage operations. The most active formed networks, transmitted messages to the Party leadership, helped prisoners to escape, established contact with the Viet Minh, and sometimes provided them with arms;[19] but most importantly with information. Probably, when they were discovered, some were discreetly disposed of for treason.[20] It was to escape this fate that an officer was to disappear and later become involved in the capture of Cao Bang.[21] But desertion for ideological reasons was rare among the French-born members of the expeditionary force.[22] All in all, French Communist activity in Indo-China was marginal, both within the army and through the intervention of the Marxist Cultural Group (GCM) which operated in Saigon from 1945 to 1950.[23] In France, however, the Party was developing a widespread feeling of guilt through its propaganda, and largely contributed to making the conflict a war of shame. In addition, it compromised the military effort with concrete action, designed to prevent the sending of reinforcements and arms, including destruction of or damage to equipment.[24] Rarely since the Liberation had the Party taken so many liberties with the law (even if, from time to time, it condemned such sabotage as provocation).

The French Communist Party's struggle against the war in Vietnam was taken up by communist parties in other countries. In 1950, a campaign against enrollment into the Foreign Legion was waged by West German communists who falsified the figures and claimed that 60,000 of their compatriots had already fallen in the Far East. In September of the same year, the Italian Communist Party called on the Romans to demonstrate in protest against an audience granted to Bao Dai and his family by Pius XII. The French Party's action was recorded as part of the general battle for peace which, according to the words of Thorez at the Gennevilliers congress, "hangs by a thread". In 1950, the dockers were persuaded to refuse to load arms for the expeditionary force or to unload equipment which the United States was delivering for the PAM (Programme of Military Aid). Action against French colonialism, against

American warmongering and German revanchists went hand in hand. Searches and arrests followed. In 1952, an attack was made on Ridgway, the NATO commander-in-chief. The communists struggled to free their heroes, Henri Martin and Jacques Duclos.[25] From this year on, the struggle against the European Defence Community (EDC) became part of the disapproval of the "dirty war'.

In this general struggle against imperialism, the Party tried to expand its audience. Political fellow-travellers were promoted in the drive for peace. These included Farge, former Commissioner of the Republic in Lyon, d'Aster de la Vigerie, a former minister under de Gaulle and Abbé Boulier, whose activities were prohibited by the Vatican. One example of a fellow-traveller was Denis, a progressive Christian and a professor at the University of Rennes, who was convicted as owner of the newspaper *Ouest-Matin* for defamatory remarks against the army; in November 1950, he was attacked by a group of paratroopers. The Indo-China issue—and especially the campaign to free Henri Martin—brought help from new quarters, in particular from Jean-Paul Sartre who devoted a long preface to the subject.[26]

The *petite gauche* as Mollet called it was no less sensitive to the Communists' arguments for the continuation of the conflict. Mollet's criticism found expression in the articles of Bourdet and Rous in *Franc-Tireur*, in Fabiani's articles in *Combat*, and in the *Temps modernes, Esprit* and *L'Observateur*, created in 1950 to defend neutralism. From 29 July 1949, *Temoignage chrétien* devoted its first page to criticizing the methods of war with the title "Tortures in Indo-China. After the typewriter, police station furniture includes a machine for making people speak." The case history had been compiled by J. Chegaray, who in the preceding issues gave picturesque and innocuous reports on his stay in the Far East. On 12 August, the newspaper resumed the subject with a long plea from Paul Mus[27] entitled: "No, not that." This was only the beginning of a series of articles on the question. By supporting the parallel campaign led by the Communists, and backing it up through a prominent university don (who was also head of the Colonial School), *Témoignage chrétien* created a stir in the Catholic world. Michelet, an important resistance fighter and a Christian, denounced "a magazine about which I have the right to say that its frightful lapse could not be foreseen when we distributed it at the risk of our lives."[28] Mauriac warned in *Le Figaro* on 23 January 1950: "Do not hope that I will lower myself so far as to borrow from the men from Moscow the slogan 'dirty war'." But the Indo-China affair was the opportunity for a group of progressive Catholics to become involved against a policy for which French Christian Democracy had borne the greatest responsibility. In February 1950, Paul Mus took part in the conference of left-wing Christians which Jacques Madaule organized in his constituency of Issy-les-Moulineaux to ask for peace in Vietnam. Professor Boulet, mayor of Montpellier, was expelled from the MRP at the beginning of 1950 for his stance which was considered too close to that of the Communists. Resignations by other members followed. A Catholic, Moiroud, was made a member of the general secretariat of the Committee of Study and Action for Peaceful Settlement of the Vietnam War in 1952. In November 1953, the committee was to organize a national conference assembling men with greatly diverging viewpoints, such as Hernu, Martinet and two MRP deputies. But by now, the idea of concluding the Indo-China affair by negotiating with Ho Chi Minh was making progress. It found a champion within the system itself, in Mendès-France who spoke out in its favour on the day following the Cao Bang disaster.

THE NEW DEAL

In his report of June 1949, Revers had recommended the evacuation of Cao Bang which he deemed to be too exposed, and General Blaizot had planned the operation for September. But Blaizot was replaced by Carpentier who was being harassed by opponents of evacuation. One of the most important of these was high commissioner Pignon and the military chief of Tongking, Alessandri. Various reasons were offered for continuing to hold Cao Bang. It was well protected so it was not at great risk; it considerably hindered communications between China and Viet Bac; if it were abandoned, the route would be open as far as the Delta; the ethnic minorities of the highlands could not be abandoned; it would be useful to remain at the frontier to disarm Kuomintang troops.

Yet since early 1950, the situation had been deteriorating. The Cao Bang and Dong Khê outposts could now only be supplied by air, and seemed like diminishing enclaves in a zone in which the Viet Minh was becoming more and more active. On one occasion, Dong Khê was even taken and held for several hours by the guerillas. The reports of the French forces were specific and unpromising: units of the revolutionary army were crossing into China where they were being reorganized; a stream of modern weapons was flowing into Viet Bac from China. The men of some units of the expeditionary force who had just confronted the Viet Minh at the frontier had been struck by the extraordinary strength of the enemy fire power. Ho Chi Minh's radio announced the imminent capture of all the outposts on the RC 4.

General Carpentier finally decided on evacuation. Cao Bang and Dong Khê would be abandoned in early autumn. To disguise the retreat, the operation would be linked with the taking of Thai Nguyen, a town on the Delta which was Ho Chi Minh's capital at the time. There was a choice between three routes: by air, by the RC 3 or RC 4. The first solution was not considered because it was feared that the last units holding the ground would have to be sacrificed; they would be content to help the maximum number of civilians leave in convoy which could return, bringing reinforcements in their place. The RC 3 directly linked Cao Bang and Hanoi through an often difficult but partly free zone. The disadvantage was that between it and the Delta the French no longer had a presence.[29] It was therefore decided to withdraw along the RC 4. Of course, they knew how dangerous the route was. But from That Khê onwards it was solidly in French hands. There were therefore only some fifty kilometres to cover. Carpentier counted on surprise for the evacuation to go well. As a precaution, he did not even advise Lieutenant-Colonel Charton, the commander of Cao Bang.

Just as the operation was about to begin, a new problem surfaced: the Viet Minh had just retaken Dong Khê. The French manoeuvre therefore changed as follows: a group (Lepage's group) left from Langson and headed west to retake Dong Khê, advancing to meet the garrison of Cao Bang which was to evacuate the town as soon as possible. Three officers were therefore directly responsible for the operation: Lieutenant-Colonel Lepage, who was not told of the changes to the operation to start with; Lieutenant-Colonel Charton, a tough legionnaire, whom Alessandri, going against orders, insisted on confiding in during a visit where the two men confessed their bitterness to each other. Finally, there was Colonel Constans, an ostentatious and ambitious socialite,[30] who directed the operation without leaving his command post in Langson.

The operation began badly. While Charton was preparing to leave, Lepage found himself unable to retake Dong Khê. Nevertheless, the evacuation of Cao Bang was undertaken anyway on 3 October. The command refused to postpone it despite Charton's request that they wait at least for the weather to improve so that the air force could take part. But the rapid advance they had planned—which was to have been like a raid—was transformed into a slow progress, because Charton left with all his impedimenta. Dozens of civilians followed a convoy already weighted down by lorries and heavy weapons. Meanwhile the Lepage column was split up and seriously damaged. It had to call for help. Charton received orders to go and aid those who were supposed to have come to his aid. Abandoning some of his equipment and stragglers, he rushed into the jungle to meet Lepage's troops. Fighting in extended order in great confusion, the various sections of the two groups were destroyed one by one, after intense fighting sometimes under the most terrible conditions.

Thus 4,000 crack troops were dispersed in the jungle and two colonels were taken prisoner. The Cao Bang evacuation had been performed without the command allowing for any backup forces, the whole of the parachute unit then being deployed elsewhere,[31] principally in Thai Nguyen. The command had organized the operation in its usual way without allowing for recent experiences, continuing to believe that the Viet Minh, who they conceded were skilled at ambushing, would avoid any significant action. The operation had been commanded 100 kilometres from where it was taking place with orders that could not be implemented. On the other side, Giap had demonstrated his tactical skill and his forces' fire power. The first large-scale battle which the expeditionary force had had to face since it had become used to the routine of guerilla warfare had been a disaster. At first, the communiqués were optimistic, then watered down. The spokesman in Saigon announced: "These vanguards are the only important units which have arrived in That Khê—no more will be arriving". That Khê had just welcomed some survivors of the battle and was now in the process of being occupied. Its evacuation, which threw together fighters and local civilians connected with the expeditionary force, became a confused stampede and led to the sacrifice of a parachute regiment which had just landed in the sector.

Now the question of Langson arose. Overestimating the danger, Colonel Constans persuaded his superiors to abandon the town immediately, even though it was not yet under threat. There was no preliminary demolition, so as not to arouse suspicions. The Viet Minh were therefore left with substantial stocks (10,000 weapons, thirteen cannons, tons of food...) which the air force only managed to partially destroy over the following days.[32] But it was not over yet. Shedding its arrogance of late, the command's attitude changed over a few days from excessive confidence to the deepest pessimism. Fearing that the most exposed French enclaves would be under threat and obsessed by the possible spread, which had been announced, of the "Viets" through the Delta, it was only concerned with concentrating its forces and spoke only of evacuation. Thai Nguyen was held for only a few days and subsequently abandoned. Lao Kay, wedged between the Chinese border on the high valley of the Red River, and Hoa Binh in the Muong country, were both abandoned. Preparing for any eventuality, plans were laid for the departure of European civilians from Hanoi, and there were even preparations to abandon the city altogether for the fortress of Haiphong! Evacuation might be skilled (like that of Lao Kay) or unlucky but heroic (like that of Langson) but in October 1950 it became—and would remain—one of the principal features of the war in Indo-China. It was no coincidence that the best film devoted to the conflict (*La 317e Section*) told the story of such an episode. At the end of the year, apart from the coastal position of Monkay, the frontier with China was completely open, and there was no longer any obstacle to the passage of men and arms. As for the retreat from Hoa Binh, it had opened up communications between the Viet Bac and the "liberated" zone of North Annam, extending Viet Minh territory into one block.

Cao Bang and Langson: for once, the newspapers carried stories on the Indo-China fighting. Sixty-five years after Ferry, Langson again figured in the headlines of the dailies and its name was again synonymous with disaster. After the shady affair of the generals, the shock of defeat and the evacuation worried public opinion and made it wonder about the nature and the basis for the forgotten fight in the Far East. Official speeches had been saying for months that peace-keeping was progressing smoothly and that the independence granted to Bao Dai was the political solution to the problem; France's total control of the Red River Delta was starving the Viet Minh troops who were destined, through the birth of the state of Vietnam, to suffer the fate of hunted gangs. On the basis of soothing reports from General Carpentier, the government, with imminent elections in mind, even managed a symbolic reduction in the size of the standing army.[33] In the spring, the troubles in the Cochin-Chinese capital must have cast doubts on these statements. Murders and demonstrations followed each other, proving the power of the Viet Minh in the heart of Franco-Baodaist Vietnam, although finally the battle of Saigon had been won. Cao Bang and Langson, however, showed both that Ho Chi Minh had not been reduced to the role of a tired communist guerilla chief and that Bao Dai's regime held on to power only through the support of the expeditionary force.

The force now found themselves facing so-called rebels who had a battle machine capable of manoeuvring and beating seasoned troops. Thanks to Chinese aid which was rapidly organized, the light arms supplied to the revolutionary army rivalled those of the French soldiers. All they lacked were tanks and planes. Again, the possibility of an offensive led by planes bearing the insignia of the Démocratic Republic of Vietnam flying out of Chinese airports could not be discounted. Until then, the Viet Minh regulars had consisted of large groups of guerillas. Now they were re-equipped, re-organized and re-trained in the vast training camps in the south of China. They returned to Vietnam in units. The famous general counter-offensive announced by Ho Chi Minh was now a distinct possibility. Cao Bang and Langson were only the brutal proof of what observers had known for months. Mao's victory had changed the nature of the war both militarily and politically.

The Indo-China conflict, which had been a Franco-Vietnamese affair within the French Union until 1949, became an integral part of the cold war when the powers of each camp began to recognize one or other of the Vietnamese governments. In 1949, Ho Chi Minh again wanted to distance himself from the Maoist revolution, insisting that the Viet Minh "contrary to the allegations of colonial propaganda" were not communists. But on 16 January 1950, China recognized the DRV.[34] Stalin, who was conferring with Mao at the time, followed suit on 30 January. Then the other people's democracies and even heretical Yugoslavia did the same. Paris protested to Moscow, speaking of a violation of international law: "Vietnam is part of the French Union, and it is to the government of Bao Dai that France has just transferred the sovereignty she possessed in this Union." Until then, France had hesitated in following Great Britain's example in recognizing the new Chinese power. Any idea of this sort was now abandoned.[35] On 7 February, Washington and London recognized the three associated states. The Commonwealth countries had discussed the issue at their meeting in Colombo the previous month. The British had not been able to convince anyone apart from the representatives of the old dominions. India showed the way. Governments which refused to be aligned refused to choose between Bao Dai and Ho Chi Minh.[36]

Since Roosevelt's time, the American position on Vietnam had been changing continuously and Washington had followed the birth of the associated states with interest. "The surrender of French Indo-China to the Reds seems likely if the United States does not move into action", was the *Evening Star*'s headline in one of its issues in December 1949. General Stratemeyer, United States Air Force commander in the Far East, was in Saigon and the State Department was announcing in Paris that it was only awaiting the ratification of the independence agreements by France before recognizing Baodaist Vietnam. As the editorial in *Le Monde* said in its conclusion on 15 December: "Let's ask the Americans to spell out their Asian policy. However, it would be useful for us to spell out ours."

The recognition of Ho Chi Minh by Moscow, then the start of the

Korean war, forced Washington to become more deeply committed. The process resembled what had just happened in Greece. After that country's liberation, British intervention on the side of the local right wing in the civil war was seen by the disapproving American government as a show of the traditional policy of an imperialist power. In 1947, when Truman took over from the exhausted British the fighting had changed its significance. It became an example of the "containment" of Soviet expansionism. Truman was successful: Markos's guerilla forces had been exterminated. The episode was in the spirit of the times. But unlike Markos, Ho Chi Minh had been recognized by Moscow—after four years—and that was a bad sign. Maurice Duverger was to publish an article in *Le Monde* of 25 June 1950, an explosive piece which aimed at demonstrating that none of the explanations for the continued French involvement in Indo-China were valid, and that the war had therefore become truly absurd. Monsieur Duverger did not believe in negotiations with Ho Chi Minh, now that the conflict had entered the sphere of bloc politics. Inspired by the Greek example, he suggested the Americans assume their responsibilities and take over.[37] No one agreed with him yet.

At the beginning of 1950, Washington promised France aid. But before it could deliver the goods, it wanted to see Ambassador Jessup's report. Jessup was touring South-East Asia after which he would confer with the French leaders. One month after Jessup's trip, on 23 February 1950, an economic delegation arrived in Saigon led by A. Griffin followed in May by R. Blum, one of the men in charge of the American economic mission in Paris. At the time, France was receiving aid in dollars from the United States (under the Marshall plan) as well as military aid (from the Atlantic Alliance). The latter had been organized under the treaty of 27 January 1950—establishing the PAM which stipulated in clause 3 that equipment supplied could not be used outside Europe without American authorisation.[38] Paris wanted to have both types of assistance, economic and military, for its Indo-Chinese policy too. A report by Douglas MacArthur Jr, American deputy director of the Office of European Regional Affairs, of a conversation with Jean Chauvel,[39] French Ambassador to the United Nations, reveals the tone of Franco-American discussions of the time:

> France could not afford the luxury of exhausting itself in Indo-China if French economic reconstruction was to be completed one day. Consequently, [Chauvel] thought that the time would soon come when the United States and the United Kingdom would share France's responsibility to block the southern route to communism in Asia or else France would be forced to relinquish

its Indo-China operations—no matter how hard this seemed—and to abandon Indo-China to Moscow. He did not know whether the United States realised the critical nature of the situation in Indo-China.

This was not the tone of the newspapers (whose information, it was true, was filtered on the spot through a watchful military censor) nor was it the tone of the official declarations at a time when high commissioner Pignon recalled the "last quarter of an hour".

In his Far East tour, Jessup made his support known to Bao Dai, but let it be known in declarations made in different capitals that his country desired that the independence granted to the three associated states be more manifest.[40] Washington was willing to help the anti-communist struggle but wanted it to be free of the stigma of colonialism. "The United States cannot support a colonial war because that would make it lose its prestige in the rest of Asia", wrote Walter Lippmann in the *New York Herald Tribune*. And more explicitly, J. M. Roberts of the Associated Press warned: "The United States wants to dispel any ambiguity. It is not its intention to help France to maintain its domination over Indo-China. It has to arrange for France to leave Indo-China completely." Robert Schuman indicated at the press conference he held on 9 May, following his meetings with his opposite number, Dean Acheson, that in exchange for the promised military aid his government was ready to make a gesture. The associated states would have a special minister, not the one for French Possessions Overseas, which was quite ridiculous for countries considered to be independent. The American authorities were embarrassed at supporting a regime which was still colonial, and they were also subjected to the demand formulated by Paris that aid be given not directly to the local governments, but to France which would assume responsibility for distributing it. The three associated states enjoyed sovereignty, of course, but they belonged to the French Union whose "general administration" was handled by the Republic.

Washington finally conceded. Interested in the dollars and the real prospect of independence which the intervention of the United States might bring about, the politicians of the three states began to play the American hand. In January 1950, Nguyen Phan Long became head of the Vietnamese government and in February, Phoui Sananikone became head of the government of Laos. They were pro-American and both attempted to keep their distance from the French. But they soon had to realise that the time for relief had not yet come. America was helping, but France intended to keep the upper hand in the peninsula. In April, Nguyen Phan Long had to give way. The trouble which had set

Saigon alight in the previous weeks was significant in this defeat. On 19 March, in fact, just after the high commissioner had transferred the police services to the Vietnamese government, the visit of American warships to Saigon gave rise to a series of incidents. There were student strikes, fires, mass demonstrations, and even mortar fire against the ships. The Viet Minh had made a date with a new adversary.[41] Diem did not succede Nguyen Phan Long, as some Americans were already wishing. Instead, he was replaced by a long-time colleague of the French, an old stager in Cochin-Chinese politics, Tran Van Huu.

United States aid was constantly being redefined in one discussion after another but had not yet materialized when on 25 June 1950 the North Korean government launched its troops against South Korea. On 27 June, in a declaration which solidly established the foundations of his country's Far East strategy, Truman announced that he was involved in defending South Korea, Formosa and Indo-China ("I've also given the order for the supply of military aid to the French forces and the associated states in Indo-China to be speeded up and for a military mission to be sent into the region to work closely with the forces"). In fact, during the following days, the first deliveries of planes and medical supplies were made in Saigon where a temporary military mission arrived, together with Washington's envoy to the three associated states, David Heath. The involvement of the United States was taking shape. But as for aid, as well as for gratitude, the Westerners had been left behind. While America was vacillating, Chinese arms were reaching the Viet Minh.[42] Moreover, the priority given to Korea and the need to supply Europe with the agreed equipment in the name of the PAM brought a slowdown in the supply in late summer.[43] Since the beginning of the year, people had been saying that France was facing the same enemy in Europe as in the Far East. Now they would add that the Americans were fighting the same war in Korea as the expeditionary force in Vietnam. In Schuman's words, "Unknown yesterday, understood today, helped tomorrow", the Indo-China war had fully entered into the strategy of global containment.

This escalation in international tension forced the Americans to rearm the Western bloc. The European military situation seemed worrying to them. On either side of the iron curtain, the ratio of conventional forces was more than 10 to 1 in favour of the USSR (which had also just become an atomic power). The United States was involved in Korea; France was already fighting in Indo-China and its powerful Communist Party made it not completely reliable. Washington therefore decided to force the Germans to re-arm. During Cao Bang, the subject of defence dominated Franco-American relations and a kind of agreement was in the process of being formed. France—which could not significantly increase its military effort—would accept the lead, even though many were still shocked that Germany had soldiers who were to be integrated into the European army, the plan for which was presented by Pleven on 23 October.

On the other hand, the United States would increase its aid to Indo-China while making it understood that the best way to fight communism was to grant full sovereignty to Bao Dai's Vietnam. The leaders of Vietnam were all too ready to follow this line. In the aftermath of Cao Bang, there were statements to the international press by Tran Van Huu on the unsatisfactory application of the agreement of 8 March and the continued maintenance of a colonialist spirit. These statements were unwelcome to French ears "at a time when France is bleeding with all its sacrifices for the safety of those here who contest her rights which have been recognized under the agreements reached" (Sarraut). On 24 October, United Nations Day, the Saigon government paid tribute to the UN. Coming after the startling declarations of Tran Van Huu, this tribute directed to an organization in whose name MacArthur was waging war in Korea became in effect a day for praising America. The Viet Minh was stronger than ever. The Vietnamese administration could scarcely impose itself and even contested its status in relation to France. The war had become internationalized just as world tension was worsening. Parliament devoted four debates to the military problems in one month.[44] It was in this context that the national assembly discussed French involvement in the Far East the day after Cao Bang.

Two days, 19 October and 22 November, had been reserved for the events in Indo-China. The Pleven government, challenged on the question on 19 October, promised the deputies a more in-depth debate after the Juin-Letourneau Mission which had gone for first-hand information, had made its report. The Communists unleashed their usual diatribes against the "dirty war", and were now especially insistent on the role played by American imperialism. "Not only do you betray the soldiers by making them fight in a war against the interests of the motherland, but you also want to deliver them to Truman and MacArthur, whose old eyes need to see corpses" (Tillon). "We already knew that the French soldiers were fighting in Vietnam principally to ensure that American strategists had an important base for their plan to start World War III" (Girardot). But their arguments were scarcely listened to. They were in the opposite camp. Pierre Cot demonstrated powerfully that there were only two alternatives: intensify the war or negotiate. The first option implied a new and enormous effort which was unthinkable since it placed too great a burden on too weak a country. All that remained was to talk to Ho Chi Minh. But Cot was too involved with the Communists to be convincing.[45] He was a member of the Progressistes, a small far left party, and had hitherto failed to manifest any opposition to his country's Far Eastern policy.[46] But Mendès-France created a stir:

> The whole concept of our action in Indo-China is wrong, because it is based both on a military effort which is insufficient and incapable of bringing about a solution by force and on a policy which is insufficient and incapable of ensuring us the support of the local population. It is a fact that our forces, even with the support of local units, cannot achieve a military solution, especially since the developments in China, and it is a fact that our policy of unsatisfactory concessions, constantly re-defined or revoked, has not achieved and will, alas, increasingly fail to achieve the rallying of the Vietnamese masses.

The criticism went unanswered. An explanation similar to the one made by Cot followed, but Mendès-France added: "If it is a question of countering communist expansion, is it France's duty to take charge in the Far East? Should she not devote her forces to the defence of her own land[47] which would also allow her to have in Europe an army superior to the German forces which are about to be remobilized?" On 22 November, he summarized the ideas developed on 19 October, and was more precise about the conditions for negotiating with Ho Chi Minh. He argued that an agreement was even more likely with the Viet Minh, who feared Chinese domination and that it could be achieved on the following bases: real independence for Vietnam, along with agreements on co-operation; the absence of reprisals; the evacuation of the French troops within a reasonable time-scale; free elections under impartial supervision and (why not?) the neutralization of the country.

This line of argument impressed the chamber and in particular the Socialists, who had always been embarrassed by Indo-China, "this constant remorse of the party" (Fauvet). Although they were loyal to the government by participating in the Bao Dai solution, they had never stopped considering it with scepticism. "We cannot manage to understand how France will succeed in making peace with its enemies if it is satisfied with signing treaties with its allies", wrote *Le Populaire* in the aftermath of the Along Bay agreements. This mouthpiece of the party went through the ritual of recommending that negotiations with Ho Chi Minh be entered into. Again, in January 1949, Mollet wrote in the name of the steering committee to Prime Minister Queuille: "The military solution has not succeeded and everyone now recognizes that it cannot do so.... If we want peace, we must deal with those waging the war and not those who represent nothing in the opposite camp." The Communists took malicious pleasure in recalling those sentences now. But for several months the Socialists had been advocating recourse to the United Nations[48] while once more unenthusiastically following the policy of the government to which they belonged.

So, apart from the Communists and some other isolated members, the deputies refused the prospect of negotiations with the Viet Minh. The arguments advanced were many: it's already been done and we ended up with the 19 December 1946 incident; it's of no use since Ho Chi Minh is a pawn in the game of international communism; the fighting should continue in the name of the sacrifices made and for the defence of our interests in Indo-China; France has obligations to those who supported her. But mostly the arguments revolved around containment of communist expansionism and around the French Union. The former governor-general Viollette warned, to great applause: "If you make the mistake of entering into negotiations, you are abdicating to Ho Chi Minh, and tomorrow we will have to abdicate in Madagascar, in Tunisia and in Algeria. Given the chance, there may be men who would say that the Vosges is border enough for France. When we pass from one abdication to another, we are approaching catastrophe and even dishonour."[49] And some evoked Munich or Vichy. "We heard a voice in 1940 which called on us to stop fighting against totalitarianism at the time of the provisional defeat..." declared Coste-Floret on 22 November. He vigorously defended a policy (which he had initiated) and rejected Mendès-France's arguments on principle. Would France be forced to deal because she could not bear the burden of an intensification of the war? Was it impossible to increase the standing army? Why, all that was needed was to appeal to Indo-Chinese recruits. Would the financial cost be intolerable? Well, they could count on their American ally. The French thus had to pursue their course of action—and Coste-Floret reminded the assembly that it had always widely endorsed the policy conducted in Indo-China—but by Vietnamising and Americanising the war. This was to become the leitmotif of the French leaders.

It was on the basis of this programme that the parties of the parliamentary majority compiled the agenda. The national assembly

> having decided to supply the government with the means to allow the associated states to set up national armies as soon as possible and to participate in the struggle of the free nations in the Far East, it has given the government the mandate to reinforce as far as pos-

sible the means at the disposal of the French forces in Indo-China to enable them to fulfil their present mission; to insist to the free nations on the international nature of the conflict maintained by the Viet Minh which is raising doubts about the future of South-East Asia, and on the need for a common effort, not only to confront the threats at hand, but also to find means to a lasting peace.

There were 337 votes in favour, 187 against. This was still a good result for the Indo-China policy. It was true that the text had been re-worded *in extremis* and that the classic formula "trust the government" had wisely been avoided.[50] Vietnamising the war had been the issue since the Bao Dai solution had been mentioned. Americanising it was what they had been trying to do for some months now. General Aumeran summed it up: "The policy we have chosen in Indo-China has produced disastrous results; so let us continue it!"[51] Having re-installed Bao Dai, proclaimed his government as the only legitimate one, refused any representation with Ho Chi Minh, solicited and partially obtained American aid for Indo-China, participated in the containment policy in Europe with the creation of the EDC and adopted a position of solidarity with the United States' action in Korea, the government was held to the logic of its choices. The logic was that of the cold war.[52] The Socialists resented this and on 22 November, one of their members, Christian Pineau, tried to explain how it had come about and his doubts about it:

The solutions which we proposed two years ago, when we asked for talks with qualified representatives of the Vietnamese people, were no longer valid a year later, when the national movement changed, partly because of our inertia and partly because the nationalists are closely allied to the communists. What was still possible when Mao Tse Tung's troops were several hundreds of kilometres from the Tongking border was no longer possible after the [Chinese] Nationalist defeat. Recourse to the United Nations was a difficult solution and was possible several months ago but would today would have no positive results. And similarly, we know that the solutions we are proposing today would be out of date tomorrow if we delay a quarter of an hour in taking the decisions. There's a sort of fatality here which frightens me.

The Socialists had ended up by taking the opposite direction to Mendès-France. For them the new nature of the war forbade negotiation; for Mendès-France it begged it. The "conversion" of Boutbien, one of the most striking anti-colonialist figures in the party, after a trip to Vietnam, was particularly typical of developments.[53] Speaking in the name of his party, the Socialist deputy, Reeb, justified the vote on the agenda by the majority: "We believe that the motion places the problem of the defence and independence of Vietnam on a level which is no longer limited to the French Union, but appeals to international circumstances. It defines a front of peace against the forces of evil, and we believe, honorable Prime Minister, that the motion corresponds to one of our dearest hopes, that the aggressor will retreat on all fronts because he will see that aggression is useless."

Cao Bang, demonstrating the seriousness of the situation in Indo-China, had forced the politicians to question, for once, the very basis of French involvement. Mendès-France's solution had the merit of clarity. But even the party which had often been in favour of it now rejected it.[54] The Third Force, with all its factions confused, decided to continue the war under the banner of the free world. To show its determination, it chose General Jean de Lattre de Tassigny, an army officer of great prestige, to carry it out.

VIETNAMISING AND AMERICANISING

The MRP deputy Jean Letourneau had since November 1949 (when he had replaced Coste-Floret in the Ministry of French Possessions Overseas), been the main architect of the country's Indo-Chinese policy and as second-in-command of the Pleven cabinet was the Minister of State responsible for relations with the associated states.[55] The choices made were confirmed; the Minister kept his portfolio and continued to keep it until 1953. Letourneau and General Juin were sent to the scene of the conflict by the Prime Minister and landed in Saigon on 17 October during the evacuation of Langson. They discovered an expeditionary force haunted by defeat and doubt and were continually struck during their stay by the pernicious climate of officialdom in Indo-China. To redress the situation, Pleven decided to change the supreme command. Juin supported Carpentier, a man from his own stable, and Alessandri was dismissed from Tongking and replaced by Latour on 8 November. This was not the wisest choice for the defence of Tongking, because it meant the army there was commanded by a man who was only interested in defending Cochin-China. Juin was prestigious and the government was happy for him to assume command of the army in Indo-China; but he was an Africa hand who did not want to be compromised in this affair.[56] Koenig also refused. Finally, it was decided to call on de Lattre, who was far from displeased with this difficult post. After requesting and obtaining an increase in civilian and military powers, he was appointed on 6 December.

This was a particularly dramatic moment. Giap was expected to attack in the Delta and the Chinese, who had just become involved as "volunteers" in Korea where they began to overwhelm the Americans, increased their threats. "Indo-China is only a platform for American aggression. We cannot tolerate this situation any longer", said Chou Enlai, whilst the alleged violations of People's Republic territory by the expeditionary force were being vehemently denounced.[57] The intelligence services noted military activity in the provinces of the south which could not be explained as mere support for the Viet Minh. MacArthur threatened China in Manchuria and China was threatening his French ally in Tongking.

"King Jean" had found his kingdom. But not everyone was so enthusiastic about it. Admired but controversial, de Lattre only had friends in the army. Revers however was not one of them, as was clear when his despatches were read several weeks later. De Lattre's opponents considered him to be a killer, or a capricious *prima donna*. His fixations, his authoritarianism and his megalomania were criticized. De Lattre consulted the main experts in Indo-China—whose general problems and climate he was familiar with because of his former functions and through his son's letters. He formed a team with officers of the First Army and former colleagues of Admiral Decoux. The first of his "marshals", Salan, seconded him in his functions as commander-in-chief; governor-general Gautier seconded him in his functions as high commissioner. On his arrival in Saigon on 17 December, the new proconsul began to dismiss people. On 19 December he presided over a parade in the streets of Hanoi in defiance of the Viet Minh, whose radio announced that the town would be captured before the fourth anniversary of Giap's coup. Like de Gaulle, de Lattre was a theatrical type and set about creating an effect. He had a taste for parades and panache, a sense of style and attitude. Feared by the higher echelons on whom he had clearly made his mark, but winning over most of the officers, the "master of command" immediately imposed himself on the expeditionary force as the leader they had been waiting for. He stopped all evacuation from Hanoi at once. He had decided to defend Tongking at any cost, and breathed new life into the resistance.

The feared attack on the Delta took place on 12 January 1951. Giap launched twenty battalions on Vinh Yen. De Lattre responded by mobilizing all available means and by surprising the enemy with napalm bombs. This first "conventional" battle in the Indo-China war was won by the French, and they managed to exploit their victory. After striking west of the Delta, Giap conducted a new assault in the north, in March at Dong Trieu, then in the south, in late May, at the battle of Day. These three reversals one after the other were not conclusive, but proved to the Viet Minh how difficult it was to win a decisive victory through large-scale attacks conducted in a zone in which the French, being close to base, could exploit their superior equipment. A general counter-offensive was not for the immediate future.[58]

To make further defence of the Delta against a possible Chinese incursion easier, de Lattre began the construction of a series of concrete bulwarks around it. Construction began in the north and was completed by the establishment of a fortified post in Hanoi to ensure the safety of the expeditionary force in case of enemy penetration. In September, a new defensive battle was won: the Viet Minh action against the Thai country was crushed at Nghia Lo by Salan's skilful manoeuvering.

At the time, de Lattre was once again absent from the theatre of operations. In February, he had returned to Paris to use his prestige to procure fresh reinforcements. No one knew where to find them. The government was under pressure from events in Africa and its obligations to NATO to re-arm in Europe. Finally, it was decided to raise them, provisionally in theory[59] from among the North African troops. In September, the General was in the United States. He met everyone who was anyone in the fight against communism, from Truman to Cardinal Spellman. He knew how important newspapers were there and conducted an active campaign in the various media. Convincing public opinion of the just nature of the conflict in Indo-China, discussing military cooperation, but above all obtaining more aid: these were the objectives of this important trip. Whether in Vietnam where he was skilled in dealing with the official leaders, or in France, Washington, London, or at the Vatican, in fact wherever he was, he worked to "sell" the war. Wherever he went, he tried to mobilize energy so that the war, like a crusade, could be waged and won. Exhausted by the effort he had put into his activities, affected by the death of his only son (killed in the Battle of Day), and afflicted with cancer which made him suffer cruelly, he left Indo-China (which he could have dominated) at the end of 1951 and quietly entered a hospital at Neuilly. In November, he managed to attend the reunion of the Supreme Council of the French Union, which had been planned since 1946 and organized two years before, but was only just having its first session.[60] On his death, on 11 January 1952, the government promoted him to the rank of Marshal of France, and he was given a state funeral. After him, the same men (Letourneau, Salan, Gautier...) continued to carry out his work. Although they had less panache and charisma, it was the same story and the same policy.

The Pau conference ended on the day before de Lattre's nomination.

Its aim was to define the methods of co-operation of the three Indo-Chinese states economically as well as militarily. France fully intended to be the beneficiary of this system. The conference had opened in June 1950, under the chairmanship of Sarraut, and had produced very tedious discussions. Despite the theoretically limited nature of its remit, basic political problems had been aired, in particular with regard to the nature of the French Union. Forceful disagreements emerged between Cambodia and Laos on the one hand and Vietnam whose leading role they feared on the other. Nor was there any love lost between the French and Vietnamese. Auriol said of them: "They are unbearable and impossible people." The three Indo-Chinese delegations insisted on increasing the sovereignty of their respective states, so the conference kept supranational bodies to a minimum. Of course, things like the broadcasting service and the running of the port of Saigon were organized on quadripartite lines. But most of the services belonged to the local governments, including customs (which did not, however, raise the question of the principle of customs union provided for in the treaties of 1949).

The Pau agreements resulted in a new series of transfers of power during 1951. The last important service to pass to the Saigon government was the Treasury (in October). Also in Pau the Vietnamese had obtained the concession that they would not automatically be involved in a conflict in which the French were involved. This was a new stage in emancipation, and the agreements gave Paris a new chance to declare the complete sovereignty of the three states. In March 1951, they were invited by the governments of the Commonwealth countries to be represented in the Council for Economic Development of South and South-East Asia. They were members of six specialist United Nations organizations, and had been recognized by the majority of its member states although the Soviet veto blocked their being admitted to the UN. In September 1951, Tran Van Huu was invited to the San Francisco Conference to take part in the signing of the peace treaty with Japan next to the victors. On this occasion, he managed to confer with the two great English-speaking allies, Truman and Attlee. Supported by France, this international opening was bound to reinforce the legitimacy of the three governments and the reality of independence.

"I have come here to achieve your independence, not to limit it. The French army is here only to defend it.... That Vietnam belongs to the French Union is not a limitation for her, but a support, because in the modern world there is no room for isolated nations." The theme of his speech in Vin Yen on 19 April 1951 was taken up by de Lattre in his speech of 11 July made to the lycée Chasseloup-Laubat in Saigon, at the prize-giving ceremony, to stir the youth of the country to involve itself: "Be men, that is, if you are communists join the Viet Minh; there are those individuals who fight well for a bad cause. But if you are patriots, fight for your motherland, because it is your war. It is France's concern only as far as her promises towards Vietnam are involved and the side she intends to take in the defence of the free world. France has not taken part in such a disinterested operation since the crusades. This war, whether you wanted it or not, is Vietnam's war for Vietnam. And France will only fight for you if you fight with her." Five days later, Bao Dai's decision to mobilize the country gave de Lattre much satisfaction. In his 11 July speech, the high commissioner criticized the wait-and-see attitude of the local middle class: "Like parasites, they take advantage of the order maintained by the legitimate government and by the army of the French Union and they do penance for all the material and intellectual comfort they do not want to lose, by expressing genuine disapproval towards the protecting authorities and a virtuous sympathy for the rebels.

Evidently, the man who became head of the Saigon government in June 1952 was not that type of man. As an official in Cochin-China, Nguyen Van Tam had brutally repressed the revolt of November 1940. This had earned him the nickname of "the Tiger of Cai Lai". Arrested and tortured by the Japanese in 1945, incarcerated during the August revolution by the Viet Minh who killed one of his sons, the *doc phu*—his title in the bureaucratic hierarchy—participated as a minister in the experiment of the Cochin-China Republic. In 1950, he shattered the terrorist offensive in Saigon, breaking up the networks, arresting his Viet Minh opposite number (Le Van Linh, the head of the "red Sûreté" in the capital). Director of the Sûreté, Minister of the Interior, Governor of North Vietnam—whatever position he held, he seemed to be the energetic collaborator of the French in police repression. When he passed through Paris in March 1952, he declared that everything was going smoothly: "We do not compromise with the Indo-Chinese Communist Party. We have to strike it down, or it will strike us down." Parodying Clemenceau, when he presented his cabinet he said: "My government will have the following programme: I will make war."

With the promotion of Tam, the involvement of official Vietnam in the anti-Viet Minh struggle was taking shape. His son, Nguyen Van Hinh, as a lieutenant-colonel in the air force, enjoyed French nationality like his father the Prime Minister. Thanks to Bao Dai, the son became a general and chief of staff of this army whose creation, as a final hope and thought, had to show the reality of Vietnamese sovereignty and to enable the French to be relieved.

Without needing to return to the subject of d'Argenlieu who had asked, in a note dated 23 September 1946, for "the organization of local armies in the states of Indo-China", there are a host of quotes by eminent Frenchmen spelling out such a need. Coste-Floret wrote, in his report of September 1949: "The formation of the Vietnamese national army must be undertaken and speeded up." In March 1950, the board of chiefs of staff recommended the organization of a Baodaist army to relieve the French forces from peace-keeping responsibilities (keeping them only for large-scale operations). Since 1945, to be sure, the command had made the expeditionary force "more and more yellow", by allowing the natives to fight both as auxiliaries and as infantry in the colonial tradition. But the French generals had always shown themselves very reluctant to embrace the idea of truly national armies. It was only after Cao Bang that such armies were finally formed. A military conference held in Dalat by Letourneau (at which Tran Van Huu and General Juin took part) organized the rapid mobilization of four divisions. De Lattre wanted to speed up the movement, so the divisions increased from four to eight. But the move was full of disappointments. First of all, the problem of officers had to be solved. In October 1950, Bao Dai set up the "Vietnamese Saint-Cyr" in Dalat. But there were few candidates—many of the officers created in haste during the politico-military reverses of the American period were trained at that time—and, in any event, promotion would not fill the higher ranks for a while yet. The French senior officers were therefore necessary (it was as commander of the Tongkingese soldiers that Bernard de Lattre was killed during the battle of Day). In fact, the distinction was not always clear between the formation of a national army and the traditional "yellowing" of the units. In 1952, however, General Hinh conceived the idea of light battalions led solely by Vietnamese officers (regiments called TDKQ) which were supposed to be equivalent to the regional Viet Minh troops. At the same time, small Laotian and Cambodian armies were being created. The French command decided to transfer the quietest sectors to the forces of each of the associated states. At the beginning of 1953, they had as many men as the expeditionary force. Minister Letourneau was then able to announce that in 1946, 88 per cent of the losses were French, but the figure had fallen to 17 per cent as against over 50 per cent for the Indo-Chinese. From the point of view of the dead at least, Vietnamisation was well on the way.

"We are not conducting a colonialist war since the total French investment in Indo-China does not represent half of the budget which we will devote to the defence of the independence of the associated states in

1952", stressed the deputy André during the debate on the budget in December 1951. Why then were they fighting? President Auriol replied on 25 October 1952, in his inaugural address in response to an attack by Donzère-Mondragon: "For our interests? No, but for a cause which is not only ours, to defend young associated states and the friends to whom we have brought prosperity. We have brought them along the road to independence to protect freedom in Asia and hence the freedom and security of Europe and the world." Explaining these matters to the United States with his usual vigour, de Lattre launched the domino theory in a outrageously shortened form: "Once Tongking is lost, there is no barrier until Suez" (Washington, 20 September 1951). As the "foot-soldier of the free world" France had to obtain its support, something the Council of NATO recognized on Schuman's prompting in December 1952, when the statement noted that the "campaign conducted by the forces of the French Union in Indo-China merits support without default on the part of the Atlantic governments".

In Malaysia, the British were conducting a struggle along similar lines to that of the French in Vietnam. The solidarity of the two powers spoke for itself. The British commissioner-general MacDonald visited Saigon on several occasions and bilateral military conferences took place in Singapore. But it was more a question of their keeping each other informed rather than really co-operating. Australia and New Zealand, as the ever-loyal partners of London, showed some interest in French involvement. The Australian Minister of the Air Force and Navy came to confer on the spot with the generals of the expeditionary force in December 1952. In March 1953, Jean Letourneau visited, addressed the parliament and obtained a small contribution in the form of equipment and supplies. In 1951–2, the creation of a mutual assistance pact for South-East Asia was mentioned on several occasions. It would have linked the three great western powers and New Zealand and Australia.[61] The project came to nothing. But the fear of Chinese intervention at the moment of the Korean armistice gave birth to the "inter-allied agency", as a result of which the chiefs of staff of the five countries would study ways of dealing with this eventuality. In fact, the French military chiefs had alluded to this danger several times since the start of the Korean war. During his trip to the States, de Lattre obtained the promise of American air intervention, with the aim of saving the units of the expeditionary force fighting in Tongking—the Damocles operation.

Both in the bilateral and trilateral (with Great Britain) discussions, and as part of the Atlantic Alliance, the Indo-China question was at the heart of the Franco-American talks. French representatives regularly insisted on the connection between the two problems.[62] So at the NATO conference held in Lisbon in April 1952, Prime Minister Edgar Faure let it be understood that "France could not enter the EDC unless freed from the special burden of the Indo-China affair". Each time Paris insisted on the need for aid and on the necessity for it to be increased in relation to the escalation of the military effort. It deplored delays, U-turns and excuses. The Americans ended up bearing the essential burden for the weaponry. In 1952, they paid half of the costs.[63]

Gifts were made to the associated states. Various items of military equipment were delivered, mainly ships and planes. It was often obsolete equipment for a war in Europe, but adequate against an enemy with only light arms. Finally, the French government was given aid in dollars. It benefited from a sort of extension of the Marshall Plan using it to prolong the favourable effects on the national economy. Some could talk of the war in Indo-China which fed the flow of American manna as the best French export. This comforted the traditional wish of Paris to control American material participation in the conflict. "What is worrying is precisely the fact that the war is a good financial relationship", noted the magazine *Esprit* with bitterness in May 1954. The Communist Party was now attacking the cynicism of Washington which was buying French blood with its dollars. It still criticized the ruinous conflict. "In one year, Indo-China has cost us what we need to solve the housing problem", maintained Giovoni to the national assembly on 5 March 1954.

The Americans were thus being gradually drawn into the conflict, and their numbers were increasing in Indo-China, with their dollars, their mania for cleanliness, and their more relaxed attitude to the neo-colonial system. They installed themselves in fine Saigon villas, where they began to have furniture built. Their Protestant missionaries surprised their Catholic colleagues with their affluence. As the Washington government's representative to the three associated states, Heath, who since 1952 had had the title of ambassador, became one of the key people in Saigon political life. After Cao Bang, a permanent military mission had been set up, led by General Brink. A delegation from MAAG (Military Aid and Advisory Group) studied on site the needs of the French Union's forces and took care of deliveries, and the maintenance of the supplied equipment. From September 1953, the Americans would be kept up-to-date with the operational plans.[64] Businessmen, generals, and congressmen came to make an Indo-China tour.[65] In May 1953, in its report on its mission to the Far East, a delegation from the House of Representatives concluded that it would be appropriate to send aid directly to the associated states, to which France had to grant total independence.

This was where the shoe pinched. Washington agreed that the expeditionary force should fight against communism. But its statements on the sovereignty of the associated states were never convincing. They were sure that if it was rid of continuing colonialism the struggle would be more effective. "They give us money, and we pay for it by way of independence. It is shocking", noted Auriol in his *Journal* on 19 October 1950. Despite apparently good relations, things were far from harmonious between the two allies. On 8 October 1952, for example, Prime Minister Pinay caused a scandal by summoning US Ambassador Dunn and theatrically protesting against his note of 6 October, concerning the way in which the aid was used, as unacceptable interference.

In Vietnam, the French suspected some Americans of undermining them—this also caused some friction. At the same time, it forced the Baodaist regime into the war. Paris invited Washington to take charge of the war materially, but insisted on running the show. However, in June 1950, Maurice Duverger mentioned it in his article in *Le Monde*: the logic of the operation now was that France had to be ousted from Indo-China, whatever the military outcome.

On the one hand American aid was coming in, the so-called troops of the French Union were being formed, Vietnam itself was officially becoming more and more involved in the struggle; on the other hand, the Viet Minh was intensifying its fight with increasing help from China. Here again, the materiel came from the United States. Tons of weapons had been recovered from the Kuomintang troops, and more were captured in the Korean offensive. The equipment was supplemented by supplies made in China, the Soviet Union or Czechoslovakia. Eight divisions were all equipped in a similar way. Their light arms often outclassed those of the expeditionary force.

Ideological alignment followed. During 1950, observers noted that the issue was shifting to the left.[66] An essential step had been taken in February 1951 when a meeting convened in the Viet Bac resurrected the Communist Party under the name of Dang Lao Dong Viet Nam (Workers Party of Vietnam). The Indo-Chinese framework of the old PCI was abandoned. Sister parties in Laos and Cambodia were formed alongside the Lao Dong. "The basis of the DLDVN was laid down and the principles which defined all its activities were the doctrines of Marx, Engels, Lenin and Mao, adapted to the realities of the revolution." The political programme proclaimed: "The fundamental task of the Vietnamese revolution is to rout the imperialist aggressors, to win genuine independence and national unity, to suppress the remnants of feudalism and semi-feudalism, to give this land back to those who work it, to develop a popular democratic regime and to lay the foundations of socialism."

Times had changed. Ho Chi Minh was no longer the head of an obscure guerilla organization, but the leader of a genuine state, with the whole communist bloc behind it. Until recently a convenient umbrella, the Viet Minh League had had its day. The Lao Dong now led the United National Front, the Lien Viet, to which all the other parties (Socialist Party, Democrat Party, left-overs of the VNQDD and the DMH) belonged.[67] As leader of the pro-Chinese wing (his name was a pseudonym meaning "Long March") Truong Chinh became Secretary-General of the new party. Reforms inspired by the Maoist model were implemented, and a purge of the cadres was started, leading to a series of defections to the Bao Dai regime. Even Nguyen Binh was affected. Of course, the General had suffered a double failure in 1950. His terrorist campaign in Saigon had failed, followed by his large-scale operations in the campaigns. But most of all, his revolutionary romanticism was disapproved of and he was not ideologically dependable;[68] he had already received several warnings. In July 1951, he was replaced by an orthodox Communist, Le Duan, and he headed for Tongking whence he had been recalled. His duties were over and all that remained for him was to be killed by a patrol of Cambodian hunters in the Annamese mountains. Once it had been taken over by Le Duan, Nambo no longer had a determining role in the conflict. The sporadic guerilla fighting had to continue to immobilize as many of the enemy forces as possible. But the war was being decided in the North where recent purges had not diminished the Viet Minh's capacity at all.

The defensive victories did not satisfy Paris; de Lattre had been appointed to take offensive action. His choice had been Hoa Binh, which had been evacuated the previous year. The town was in the mountains, in the heart of the Muong country, but only eighty kilometres from Hanoi from whence it could be reached by the RC 6, by the Black River and by air (the town had a small airport). The operation had three objectives: to disrupt the links between the Viet Minh zones of Viet Bac and north Annam (and to secure the Thai country at the Delta); to divert the maximum number of Tongking forces; and finally to strike serious blows against the enemy by making its battalions fight. Hoa Binh was taken without difficulty in November 1951 and propaganda spoke of "the pistol pointing at the heart of the enemy". But things very quickly took a turn for the worse. Giap concentrated a major effort on cutting French communications in this difficult zone. The airport was rendered useless, and the river was dammed; eight days of fighting had to be sustained with the support of all available planes to re-open the route which the Viet Minh had just cut off (18–29 January 1952). Finally, in February 1952, Salan decided to evacuate. This was done professionally and without any losses. The results were moderate. Of course, the enemy had suffered heavy losses, but supply lines had not been interrupted. As for the role of the battle in the war for the Delta, it was debatable as to who was holding whom.[69] The re-occupation of the town had been celebrated as a victory. Any withdrawal could only be considered as a reversal by a public who saw the war from the European point of view, as a series of positions taken by one army or the other. "Ah, we shouldn't, we shouldn't have gone", sang the soldiers on their return to Hanoi.

In the autumn of 1952, there was another evacuation. The Viet Minh repeated its offensive in the highlands but with more power and having learnt from the previous defeat. This time Nghia Lo fell. Outposts had to be closed, the Thai country was occupied. Salan responded by setting up entrenched camps. Two positions were organized in West Tongking, one at Laichau (capital of Deo Van Long) whose site was hardly advantageous and the main one at Na San. The "hedgehog"[70] at Na San was supposed at least to put the brakes on the Viet Minh march towards Lao, if not stop them, and allow French forces to control part of the Thai country. The camp was set up at the bottom of a narrow basin, and was totally dependent on the air bridge for its supplies. The defenders held the surrounding ridges and broke the attacks started by the Viet Minh through sheer firepower. This took place between 30 November and 2 December and forced Giap to abandon the siege during the following days. During the construction of Na San, Salan launched heavy delaying tactics to cut the enemy communication lines. The 30,000 men in the "Lorraine" operation went up the Red River and the Claire River without encountering great resistance on the way up, but they suffered violent attacks when they were striking camp. At least the enemy's logistics had been disrupted for a couple of weeks. Salan also intended to hinder the Viet Minh push towards the west by reinforcing the underground troops being organized in the highlands. The French too were considering using guerilla tactics, counting on the ethnic minorities. The first groups had been created around some Tongking outposts during de Lattre's command and under the auspices of the SDECE. Since the start of 1952, the GCMA (groups of mixed airlifted commandos) were operating throughout the Viet Minh zone. After a reconnaissance stage, officers and equipment (an estimated ton of materiel a month for every ten men) were parachuted to the men chosen to fight the guerillas. In June 1952, Giap had to appeal for Chinese aid to liquidate the underground in the region of Lao Kay. The affair remained secret, the command of the expeditionary force not wishing this incursion by some of Lin Biao's battalions to disturb public opinion in mainland France.[71]

Subjected to the ups-and-downs of almost general guerilla warfare, and faced with an increasingly powerful battle force, the French were on the defensive everywhere by the end of 1952. More than ever what de Lattre said in September 1951 in a report to the government was valid. "There may be a catastrophe in Indo-China; there is little chance of a miracle."

6

Liquidations

CRISIS

On 16 February 1951, in his *Journal du septennat*, Auriol wrote the following about the Vietnamese head of state: "When someone buys the villa of the Count of Paris in Morocco, when he has his own aeroplane so that he can get about more quickly if need be, when he has tennis courts built so that he can take women there, how can you expect him to govern a country properly? What has he achieved in the last two years?" In the entry for 17 November 1952, he reported the opinions expressed by the Secretary of State for War, Chevigné, "Bao Dai is unknown in Tongking and Cochin-China and discredited in Annam where they know him. He has no contact with anyone and no authority." One certainly could not say that his protectors had any illusions about their protégé. The international attention that the regime had managed to attract was not matched by its popularity. The organization which the French referred to as the Viet Minh was called "the resistance" by the vast majority of the Vietnamese people. Its successes had aroused the patriotism of individuals who were far from being classed officially as "rebels". The term "rebel" in this context was an extremely ambiguous one. As far as the government of the Democratic Republic of Vietnam was concerned, the Saigon government was a regime of usurpers put there by the French and therefore out of line with public opinion. So where did Bao Dai's legitimacy lie? In tradition? But he had abdicated in 1945 in favour of the revolutionary government and had only been restored in an illusory sense in 1949. Certainly, he was referred to as "His Majesty Bao Dai", but the Annamite Empire had had its day.

The only way in which the Vietnamese head of state could claim to resemble the "son of heaven" was in his desire to remain unseen. When he was not in Cannes, he resided far from the real Vietnam, in Dalat or in his retreat at Ban Me Thuout in the Moi country. He was constantly surrounded by an entourage, headed by his confidant, the Catholic

Nguyen Dê, who was also the head of the imperial cabinet. Apart from gambling, women and hunting, Bao Dai also enjoyed complicated intrigues; his keenly malevolent intellect delighted in them and Nguyen Dê was used to implement them. The Saigon government was answerable to no one but Bao Dai. All the main parties that supported the regime were represented, but they were divided and opposed to one another in matters of tactics, ideology and the interests of the country. None of these forces, Catholics, Cadaoists, Hoa Hao or VNQDD, supported the Tam cabinet fully. The sects were busily plotting because they did not like the fact that the government wanted their fiefdoms to be subject to the common law. The gradual rallying of the Catholics did not make them any more united politically, and they represented every shade of opinion ranging from supporters of the Viet Minh such as Nguyen Manh to the pro-American Ngo clan.

Even though it was represented in the Tam government by Vu Hong Khanh, who had been one of the signatories of the Sainteny-Ho Chi Minh accords, the VNQDD conducted itself with extreme reserve. As for the newly re-formed ultra-nationalist extreme right-wing movement, the Dai Viet, which had sided with the Japanese during the war, it was now counting for the most part on American support. The Dai Viet was the most powerful force in Bao Dai's time. A semi-clandestine, centralized party split into divisions and cadres, it delighted in ambiguity. "The theoretical organization, which was extremely mysterious, became even more so when it split into two groups, in order to meet the political and tactical needs of the moment and so as to enable the movement to be both in government and in opposition, to deal with France and yet fight it at the same time and to struggle against the Viet Minh and yet maintain contacts with certain of its members and sympathisers" (Dabezies). The party was well established in Tongking, and took advantage of the fact that its leader, Nguyen Huu Tri, was in charge of the region, to form cells within the police and the administration. It was thus able to exercise a regime of terror.[1]

The first elections held by the regime were the municipal elections of 1953. They gave very little indication of just how representative the various political forces really were, mainly because only a million electors were involved. For the most part, polling took place in towns and cities. On the Red River Delta, voting took place in less than one village in ten. Due to the lack of voters, the fact that the Lien Viet did not participate of course, and also the confusion over political labels, there was no certain way of analysing the results, although it was noted that a number of the winners had expressed harsh criticism of the government. Next came the election of provincial councils in the autumn and finally the general elections. Nguyen Van Tam felt it was important to lend a certain democratic legitimacy to what was actually a monarchy, if only to improve the official Vietnam's image in the eyes of the West, particularly the United States. He also launched agrarian reforms, granted freedom to the trade unions and put together an employment code. His initiatives won him support here and there from politicians who had previously pursued a centrist or wait-and-see policy. But it also led to veiled hostility on the part of the most conservative factions in the government. Tam abandoned his previous lethargy and attempted to build up a nationalist Vietnam. Since this happened at the very moment when the Viet Minh, who were so much more united and powerful, were preparing to counter-attack, the effort was doomed to failure. Furthermore, despite his ability and determination, Nguyen Van Tam still looked like France's man, even to the anti-communist camp.

The legitimacy of the two monarchies of western Indo-China, rooted as they were in long tradition, was more assured than that of Bao Dai. Here, there was a better case for describing the guerillas as "rebels". Nevertheless, the powers that reigned in Phnom Penh and Vientiane came under increasing threat as the war spread throughout Indo-China.

The 1951 elections in Laos, for which there was an extremely low turnout, resulted in a victory for the party of Souvanna Phouma, who then took over from Phoui Sananikone. His government found itself faced with growing activity on the part of the revolutionaries of the Pathet Lao. In August 1950, Souphanouvong had created the provisional government of the state of Laos. The Prince attended the inaugural conference of the Lao Dong, during the course of which a treaty of alliance, on the basis of equality and independence, was signed by the three Indo-Chinese revolutionary movements. Considerably strengthened by the support of the Viet Minh, Souphanouvong was also able to recruit from the mountain-dwelling minorities, such as the Sithone Komadan who were one of the most important *kha*s of the Boloven Plateau.[2] The Pathet Lao grew in strength, while Giap's army pushed westwards. By early 1953, the Viet Minh had established a presence along most of the long Laotian border. With its support, the Souphanouvong government was installed in the red Thai capital, Sam Neua. A large area of jungle stretching from China as far as Cambodia, in which the rebels were more or less guaranteed freedom of movement, became totally isolated from the authority of the government in Vientiane. Thanks to the strong backing of its Vietnamese ally, the Pathet Lao now had a real territorial base. Souphanouvong denounced the monarchy as French puppets. The government hit back by calling the revolutionaries traitors and tools of the Viet Minh.

The autumn of 1951 saw the beginning of a turbulent period in Cambodia. Two years later, constitutional order was restored by the election of a new assembly, dominated once again by the Democrats. In October, the deputies placed Huy Kanthul at the head of a government which immediately expressed its opposition to the king and the French. That month, the French commissioner Raymond was assassinated by a servant who was a Viet Minh member, and Son Ngoc Thanh, the strong man of the Japanese period, returned to the country after Paris had confirmed his appointment at Sihanouk's request. Son Ngoc Thanh immediately joined the nationalist bid for power.[3] When Risterucci arrived to take over from Raymond, he found the kingdom in total disarray. Son Ngoc Thanh had joined the guerillas near the border with Thailand and was calling for a general uprising and trying to federate the various Issarak bands under the very noses of the American forces. Thanks to the support of the Viet Minh, the communist guerrilla movement was otherwise strong.[4] Although few in number by comparison with the Franco-Khmer forces, the partisans managed to cause an increasing degree of destabilization. The equivalent of the Pathet Lao in Cambodia was the FUNC, or United National Front of Cambodia, one of the signatories of the triple alliance of March 1951. Torn apart by divisions and increasingly discredited by corruption and patronage, the ruling Democrats were disinclined to collaborate with the French, whom they wished to see removed immediately. Furthermore, they were rendered still less able to fight the guerillas since some of their own leaders were in contact with them. As in 1949, the king was prompted to defy the ruling party. In June 1952, he sacked Huy Kanthal, put together a cabinet of his own supporters, and appointed himself head of the government. In January 1953,[5] he decided to dissolve the assembly and declare a state of emergency, throwing several of his opponents into prison.

Now that he had carried out this legal, two-part *coup d'état*, the king had all the power he needed to carry out his plans. He had first outlined them in 1952 when he made a proclamation to the people asking them for three years in which to implement a whole series of reforms and achieve "full and complete independence". Until then, Sihanouk had steered his way between the disorganized agitation of the Democrats and the protection of France, not wanting to enter into open conflict with the former or to appear to be a yes-man. Now that he was complete master of the situation, he was in a position to take charge of the nationalist movement in order to restore total sovereignty to the country without having recourse to armed struggle. So, the final showdown with Paris was instigated at the beginning of 1953 by Cambodia, the least vulnerable to the Viet Minh of the three associated states.

In February, Sihanouk left for France where he wrote to President Auriol and met those responsible for French policy on Indo-China. He put his argument to all of them, namely that it was necessary to proceed with the final transfer of power in Indo-China in order to prevent the situation from worsening and to combat the Viet Minh. An independent and united Cambodia would soon put an end to rebel activities and would retain friendly links with France. However, he was granted no concessions so in April he flew to North America. He hoped to play on America's traditional anti-colonialist feelings towards France. But he was disappointed by the attitude of Dulles, the recently appointed Secretary of State, who was deaf to his arguments and told him that "any dispute with France would mean playing into the hands of the communists". So Sihanouk went to the newspapers. In a famous interview with the *New York Times*, he complained about France's attitude and threatened to side with the Viet Minh against her. The crisis in Franco-Khmer relations was now out in the open. It lasted seven months, fuelled by the tirades of the "little king" as he carried out his "crusade for independence" in his own skilful, determined, tragi-comic way. On his return home, he left the capital and took refuge in a sector assigned to the national army and then exiled himself in Thailand, where his activism was not welcomed by the local authorities. On 21 June, he returned to his own kingdom and went to the province of Battambang, where he was surrounded by Khmer troops. There, he called upon Cambodia to mobilize and refused all contact with the representatives of France.

It was not long before the Saigon government followed Sihanouk's example, although in a different way. On 10 May 1953, René Mayer proceeded to devalue the piastre to a more realistic figure of 10 francs, thus sparking off a crisis in Franco-Vietnamese relations. The French Prime Minister had plenty of good reasons for proceeding with the measure, but in order to avoid speculation he made the decision without first consulting the Indo-Chinese states. Apart from the fact that it put a stop to some lucrative shady deals, the devaluation caused a certain amount of economic upheaval. But most important of all, France's cavalier methods demonstrated its true attitude towards the sovereignty of its associates and towards past agreements.[6] The three Indo-Chinese capitals raised a chorus of protest over the move. Haphazard safety measures were taken in order to cushion its effects. Price rises followed. Saigon called for a re-examination of "the concept of the French Union and quadripartism". In June Tam stated, "It is clear that the constitution laid down by France in 1946 no longer responds to the needs of the nations which have to abide by it." He expressed a wish to see the end of the customs union[7] and the monetary union, with a transfer of the foreign exchange office. He also said he would like to see large sectors entrusted to the national army. In his conversations with Letourneau, Bao Dai added that the latter should also have supreme command over the forces of the French Union in Vietnam. Without doubt, devaluation had given excellent ammunition to Sihanouk's campaign and had actually helped to relaunch it.

This intensive campaign prompted the newly-formed Laniel government to issue a memorandum on 3 July 1953, stating that as far as France was concerned, "in view of the perilous circumstances brought about by the current state of war, there is every reason to finalize the independence and sovereignty of the states of Indo-China and come to an agreement with the three governments concerned over the transfer of the powers France had retained in the interests of those states." The concession was accompanied by a symbolic change in that a diplomat, the ambassador Dejean, was appointed general commissioner in Indo-China.[8] His predecessor, Letourneau, had been in Saigon for a year while still remaining a member of the French government, and he had been answerable to no one. Dejean was placed under the supervision of the Secretary of State for the Associated States, Marc Jacquet. However, in order to simplify things, Laniel's cabinet also appointed a Minister for Indo-Chinese Affairs, namely Paul Reynaud, the man behind the declaration of 3 July. Even though there was no clear division of responsibility,[9] at least the two men were in agreement that the three states should have real independence, unlike other ministers such as Bidault and President Auriol, who were of the opinion that it was impossible to deviate from the framework imposed by paragraph VIII of the constitution.

Open negotiations were conducted with the governments of the associated states in order to determine the status of each one. These proved more complicated in some cases than in others. Laos was vulnerable and threatened by invasion and soon agreed to a treaty of friendship and association, according to which, "it willingly reaffirms its membership of the French Union".[10] However, the atmosphere remained tense between Paris and Phnom Penh. Sihanouk's representative Penn Nouth demanded "status within the French Union at least equal to that of India within the Commonwealth". In concrete terms, he asked for the immediate devolution of all the powers exercised by France and by the quadripartite system laid down at Pau. In August, agreement was reached over the transfer of France's remaining police and judicial powers. It was much more difficult to come to an agreement over the army since, in view of the general situation, the demands of the Khmers seemed unrealistic. Worried by Cambodia's declaration that the country might move towards neutralism, the Americans put pressure on Penn Nouth. The agreement was finally signed on 17 October. The basic groundwork was complete. Sihanouk was now able to resume contact with the French. Leaving his internal exile, he made a triumphant return to the capital on 8 November. Negotiations continued, but quietly this time, and with none of the tension of the preceding months. At the beginning of 1954, they culminated in further transfers of economic and diplomatic powers, thus making the kingdom completely independent.

Bao Dai's demands were very similar to those of Sihanouk, but his regime was weaker and the military situation was much worse in Vietnam than in Cambodia. The ex-Emperor left Vietnam in July 1953 to open negotiations in connection with the Laniel cabinet's declaration of 3 July. Nguyen Van Tam joined him in September. The departure of the head of the government led to a revolt instigated by the sects. On 5 September, their representatives got together with a leading Buddhist and a Catholic prelate and signed a document denouncing the government in the strongest of terms. The bishop in question was Diem's brother, Ngo Dinh Thuc. Thus the Ngo clan had now entered the picture. On the next day, the intellectual of the family, Ngo Dinh Nhu, led a gathering of about fifty people which culminated in the formation of a front aimed at achieving unity, independence and peace. It intended to group together the forces oppposed to Tam and set itself up as the uncompromising defender of Vietnamese sovereignty.

It was in this heightened, impassioned atmosphere that the commissioner-general, Dejean, was prompted to make the following statement on 10 September:

> If the principle of a single commander in wartime is not recognized, if the associated states do not allow the French supreme command the same prerogatives that France and the NATO states have granted to an American general, then there is no French Union. In a world which is returning to coalitions and in which free nations need to unite in order to survive, if the member states of the Union are not linked by treaties of alliance and constant diplomatic co-operation then there is no French Union. If the mutual economic advantages offered to one another by France and Vietnam are insufficient to counter the attraction of foreign

markets, if France is unable to obtain from Vietnam even a part of the benefits that a certain other power has been granted by the Philippines, then there is no French Union. If the French language does not retain a privileged place at secondary school level, if the Vietnamese, who have so many intellectuals among their number, do not feel the same responsibility as we do towards a culture which has become their own, then the whole situation will become a tower of Babel and there will be no French Union in Indo-China.

Unable to obtain the constituent assembly demanded by Nhu's Front, Bao Dai agreed to an assembly of an appointed congress, so as to involve all the anti-Viet Minh forces in the definition of the new relationship with France. The congress met on 14 October under the chairmanship of Kim, who had been the head of the government during the Japanese period. The tone was set right from the beginning. The drastic proposals made by the first speakers led on to greater and greater demands. The congress ended with a refusal to give Bao Dai a list of twenty people who would take part in the negotiations with France, as was originally intended, and demands for a constituent assembly and for complete independence outside the French Union. Auriol complained in his *Journal*, "It is scandalous, a terribly ungrateful gesture. We must take drastic action." Certainly, the Vietnamese head of state dissociated himself from all this and his representative, Prince Buu Loc, managed to obtain an amendment to the final document, stating, "We reject the French Union in its current form." But the Saigon congress was a revelation. It showed the ruling French politicians how weak Bao Dai was, even within anti-Viet Minh circles. It revealed to them the existence of a pro-American group. It made them aware of the futility of their own efforts, given that they would inevitably have to grant unconditional sovereignty to the country. Tam was now branded and there was too much opposition to him, so he was removed in December and replaced by the king's cousin, Buu Loc. With independence already granted to Cambodia and about to be granted to Vietnam, the French Union underwent a complete change even before the war was over. Section VIII was now null and void and there was a return to the progressive concept expressed in the preamble to the constitution. On 18 January 1954, Ambassador Dejean explained to the Vietnamese government that the French Union was based on two concepts: "The first, which is expressed in the preamble to the constitution, is basically bilateral and egalitarian. The second, contained in paragraph VIII, is federative and bestows a coordinating and administrative role upon one of the partners. I am now permitted to tell you that

France has decided on the former in the case of its relationship with the associated states." The declaration of 28 April 1954 proposed two treaties, one "granting independence and full and complete sovereignty to Vietnam" (for the fifth time, but this time for real), the other establishing a system of cooperation between the two countries. The treaties were finally signed on 4 June. However, this whole procedure was something of a farce, for the point was that armed struggle had prevailed. In the meantime, Dien Bien Phu had fallen.

HONOURABLE WITHDRAWAL?...

The political and the military crises both began at the same time, early in 1953, when Mayer was in power. While Sihanouk was launching his campaign for independence, Giap was attacking northern Laos. Two attacks were launched, one from Thailand, which was aimed at the royal capital of Luang Prabang, and another from Hoa Binh and North Annam, which threatened the Plain of Jars. In aiming for the Mekong Delta, Giap undermined all the accepted ideas about strategy that had so far been built up during the war. He threatened to take Cambodia from the rear and to upset the pacification of South Vietnam. Some French generals were of the opinion that he might even overthrow the government of Thailand.[11] Since the time of de Lattre, it had been understood that Tongking was a useful barrier protecting the whole of South-East Asia. The offensive of March-April 1953 showed this conclusion to be false and proved that, by holding onto the Red River Delta, the French were merely occupying a sort of bridgehead. Here, as in the defence of Thailand, Salan was counting to some extent on the developing underground forces and on raids aimed at disrupting the enemy's movements. Most of all, however, he was relying on the technique of fortified camps. Three had just been set up, one on the Plain of Jars, one at Luang Prabang and one at Paksane on the Mekong. Things began badly for the expeditionary force. The withdrawal from Sam Neua turned into a rout in which many of the Laotian troops deserted.

Souvanna Phouma appealed to the United Nations to condemn this invasion of sovereign territory. The Americans supported such a measure. However, the French government hesitated, then finally opposed it on the advice of Bidault, the Minister for Foreign Affairs, who did not want the problem to become an international issue in this way. Nevertheless, the Americans took the precaution of stepping up their aid to Thailand. But in the end the invasion came to a halt before the two major obstacles of Luang Prabang and the Plain of Jars. Exhausted and far from their bases, the Viet Minh divisions had to turn back in

May, so as to be able to spend the rainy season away from the Delta as was customary. However, mobile units and political agents were left in place in anticipation of a further attack, and in order to ensure the strength of their ally, the Pathet Lao. The occupation of Laos had merely been postponed. In May 1953, the Lao Dong launched revolutionary agrarian reforms based on the slogan "Give the land to those who cultivate it."[12] It was certainly an attempt to copy the policies of China. But, given that these men had always associated social struggle with nationalist struggle, it was also an attempt to rouse the rural masses into a final struggle against France and its "puppets".

The new face of the war convinced the French Prime Minister, René Mayer, of the necessity of seeking "an honourable withdrawal" from Indo-China as quickly as possible. Since a way could not be found immediately, he appointed a new commander-in-chief who was to be charged with the task of ensuring the necessary conditions for such a withdrawal. In the upper military echelons Salan, nicknamed the "mandarin", was the man who knew Indo-China best. He was removed and replaced by Navarre, who had never served there at all. A new commander was needed for a new phase, someone who would see things from a fresh point of view. Navarre had been a brilliant chief of staff for the Centre-Europe sector and had impressed Mayer, the then deputy for Constantine, when he had been in command there. Besides the "mandarin", de Lattre's other "marshals" were replaced too, all except for Cogny, an engineer and committed fighter, who was placed in charge of the North Vietnamese troops. The departure of Letourneau in June completed the changeover. The piastre was devalued and the MRP ceased to be in charge of policy in Indo-China. It was definitely the end of an era.

The new commander-in-chief painted rather a grim picture of the situation he found on his arrival in Saigon. The forces said to be of the French Union slightly outnumbered those of the Viet Minh, 450,000 men as against 400,000.[13] In the early stages of the war, General Leclerc had estimated that 500,000 soldiers would be needed in order to ensure a military solution to the question, and so they were not far short of this. Later calculations made by the Americans proved that, given the nature of the conflict, the forces of repression had no chance of winning unless they outnumbered the guerillas 10 to 1. On the French side, the quality of the troops varied greatly. Events at Sam Neua had already shown that the combativeness of Indo-Chinese soldiers often left much to be desired. It was a motley army with an ever-decreasing minority of French troops and its soldiers had a variety of reasons for fighting. Many of them had very little apparent reason at all.[14] Furthermore, it had to face the APV (Popular Army of Vietnam), a homogenous force[15] whose sole aim was war. The command also fell short of what was to be desired. The officers only stayed in Indo-China for a limited period of time: therefore they had less experience of the type of war in question than their adversaries. Above all, there were too few of them. To take a typical example, a few months later, one colonel was placed in charge of the equivalent of a whole division, at Dien Bien Phu. The most worrying thing of all, without a shadow of doubt, was the fact that Navarre's troops were at the mercy of a widespread guerilla force which was immobilizing them and all he could find to oppose the eight divisions of Viet Minh[16] were six mobile units[17] and eight battalions of parachutists. In other words, the French fighting corps (and Navarre was not the first to deplore this) was equal to about one-third of the enemy fighting corps.

The Viet Minh also had clear superiority when it came to intelligence. It could easily predict the movements of the expeditionary force. This was partly because the latter relied on heavy transport vehicles, and partly because the whole population was there to spy on them. In order to understand the general outline of the way in which the war was being conducted, all one had to do was read the newspapers and accounts of various parliamentary debates. There were also leaks. *L'Observateur* gave a faithful report of the defence committee meeting of 24 July 1953. As a former intelligence officer, Navarre was extremely aware of this aspect of the operations and he took the maximum precautions. On the other hand, the French got very little information out of the Vietnamese people. Many supported the Viet Minh, and those who did not were afraid of them.[18] For the most part, information was obtained by breaking codes. Needless to say, they had no information on negotiations with China, or on the content of private discussions among Viet Minh leaders, or on how the latter envisaged the rest of the war. Furthermore, on the Democratic Republic of Vietnam side the war had been led from the very beginning by the same men, who could thus ensure that it was conducted in a continuous and coherent manner.

By May 1953, much of northern Indo-China was controlled by the enemy, a situation which gave the French commanders double cause for concern. Laos, with its wide open spaces and lack of roads, looked as if it would be difficult to defend. The habitable areas of Tongking had not been subjected to any large-scale attacks since the beginning of 1951. On the other hand, ever since Alessandri had won back the Red River Delta on the eve of Cao Bang, the Viet Minh had made regular and methodical attempts to undermine it. The Delta was the size of two

French *départements* and had 10 million inhabitants, so it was an important prize. It provided the Viet Minh with the bulk of its troops, rice and other provisions. France concentrated over a quarter of its troops there, stationing them in dozens of outposts covering almost the entire area. These outposts alone accounted for 20,000 men, who were thus immobilized.[19] Although this defence line set up by de Lattre did disperse any major attacks, it did not stop the enemy from getting through in one way or another. So, while the mobile units were fighting at Hoa Binh, Giap took advantage of their absence to move in major reinforcements. The men of the expeditionary force drew a map of the type known in military terms as a *carte vérole* or 'pox map' (translated into MRP terms as *carte rougeole* or 'measles map'), on which villages held by the enemy were represented by a red dot. In 1953, 5,000 of the 7,000 Delta villages were in the hands of the Viet Minh. So, now the latter had more than 60,000 suitably armed men inside the French lines.

The People's Army of Vietnam established hideouts near the remotest of the 900 enemy garrisons. The villages there were fortified and used to store arms and food. So, first Linarès, then Cogny, had to deal with the problem of repeated night raids on their garrisons by an increasingly well-equipped enemy,[20] and all attempts to root out the guerillas and surround them proved fruitless. The part of Tongking in which the French were based was now surrounded by an area totally controlled by the Democratic Republic of Vietnam and Giap was in a position to concentrate his entire fighting force there. Menaced from within by a progressively deteriorating situation, Tongking was all the more worrying to the French generals because they could not ignore the Chinese threat. The forthcoming armistice in Korea gave rise to fears that the People's Republic of China would direct its efforts southwards again. Only the expeditionary force had tanks and aeroplanes, and these constituted its one undoubted claim to superiority. The military commanders felt that the war would become protracted, and this led them to economize on certain types of equipment such as anti-aircraft and anti-tank weapons.

The imminent end to hostilities in Korea threatened to bring about changes. The Chinese would probably step up their aid to the Viet Minh. Furthermore, the possibility of a raid by Chinese "volunteers", and more probably of an air raid, could not be ruled out. It was not long before the intelligence service spotted Vietnamese pilots undergoing training across the border. However on 28 March 1953, just when it seemed that the Panmunjom negotiations were about to reach their conclusion, the final communiqué of the Franco-American talks was issued, which deterred the Chinese from taking any action In Indo-China.

Navarre was now facing a situation which he felt was critical. Like his predecessors, he began by asking for reinforcements. They were sent, but in niggardly numbers. It was a question of just holding out and speeding up the process of forming national armies, so that these could bring relief. The 1953–4 campaign promised to be difficult. Therefore, the "Navarre plan" advocated a strictly defensive attitude in the area where the Viet Minh was strongest, north of the 18th parallel. On the other hand, an active peacemaking policy was pursued in the south. The idea for operation "Atlante" came into being, an exercise intended to clear the southern part of Annam, where there was a large concentration of enemy forces. The aim was to place South Vietnam under the control of General Hinh's recently formed army as quickly as possible. The commander-in-chief felt that this army was now strong enough to make it possible for the situation to be turned around during the 1954–5 campaign. Some time during that period, he could then try to bring about a decisive battle and create the right conditions for an "honourable way out", as he had been requested to do by René Mayer.

During the usual rainy season lull, Navarre managed to carry out two timely operations. He took Langson and occupied it for several hours (the effect of this was mainly psychological) and withdrew from Na San without incident. The Na San operation showed the effectiveness of the fortified camps (which could be dismantled if necessary) and also their limitations. The Viet Minh built a track suitable for vehicles which enabled them to bypass the valley completely, thereby depriving the base of its main reason for existence, so it was abandoned. In October, the French attacked and routed Division 320 as it moved in from the Annamese border and prepared to infiltrate the Delta. At that point Giap made a choice. He decided to concentrate most of his efforts on Laos, not on the Plain of Tongking. The latter would be a secondary theatre of war, used for minor raids aimed at diversion and destabilisation. As soon as Navarre received the first intelligence reports, he decided to occupy Dien Bien Phu as Salan had in fact suggested in his final report. The road to Luang Prabang ran through the valley in the extreme west of the Vietnamese highlands. Navarre took it upon himself to defend the kingdom by setting up a powerful line of defence along the perimeter of this valley. The position would also serve as a base for operations in Thailand, where Laichau was still holding out. A few officers raised objections to the setting up of a fortified camp. These were basically of two types. First of all, it would not prevent the Viet Minh from getting through. With its logistics, the Viet Minh could get past anything. However, came the reply, it would need heavy equipment for an attack on Laos and that was where Dien Bien Phu could come in useful. The most relevant criticism came from the fighter pilots, who said that weather conditions over the area would often make air raids impossible, and fighter planes taking off from Hanoi (300 kilometres away) would only just be within their radius of action.

On 20 November, the French succeeded in occupying the basin by means of a massive airborne operation commanded by Colonel Gilles, the man responsible for Na San. Headquarters had made its calculations. Given that its bases were so far away, the enemy would only be able to maintain two divisions in the area. It would only have limited artillery at its disposal and would only be able to carry out brief skirmishes. Giap mobilized the local inhabitants, and was able to surround the area with four well-equipped divisions. So, straight away, it seemed as if one of the functions assigned to the fortified camp, i.e. to serve as a base for operations in Thailand, was no longer valid. While Laichau was being evacuated,[21] Dien Bien Phu prepared itself for a regular siege. Had he been well informed by the Deuxième Bureau concerning the huge scale of the Viet Minh operation, the commander-in-chief could have proceeded to withdraw. But, by the end of December, this had become impossible because the position was totally surrounded. So, the French commanders were condemned to the kind of confrontation that their initial plan had rejected. Navarre's subordinates were not altogether unhappy about this. Navarre had not set up this blockade to break the Vietnamese but to protect Laos. He feared the battle to come, but many of the officers of the expeditionary force looked forward to the opportunity of destroying the elusive enemy forces at last, by the sheer superiority of French military equipment.

Despite the likelihood of a large-scale confrontation at Dien Bien Phu, operation "Atlante" went ahead in January 1954, as planned. It was essential if the handling of the war was to be transferred to the Vietnamese themselves.[22] At the time, the French press had recently been full of alarming stories describing Indo-China as having been cut in two, following a successful raid by the Viet Minh which had enabled them to occupy the town of Thakkek on the Mekong. This action was part of the Giap's diversionary tactics in central Laos and on the Delta. Meanwhile, huge efforts were being made to supply the forces stationed around Dien Bien Phu. Roads were repaired or even specially built, so that supplies could be brought in by truck. Supplies were also brought in in the traditional way, and thousands of coolies were mobilized for the purpose. The bulk was transported via Langson or Cao Bang, more than 500 kilometres from the fortified camp. The fact was that the Maoist regime had been able to increase its aid since the signing of the armistice at Panmunjom on 27 July 1953. On 3 September, Dulles issued a clear warning, "Communist Chine has trained, equipped and supplied the communist forces in Indo-China and is continuing to do so. There is a risk that Red China will send its own armies into Indo-China as it did in Korea. The government of Communist China must understand that a second act of aggression would have grave consequences that might reach beyond the boundaries of Indo-China. I state this calmly, in the interests of peace and in the hope of preventing the aggressor from committing another error of judgment".

Negotiated for two years and awaited for four months, the end of the Korean war was seen by the French government as a major event but a mixed blessing. Although it enabled China to strengthen its alliance with Vietnam, the settlement of the conflict also raised hopes for peace throughout the whole of South-East Asia. As Maurice Schumann stated to the United Nations, "Korea is not alone in the world, peace is not divisible. It is difficult to imagine real, lasting peace in the Far East while there is war in other parts of Asia." Anyway, when looked at in conjunction with the worsening military situation and the conviction that a victory on the ground was impossible, the crisis in relations with the associated states and public indifference as revealed largely by opinion polls,[23] this new development seemed to make it imperative to find a way out of the war by means of negotiation. This viewpoint was expressed in the nomination speeches of five new prime ministerial candidates,[24] which were delivered between 21 May 1953 and 26 June 1953, during the crisis that followed the fall of the Mayer government. Mendès-France, who was standing, although without any great conviction, remained vague on the topic. However, it was generally known from an interview he had recently given to l'Express that his opinion had not changed. Since 1950, Mendès-France had stood for the body of opinion that wished to seek a compromise with Ho Chi Minh. He won a respectable proportion of the vote, and it was this fact that prompted Letourneau to write the following in a letter to General Navarre: "I am somewhat worried for the future when I see that 300 members of parliament have voted for the nomination of M. Mendès-France, thereby practically stating that they are ready to envisage some way of pulling out of Indo-China. It is even more worrying when you think that 100 communist deputies voted for him too."

Bidault, who also lost the election, had an extremely limited view of the opportunities for negotiation. "On an international level, we shall not fail to use any conference called after the Korean armistice as an opportunity to mention the problem of the outside aid that the Viet Minh is receiving." Bidault was to be Minister for Foreign Affairs in Laniel's cabinet. Laniel opened up much broader possibilities in his nomination speech:

> Who would dare stand before this house and say that, given the chance, he would not put all his energy into ending this bloody war should the opportunity arise? My government will tirelessly seek such an opportunity, either during the course of the negotiations that are to follow the signing of the armistice in Korea or else by means of completely separate talks conducted in agreement with the governments of the associated states.

Handing over the war to the Vietnamese themselves and to the Americans had not proved adequate as a solution to the Indo-Chinese question. It was necessary to negotiate an "honourable way out". The idea was steadily taking hold, and a large majority of French politicians seemed to be in favour of it during the parliamentary debates of May–June 1953. The former Prime Minister, René Pleven, had been saying since 16 November 1951 that "the conclusion of an armistice in Korea would establish a favourable climate for talks with China". Furthermore, Letourneau made the following statement on 25 February 1952: "If there were to be an armistice in Korea, the government would agree to take part in setting up an international conference aimed at seeking a diplomatic solution to the conflict." He even went so far as to admit that Ho Chi Minh might be included in this vast discussion, along with the associated states. The idea of seeking peace on an international level cropped up again and again throughout the course of 1952. But, officially at least, the French leaders ruled out the possibility of any direct negotiations with the enemy. In private, however, some politicians from the right and the centre who were involved in running the economy were admitting it would no doubt have to come to that. Contact was made with the enemy shortly before the end of the Pinay government. It was arranged by a deputy of the assembly of the French Union called Raphael-Leygues, together with other radical figures, such as Sarraut and Mendès-France, who were equally worried about the way things were developing in Indo-China.

The man who carried out these secret preliminary talks was Prince Buu Hoi, a famous Vietnamese figure who was not, however, involved in the war. A cousin of Bao Dai, he lived in France where his work was highly regarded. He was a scholar and still retained the vague title of overseas cultural representative of the Democratic Republic of Vietnam. He seemed to possess all the right qualities to act as peacemaker. Under cover of his professional activities, the prince went to Rangoon to meet local representatives of the Viet Minh. The mission was approved by Auriol, Pinay and other former Presidents. Bao Dai was informed of it. Buu Hoi returned from the Burmese capital in March 1953, mission accomplished. However, these initial discussions had no immediate consequences.[25]

The following motion was presented to the congress held in May 1951: "Indo-China is now in the international forefront of the struggle against Stalinist imperialism. It behoves France to make a contribution to the defence of the free world within this theatre of operations, by striving to guarantee the security of South-East Asia and the East Indies." Until the end of that year, the Socialists had always been staunchly with the various governments on policy in Indo-China. In December 1951, the party voted in favour of the budget for the associated states, only the Communists and the small Progressistes fellow-travellers party voting against it.

But the recent parliamentary elections had brought a swing to the right, and after the formation of the Pinay government in March 1952, the Socialists moved into clear opposition, thus enabling them to distance themselves from the government. In April, they refused to take part in the vote on military supplies. Gaston Defferre gave the following explanation for this: "Our abstention is a way of asking the government to use every opportunity of bringing the war to an end and make every possible peacemaking initiative in every possible sphere." However, the party continued to be troubled and divided over the Indo-Chinese question. On his return from Vietnam, Christian Pineau expressed concern, but said that he hoped matters could be put right by the introduction of judicious reforms. Alain Savary, on the other hand, had always been most critical of the situation.[26] He urged his friends to come out clearly in favour of opening negotiations with Ho Chi Minh. The National Council of November 1952 declared itself in favour of this and demanded a parliamentary debate on Indo-China. During the course of this debate, Savary put forward the Socialists' point of view as follows, "Since we are not in favour of withdrawing troops without prior negotiations, nor of making the war an international issue, we remain firmly convinced that there is always the option of negotiating with the enemy and making every effort to come to a truce. This would be followed by free elections. There has not been a genuine, *bona fide* attempt to do this for six years." In short, "ceasefire, elections, negotiations". Before long, another Socialist was to press for just this kind of solution in yet another colonial war. It was a position that had been advocated up to 1949.

In March 1953, the Socialists voted against military supplies. Now, more and more ministers of the centre-left declared themselves in favour of conducting direct talks with the Viet Minh as Sarraut had done. At the 1952 conference of the UDSR (Union démocratique et socialiste de la Résistance—a centre-left party), François Mitterand attacked French involvement in the Far East in the strongest terms and put forward an opinion that some others shared with him at the time, namely that Europe and Africa should take precedence over Asia.[27] The situation deteriorated in the North African protectorates throughout the course of 1953, lending weight to this argument.

From the moment Laniel took office and the Korean war came to an end, everyone was talking in terms of negotiations. So the question now was not should we talk, but what should we talk about, with whom and how? Right and left were basically divided on this point, as was shown by the parliamentary debate of October 1953. The left wanted to put an end to the war by coming to some immediate arrangement with the Viet Minh. The right wanted to settle the affair within the framework of a general peacemaking initiative covering the whole of South-East Asia. But in the meantime the war continued, the Americans and the Vietnamese themselves playing an ever-increasing role in it. If the peace could not be internationalized the war would have to be internationalized. On 28 October, the national assembly voted on precisely this issue. There were 315 votes in favour and 251 against.[28] Those who voted against were the Communist Party, the Socialists, some Radicals, some members of the UDSR and a few members of the MRP. On 30 December 1951, Mendès-France, who supported direct negotiations with Ho Chi Minh, made the following reply to Pleven: "Today, ministers are talking vaguely about fighting the war on an international scale or opening up multilateral or indirect negotiations. This way, we will only lose what little we have left to lose in Indo-China." Savary made the following statement in the debate of October 1953: "Peace will not wait, it must be actively sought. You can talk to Moscow, Peking, London and Washington, but this will not help you to deal with the real issue. The only thing that will lead to an armistice is negotiation with Ho Chi Minh." The left accused the right of not really wanting peace, and of just trying to keep the assembly happy. Philippe Devillers wrote in *Esprit*: "In opting for a solution to the problem by putting the war on an international footing(?), the Laniel-Bidault government is deliberately taking the most dangerous course."[29] He added, "For him, negotiation with

China is merely a prelude to intensifying the war against the Republic of Vietnam. In a word, he only wishes to negotiate in order to obtain a better victory."[30]

In November 1953, Ho Chi Minh replied to the questions sent him by the Swedish newspaper *Expressen*. To the question, "Would it now be possible to seek a truce or an armistice?" he replied, "Let the French government call a halt to the war, then armistice would become a reality. The grounds for such an armistice are for France to respect Vietnam's independence." The Democratic Republic of Vietnam then confirmed several times in radio broadcasts that the revolutionary powers were ready to negotiate. Such overtures on the part of the Viet Minh made the position of those in favour of direct negotiation much easier.

Laniel's cabinet was divided and unsure of which route to take. However, the prevailing hostility to settlement by means of a Franco-Viet Minh conference won the day. The argument was always the same, and René Pleven repeated it in a report he compiled in February 1954, shortly after his return from a mission to Indo-China. He claimed that it would be bad for France's prestige and that it would cause trouble for the Saigon regime. Official talks would lead to the collapse of the Bao Dai government and undermine the safety of the expeditionary force by creating the risk of a general uprising. To exonerate themselves, Vietnamese troops might turn on their fellow soldiers, particularly their French officers. The war in Indo-China was now an integral part of the cold war, in fact it was one of the major issues. Therefore, any solution would have to be on a global scale, involving the two great communist powers. Since the death of Stalin on 5 March 1953, the USSR had shown a desire for détente. It was giving priority to European questions, calling above all for rejection of the EDC. Paris had not yet ratified the treaty, and there were growing divisions on the subject in political and even government circles. However, the most important thing to look for was a compromise on the part of China. In May 1953, a French economic mission headed set out for Peking, thus raising hopes of a reconciliation.[31] This was the first such western mission to visit the country. That same month, Reynaud promised in his nomination speech that "If China shows by its actions that it wants peace in the south, as well as in the north, France might be induced to reconsider certain diplomatic stances." As Laniel remarked to the chamber on 17 October 1953, "Moscow and Peking have made a number of references to the possibility of negotiations, both in the press and on the radio." The only thing that remained to do now was set these negotiations in motion.

On 11 May 1953, Churchill took advantage of the incipient thaw in

Soviet attitudes and proposed a four-nation summit conference. However, for months the Soviet Union had been requesting a five-nation meeting, and they reiterated this demand in their reply of 4 August. A few days after the treaty of Panmunjom, Moscow put forward the opinion that the agreement of 27 July was no more than an armistice, and that a political solution to the problem would have to be achieved by means of a concerted plan, in which Peking must be allowed to participate. Predictably, the United States rejected the idea, since it did not recognize Communist China. Furthermore, it condemned Chinese aggression in Korea. Such a proposal would be tantamount to granting China the status of a great power in its own right. In November 1953, the USSR finally agreed to a four-nation summit, to be conducted by the foreign minister of each of the countries involved. However, it reserved the right to request the participation of the People's Republic of China in the next conference.

So Molotov, Bidault, Eden and Dulles met in Berlin on 25 January 1954. The heads of the French, British and American governments had already attempted to co-ordinate their approach at the Bermuda conference held from 4 to 7 December 1953.[32] They failed to agree on the central issue of the talks, that of Germany. But, with the backing of Eden, Bidault managed to get what he wanted with regard to the Far Eastern question. The communiqué of 18 February announced that a conference aimed at finding an in-depth solution to the Korean affair would convene in Geneva on 26 April. It went on to state: "The problem of re-establishing peace in Indo-China will also be examined at the conference, to which representatives from France, Great Britain, the Union of Soviet Socialist Republics, the People's Republic of China and other interested states will be invited." So the French government had finally managed to get the settlement of the Vietnam war and the Korean problem lumped together. Dulles made a major concession by accepting the presence of the Peking regime at a large international conference. Bidault made him understand that, in view of growing pressure from the French public to open negotiations, this would be the least of all the evils. For its part, the USSR accepted the restrictions imposed by the Americans. A stipulation was made that the presence of a delegation from Communist China at the conference did not imply acceptance of the regime. Furthermore, the aim of the conference was strictly defined so that the heated question of Formosa, which was most important to Mao's government, would not be broached.

The fact that the machinery was now in place gave Bidault a number of arguments against any other form of negotiated solution. Several weeks previously, there had been serious talk of India acting as a mediator, an idea which had been vaguely discussed for a number of years. There was no longer any question of this happening.[33] Nor was there any question of giving in to the Minister of Defence, who was growing increasingly concerned about the situation and had been calling for direct contact with the Viet Minh, even if only on a secret and exploratory level. In fact, Pleven had contacted Alain Savary in connection with this mission. But divisions within the government and delays prolonged the operation. Savary did not set off until April, a few days before the Geneva Conference, and he got no further than Moscow. In his *Commentaires*, Jean Chauvel provides an insight into these constant disagreements within the French government. As ambassador to Switzerland, he had been given the task of setting up the conference, and so he called on all of the most important ministers. Of Reynaud he remarks, "He was of the set opinion that we should negotiate against the ratification of the EDC and for Indo-China to be placed entirely in the hands of the United States." Of Edgar Faure, "He was of the equally set opinion that we should seize the opportunity to negotiate with the USSR against rejection of the EDC and for a peace settlement in Indo-China." And of Pleven, "He saw the conference as a means of getting to the Viet Minh and appealing to their spirit of nationalism in such a way that it would be possible to negotiate an arrangement that would free them from the Chinese without putting them into the hands of the Americans." As for Bidault, "He envisaged direct talks with the Chinese, saying that he had his own reasons to believe that, in exchange for equipment that they needed, they would be willing to offer Ho Chi Minh a chair in politics at Peking University." If the Minister for Foreign Affairs thought that Ho Chi Minh would turn into another Markos, subsequent military developments would make him think again.

... OR LIQUIDATION IN CATASTROPHE?

In the months that followed the news of the forthcoming negotiations, Giap pulled out all the stops to try and win a decisive victory before the talks began. The diplomatic arrangements were made by 18 February 1954. The announcement of the conference meant that the stakes were now higher. Giap was now receiving more aid from China. He brought much of his new equipment into use around Dien Bien Phu, which he was now determined to take at all costs.

On the French side, this ground and air base had become one of the most visited places in the Far East. Ministers, generals and officials succeeded each other, to be told how wonderfully strong the position was.

The Minister of Defence said in his report, "No one expressed any doubts whatsoever as to the impregnability of this fortified camp." The basin measured sixteen kilometres by eight, much larger than that of Na San, with which it was constantly being compared and contrasted. There were 11,000 soldiers concentrated within it, who were of seventeen different nationalities. They were commanded by Colonel de Castries. Since the enemy held the jungle-covered peaks overlooking the wide open valley, this composite force had been placed right under its nose. Visitors to the site were always alarmed by this, but it was explained to them that the peaks surrounding the camp were too far away for enemy artillery to constitute a danger. In order to carry out an effective raid, the Viet Minh batteries would have to come halfway down the slopes, particularly if they wished to threaten the airfield, which was the most vital part of the base. The artillerymen would also explain that, if such a thing should happen, the enemy guns would be spotted as they moved into position and put out of action by shellfire from above and powerful artillery fire from inside the fortified camp.

Meanwhile, the situation meant that the French were scarcely able to bring in any reinforcements. Thanks to its position, the camp could only be supplied by air-lift, and this made it impossible to increase the numbers of the garrison. Furthermore, the only way to disrupt the long enemy lines of communication was by aircraft, and it was extremely difficult for pilots to see the Vietnamese convoys under the thick cover of the jungle. It was a futile exercise trying to cut off roads, as any damage was soon repaired by gangs of coolies, and besides, the paths had numerous forks and branches. Bombing was also useless on account of the terrain, the tenacity of the enemy and the simplicity of enemy means of transport. The more sophisticated means used later by the Americans to try and cut off the "Ho Chi Minh trail" also proved similarly ineffective.

The revolutionary government had mobilized tens of thousands of men and women, who then spent weeks making sure that a large proportion of the Viet Minh fighting corps had enough arms and food to carry on a long battle some distance away from its bases. This they achieved by driving the 700 trucks which the Democratic Republic of Vietnam now had at its disposal, by pushing heavily loaded bicycles[34] or by carrying the supplies on their back in the traditional panniers. Night after night, paths were made down the mountainside and shelters were built. Four infantry divisions, plus heavy infantry division No. 351, over 50,000 men in all, were now ready to attack.

The battle of Dien Bien Phu began on 13 March 1954, just as

Navarre was launching the second stage of operation "Atlante". The strength of the Viet Minh artillery, including their anti-aircraft equipment, immediately became clear. The guns were installed singly in well-concealed concrete bunkers (after the fashion of the Chinese), all up and down the sides of the valley. This made them practically impregnable, and yet they could threaten the French cannon which were clearly visible at the bottom of the valley. The officer in command of the artillery, Lieutenant-Colonel Piroth, committed suicide considering himself responsible for an error of judgment that had placed the camp at the mercy of enemy fire. Two forward outposts were subjected to heavy shellfire and overrun by Giap's men before Colonel de Castries, who was completely overwhelmed by the turn of events, could even organize the necessary counter-attacks. Once they had conquered "Beatrice" and "Gabrielle", the Viet Minh rendered use of the airfield impossible. From 17 March onwards, the air-lift ceased and the garrison could only be supplied by parachute drop. Already, it looked as if the fate of Dien Bien Phu was sealed.

The chief-of-staff, General Paul Ely, was sent on a mission to Washington. He and his opposite number, Admiral Radford, came to an agreement on the launching of operation "Vautour" (Vulture), a plan to save the fortified camp by carrying out massive bombing raids from the fortified airforce bases at Okinawa and in the Philippines. The French government agreed to this, even though it was in a difficult position. Without the aid of American planes, Dien Bien Phu would fall, and such a defeat would have serious consequences for the Geneva conference and for the French Union. With American aid, the war which the government hoped to put an end to at last might start all over again. Washington was more hestitant. Engineers such as Ridgway pointed out that the Korean war had shown operations of this kind to be futile. Politicians warned of the danger of escalation. America had just emerged from a confrontation with China and did not want to launch itself straight into another. When consulted, leading congressmen, including Lyndon Johnson, advocated caution. However, for over a month, the hawks, headed by Radford and backed up by Vice-President Nixon,[35] pressed for intervention and preparations were soon underway. Various possibilites were considered. There was even vague talk of using tactical atomic weapons. The justification the Americans gave for their actions was "Chinese involvement in communist aggression in Indo-China", and Dulles quoted several examples.[36] Although he was a former military commander, Eisenhower was more circumspect than his predecessor. Operation "Vautour" was abandoned at the end of April.

The British wanted an overall peace settlement in South-East Asia and had declared themselves against any untimely action. The Americans took refuge behind Britain's refusal to participate in order to justify their own non-participation. Left to their own devices, the French carried on with operation "Atlante" regardless, but made no attempt at any large scale manoeuvres aimed at bringing relief to the besieged camp. Cogny considered carrying out various raids from the Delta with a view to cutting off the enemy lines of communication, but none of these was put into practice.[37] Instead, an operation was planned which would use Laos as a base. It was an attempt at diversion rather than at liberating the camp. The situation worsened and, in the end, it was decided that the troops concerned would carry out a simple reconnaissance mission. But, in view of the conditions that prevailed at the fall of Dien Bien Phu, they were not even able to do this.

For nearly two months, Giap proceeded to close in on the camp methodically, alternating his attacks with periods of rest which enabled him to replenish his forces. Dozens of kilometres of trenches were dug in the basin so that the Viet Minh were able to get closer and closer to the French bases and capture them one after the other. They now had even more anti-aircraft equipment than ever, and this made movement by air difficult, apart from which all the available planes were involved in the battle. Reinforcements, in the form of troops and equipment, were regularly and easily being sent to the Viet Minh, whereas it became more and more difficult for the commanders of the expeditionary force to provision the garrison and compensate for the loss of men. Parachute drops became more and more risky, and it became increasingly difficult to retrieve the supplies as the enemy closed in. Yet right up to the end there were volunteers ready to go to the assistance of the besieged troops. For the last of these, it was their first jump. Such acts of bravery came to the notice of the French public, who took a detailed interest in the daily progress of this exotic Verdun, as it resisted to the bitter end.

The holders of Dien Bien Phu had been galvanized into this desperate resistance through the efforts of Colonel Langlais, who had taken matters in hand, with the help of Bigeard, after the first setback. On May 1, Giap launched his final attack. The last French outposts fell one after the other under the terrific human onslaught. The rains came early that year, so the French had to fight in the mud under incessant bombardment. In the end, it was down to man-to-man fighting. By 7 May 1954, the fortified camp no longer existed.

The French commanders had sent 15,000 men to defend Dien Bien Phu, 11,000 at the outset plus 4,000 parachutists during the siege. A few isolated individuals managed to escape in the direction of Laos. There were 2,000 deserters, most of them Thais, who came to be known as the "rats of Nam Youn" because they dug themselves in along the banks of the river. Three thousand soldiers were killed during the battle and 10,000 were taken prisoner. Half the prisoners were wounded. Meanwhile, the self-appointed strategists in the cafés back home were constantly asking the question, "What could they hope to have achieved stuck in that basin?"

Navarre did his best to play down the situation. Only a third of the forces of the French Union had been lost, and reinforcements had been sent to replace them. The battle had been extremely tough on the enemy, they had lost three times as many men and their morale had wavered at times. The fortified camp had fulfilled its intended purpose of holding up the enemy, so Laos had not been invaded. However, this did not alter the fact that the spearhead of the expeditionary force had been destroyed and that the eminently symbolic battle of Dien Bien Phyu was a resounding defeat. A model base, which the French high command had always made a point of showing to important visitors, had been utterly destroyed. People had followed the various stages of the siege day by day, not just in France but the world over, and it had ended in defeat. The incident captured the imagination of both sides, and each extolled the heroism of its troops, almost making a crusade out of the whole thing at times, as did the *Osservatore Romano*, for example. The long column of prisoners, filmed from above by a Soviet camera crew, came to be a popular image of the disaster. Dien Bien Phu was a victory of the East over the West. It also represented the confrontation between North and South Vietnam. It was an unusual case in the history of decolonization. A reputedly great power had been defeated in a large-scale battle by a national liberation movement, despite all its tanks and aeroplanes.

The French defeat gave encouragement to the freedom fighters of other colonies, particularly in North Africa, from which large numbers of troops had been withdrawn to meet the needs of the struggle in the Far East. There was increasing unrest throughout the protectorates, and some saw this as a sign of new wars to come. In Algeria, there was apparent calm, but the *Messalistes*, who had been saying that France was finished ever since World War II, now saw their judgment confirmed. Dien Bien Phu stirred the most determined of them into taking action on 1 November. Dien Bien Phu sounded the knell of the French Union.

The war lasted for another three months. After the defeat, General Ely went over on a tour of inspection accompanied by Salan. In June, Ely took over from Navarre. As both commissioner-general and commander-in-chief, Ely had been appointed to act as a kind of official receiver. The majority of the French army officers did not share Navarre's cool, optimistic analysis of events. They feared the worst, particularly as far as Hanoi was concerned. The situation throughout the Delta was steadily deteriorating,[38] and they felt that the People's Army of Vietnam would probably attack it while still intoxicated by its recent success. Defeat brought with it a series of withdrawals, as it had done after Cao Bang. The government gave orders that the safety of the expeditionary force was to be treated as top priority, and so it was necessary to concentrate resources to this effect. An Khê, a large town in the southerly part of the Mois plateaux and a vital strategic point between Cambodia and the coast of Annam, was held by mobile unit 100, which consisted mainly of the prestigious Korean regiment. The Viet Minh had been stepping up its activity in the area all that year, forcing the French to abandon Kontum in February. Although isolated and harrassed, the powerful An Khê garrison was not under any immediate threat. However, it was evacuated just the same as a precautionary measure. The operation was badly conducted and ended in another Cao Bang. The garrison came up against a series of deadly ambushes and lost a third of its men on the way to the base at Pleiku, which was situated 100 kilometres away.

Things went better in the Delta, where the French forces were positioned along the main route between Hanoi and Haiphong. Colonel Vanuxem was skilful in his evacuation of the bishoprics, an operation involving 100,000 civilian and military personnel. Taking advantage of this withdrawal, Giap launched an attack on the new base before it was fully in position. Cogny responded vigorously and dispersed the Viet Minh with tanks and aeroplanes. In the summer of 1954, the French were still in a position to inflict some savage blows on the enemy. They held most of the strategic parts of Laos and Cambodia and were soundly established in Cochin-China, so there was no need for them to go home yet. However, the situation in the Delta was critical. The People's Army of Vietnam had chalked up victories that opened up the way to the south. It would not be long before Laos, Cambodia[39] and Cochin-China were threatened too. So much hope rested on the recently formed army of South Vietnam but throughout the course of the year its strength had been steadily undermined by desertions. Faced with a Viet Minh that could sense imminent victory, the expeditionary force was in difficulties everywhere. However, in late July 1954, the Geneva conference agreed on an armistice.

The Geneva conference began to discuss the Indo-Chinese question on 8 May 1954, the day after the fall of Dien Bien Phu. Giap had calculated his moves well. As arranged, the delegations first met on 26 April to discuss Korea. Talks on this subject proceeded in an atmosphere of general indifference and, in the meantime, the conference began to tackle the problem of Vietnam. A list had been drawn up of the countries which were to take part, namely, the five major powers plus the associated states and the Democratic Republic of Vietnam. Even the layout of the meeting room had given rise to a laborious bargaining process because discussions were to take place between delegations from governments that did not recognize one another. The People's Republic of China was to make its international debut in the person of Chou En-lai. The other four "great powers" were to be represented by veterans of international diplomacy. The imperturbable Molotov, "Mr Nyet", and Sir Anthony Eden co-chaired the conference. It was general knowledge that the latter had played a decisive role in restraining the Americans. Dulles made no secret of his reservations. He only made a brief appearance in Geneva. His place was taken by General Bedell Smith, who was obviously worn out by illness.

Bidault was now a controversial figure, and it had become clear since the fall of Dien Bien Phu that his government was living on borrowed time. The delegations from Indo-China arrived in the first week of May. The Democratic Republic of Vietnam's delegation was headed by Pham Van Dong. Now that things were getting serious, Giam had been removed from the ministry for foreign affairs. Pham Van Dong began by demanding that the revolutionary governments of Laos and Cambodia should be present. His request met with a determined refusal on the part of the western powers.

At the beginning of the conference, general accounts of the situation were given. Bidault presented a history of the conflict as he saw it and then put forward the general outlines of his plan. He said that it was necessary, first of all, to distinguish between the two western kingdoms and Vietnam. In the case of the former, the problem was one of foreign aggression, and the only solution was for Viet Minh troops to withdraw. The latter, however, was a case of civil war. He advocated a ceasefire, and that troops should be regrouped bearing in mind the state of the war. It would then be up to Vietnam to solve its political problem on the basis of unity and independence. Pham Van Dong's plan contained two main points. First, the complete withdrawal of French troops from Indo-China after the armistice and secondly the reunification of all three countries by means of elections organized by "governments on both sides, in each of the states". The plan was accompanied by a promise to become part of the Union of Indo-China. Some people treated this as a joke.[40] The western powers felt that, if the plan were to be adopted as it stood, it would lead to the creation of three peoples' democracies. But, although the two plans were so different, they were not irreconcilable. For example, they both envisaged the ceasefire in similar ways, i.e., the redeployment of troops in spots according to what was known as the "leopard skin" principle. On the other hand, the proposals put forward by Bao Dai's delegation were judged to be completely unrealistic, since they called for the virtual surrender of an enemy that had just proved how strong it was.

Negotiations began on the basis of the plans put forward by the two main contenders. During the plenary sessions the delegates all stuck to the same arguments, but when they met in committee or on the sidelines, progress was made. As the military men of France and of the Viet Minh became accustomed to talking to one another, they began, first of all, to discuss the wounded of Dien Bien Phu (evacuation had been refused during the course of the battle). Eden was anxious that the war should not spread, as that would mean the failure of the talks, and he employed his skills to try and reconcile the various points of view. For weeks it had been rumoured that British diplomatic circles were in favour of dividing up Vietnam. The country itself had already paved the way for it, and in this way Laos, Cambodia and South Vietnam would become a bulwark protecting Thailand, Malaysia and Singapore.

This was the same kind of solution that had been adopted in Korea, even though the problems involved were not the same, for there was no actual front; the troops were simply dotted about. The newspapers had imagined that there would be more detailed plans than that. Bao Dai warned against such a division and the prospect even provoked nationalist demonstrations in Hanoi. France had never been a party to the idea. Bidault made the following promise to Bao Dai in a letter dated 6 May 1954, "France has no intention at all of paving the way for two internationally-recognized states, at the expense of Vietnamese unity."

Strangely enough, it was Pham Van Dong who first showed signs of coming round officially to the idea of division. On 25 May, he declared himself in favour of deploying the troops in individually-held zones rather than dotting them about. That same day, a conciliatory interview with another delegate from the Democratic Republic of Vietnam (namely the ambassador to Peking) appeared in *Le Monde*. It said, "First of all we must bring about a ceasefire. We lay down no preliminary conditions for this." Thus, negotiations proceeded one step at a time. Progress was so slow, however, that there began to be fears that the talks would go on forever as they had at Panmunjom, or that they might even break down. On 14 June, Senator Knowland called for an end to the talks on Indo-China, with the excuse that they were merely serving as enemy propaganda and the communists were only after an "abject surrender" on the part of France. Next day, at the instigation of the Americans, the Geneva conference on Korea was brought to an end. Chou En-lai was anxious to make his mark on the international scene, and even more anxious to ward off American intervention; so in order to prevent the talks on Indo-China from collapsing he made a concession. Having first discussed the matter with Eden, he agreed that Cambodia and Laos should be discussed separately from Vietnam, thus echoing the French argument. In the hours that followed, the deadlock seemed to break.

It was too late for Bidault. In May, the government had used the Geneva conference as an excuse for refusing to enter into any in-depth discussions on Indo-China. In order to achieve this, it had twice had to ask for a vote of confidence, once on 6 May and once on 13 May. The second time, it only received a majority of two votes. On 2 June, despite continual heckling, a debate was launched. It was interrupted for a few days, but restarted on 8 June. Laniel was now in a difficult position. He asked for another vote of confidence, which was taken on 12 June. This time he lost by 306 votes to 293.[41] The argument over the EDC and the disastrous military defeat had weakened the government. The prospect of a failure at Geneva was the final blow. There were fears that the war would escalate and that there would be a general mobilization.[42] Furthermore, the Americans had been pressing for "concerted action" for weeks and there were also fears that this might lead to the formation of a coalition and the prolonged presence of General Van Fleet in the Far East.[43] These were the threats that motivated Bidault to reach an agreement at last. In order to keep himself in office, Laniel had argued that a government crisis would delay the Geneva talks. In fact, everyone was thinking about the events of May–June 1953, just before the present government took office, and Bidault felt he had plenty of time to continue with the negotiations on Indo-China at will.

Actually, his career as a statesman was finished. Exceptional circumstances require exceptional methods. The Fourth Republic abandoned its usual practices abruptly. President Coty called upon Mendès-France, who had recently launched a virulent attack on the Minister for Foreign Affairs, accusing him of not doing everything he could to hasten the necessary agreement.[44] This was a completely fresh start, because the Prime Minister-designate had not been a government minister since

1945. Mendès-France resolved the crisis in record time. What the government needed was, if not a saviour, at least a liquidator.

On 17 June, Mendès-France attended the investiture of the assembly. The Communists declared that they would support him, as he had been advocating negotiations with the Viet Minh for years. However, he dissociated himself from them, saying that he wanted to be able "to negotiate independently with the enemy".[45] In his speech, he pointed out the dangers of a world war and gave himself one month to reach an agreement on Indo-China, saying: "I shall present myself before you on 20 July and give you an account of the results I have achieved. If there is no satisfactory solution by that date, you will be free from the agreement that binds us." He did not want the talks to get bogged down as they had done in Korea, particularly as he had consulted some of the military commanders and they had told him that the situation was critical. The report by General Blanc, the commander of the land forces, was particularly worrying. The tight deadline also prompted the enemy to try to reach agreement for, of all the French statesmen, Mendès was the one most likely to compromise and, if they failed, it might mean that the war would spread. The new Prime Minister appointed his team without bargaining with all the parties, as was the usual practice. He made the moderate, Guy La Chambre, responsible for the associated states[46] and appointed himself Minister for Foreign Affairs. It was a post that was usually the prerogative of the MRP. It was a sign of the times. The group which had hitherto borne most of the responsibility for policy on Indo-China was not invited into the new government,[47] whose first task was to end the war. Mendès-France decided to head the French delegation at the Geneva talks himself, but he retained Bidault's principal assistants, namely, Ambassador Chauvel, General Delteil and Colonel de Brébisson, so as to ensure continuity.

On 23 June, Mendès-France ("Prometheus Chained", as he was dubbed by the similarly named satirical weekly, *Le Canard Enchaîné*) began his task by talking to Chou En-lai. They managed to map out the general outlines of a possible agreement. Mendès-France ended the conversation with a threat to send in the troops if talks failed. The method he was to adopt consisted of direct negotiations with the Viet Minh. In fact, as under Bidault, there were two parallel sets of negotiations. Given Mendès-France's reputation and the deadline he had set himself, the enemy could rest assured that France wanted to extricate itself from the war at all costs and it was important to reach a compromise that would be acceptable to the enemy. But it was also necessary to reach an understanding with the western allies. Mendès-France was said by some to be in favour of peace through surrender. He was even suspected of neutralism. Consequently, Washington was most unhappy when he came to power. He had to make himself accepted, clear up misunderstandings and gain the support of the Americans. In the words of Chauvel: "When the Laniel government fell and a man came to power who was openly in favour of negotiation, the tendency was to wash their hands of the whole thing, feeling that the outcome was inevitable and that it would inevitably be bad." The new French delegation was helped by Eden, who pleaded their cause skilfully during the course of his talks with the Americans. General Bedell Smith had left Geneva at the end of June along with the other heads of the American delegation, and he had not expected to return. He was prompted to do so, however, and Mendès-France was finally able to speak on behalf of the West and obtain a compromise that was very close to the seven-point document which the British had recently stated as their conditions for an acceptable agreement.

As far as the other side was concerned, China and the Soviet Union put pressure on Pham Van Dong to climb down a little. The arrival of Mendès-France turned the possibility of a divided Vietnam into a definite idea. The French suggested dividing it at the threshold of Annam, that is to say at the 18th parallel. It was a solution that made sense geographically, and it had already been put forward by Navarre in the report he made after Dien Bien Phu.[48] It had also been suggested in a plan outlined by R. Guillain in *Le Monde* just before the conference. The delegation from the Democratic Republic of Vietnam argued for the 13th parallel, then agreed to the 16th. It was finally decided that the division would be drawn at the 17th parallel.[49] Some final compromises were made in order to resolve two more delicate questions, the date of the Vietnamese elections and the deadline for the withdrawal of the French troops. Pham Van Dong wanted elections to be held six months after the armistice. Mendès-France was against fixing a date at all. A compromise date was fixed for July 1956. The Viet Minh wanted the French troops out in three months, the French asked for 380 days, the compromise was 300 days. Agreement was reached within the allotted time. However, Cambodia did not want any restrictions on its independence and made some last minute claims. This did not jeopardise the success of the conference, and matters were settled on time. Molotov gave in, saying that such obstinacy on the part of such a country was laughable. Mendès-France had won his bet. The war in Indo-China was over.

Apart from the final declarations and speeches, the agreements were set out in four documents. The first three were military in content. They concerned the ceasefire, the regrouping and withdrawal of troops and the role of the joint committees which were to be appointed to assist with the application of the accord. Three nations, Poland, Canada and India, were called upon to supervise the proceedings. All three documents were signed by the Minister of Defence of the Democratic Republic of Vietnam, Ta Quang Buu, those concerning Laos and Vietnam were signed by General Delteil and those concerning Cambodia by General Nhiek Tioulong (in view of the recent military autonomy obtained by Sihanouk). The Viet Minh troops and those of the expeditionary force were to withdraw from the Khmer kingdom within 90 days. In the case of Laos, the withdrawal period was to be 120 days; however, there was to be a temporary regroupment zone in the mountains of the east for the Pathet Lao guerillas. In the case of Vietnam, a deadline of exactly ten months was set for the troops of the French Union to withdraw south of the 17th parallel and those of the Viet Minh to move back into the north. There was a total ban on bringing in new troops or new arms or taking part in any military alliances. Such restrictions were not imposed in Laos, and certainly not in Cambodia.[50]

The most general of the documents consisted of a "final declaration"[51] which summarized the previous documents and outlined a political solution. The independence and unity of each of the three states were formally confirmed and the following stipulation was made in the case of Vietnam: "the military demarcation line is a temporary one and should in no way be interpreted as a political or territorial boundary." The three countries were to be re-unified by means of free elections. In the case of Laos and Cambodia, these were to be held in 1955. In the case of Vietnam, they were to be held before July 1956 under the supervision of a tripartite international committee. The United States did not want to associate itself with the Peking government. The American representative insisted that the final accord should be left unsigned, while declaring at the same time that the American government would "refrain from threats or from using threats to bring about any changes in the accords". The Saigon government, now headed by the intransigent Ngo Dinh Diem, protested vehemently against this settlement, which it had been powerless to prevent. In particular, it denounced the territorial division and complained of abuse of power on the part of Mendès-France.[52] The fact that the final declaration was not signed, that the South Vietnamese government did not consider itself bound by the accord and that Washington's attitude was ambiguous placed a question mark over the application of those parts of the declaration that were not simple reiterations of the clauses of the armistice.

The French national assembly was relieved at the outcome of the Geneva talks and accepted the agreement by 462 votes to 13, with 134 abstentions. All the newspapers approved. On 21 July, *l'Aurore*, which could never be accused of pro-communism or anti-colonialism said, "It was a painful, but inevitable solution to a situation that had become sterile." *Le Figaro* acquiesced in the same sort of way, "M. Mendès-France has done a good job for the country. It would be unjust to blame him for a withdrawal that was already on the cards when he took power. It would be equally unjust to forget (and we can be sure that he himself has not done so) that his predecessors at Geneva had already begun the task by setting up negotiations and outlining solutions." These two newspapers set the tone of right-wing opinion on the subject, although a few lone voices called the whole affair the "Asian Munich".[53] Mendès-France liked to deal with problems in series, and he was now able to direct his efforts towards settling another de-colonization question. Tunisia had to be prevented from turning into another Vietnam. Then, on 30 August, came the final shelving of the EDC. The Indo-Chinese question and the question of the European army had been closely linked, and so one solution followed another.[54]

First Korea, then Indo-China. The world press dwelt upon this new step towards detente. In the spring of 1954, there had been a real danger of escalation and the situation was slightly reminiscent of the threat to peace posed by the Korean situation in 1951. In both cases, western armies had found themselves in difficulties because Mao's regime was giving active assistance to the enemy. In both cases, certain American figures had been tempted to attack China directly. But, in the same way that Truman had refused to go along with MacArthur, President Eisenhower did not want to take such a massive risk. The relief generated by the Geneva agreement was no greater than the fear aroused by the warlike noises that had been emanating from the United States. A year after the success of the talks on Indo-China, the "four great powers" found themselves in Geneva once again, this time for a summit conference. In May 1955, they achieved a final settlement of the Austrian question. All four countries withdrew their troops and Austria was re-unified. Was the cold war a thing of the past?

In the Far East, the idea of peaceful co-existence was readily put forward. The People's Republic of China had dropped the attitude it had taken during the first few years of its existence and was talking in these terms. During the period from 1949 to 1950, China had set itself up as a leader, an example for all other revolutionary forces in Asia to follow. It had called upon each country to choose sides. Now, it was intent on winning over the non-aligned countries. This was clear at the time of the Geneva conference. Chou En-lai visited India while the talks were in full swing, thus confirming the growing friendship between the two countries. With regard to Indo-China, China demonstrated its new policy by upholding the two monarchies of Laos and Cambodia, thus helping to confirm their legitimacy. It was an action which caused one of a number of differences of opinion between Hanoi and Peking.[55] During the Geneva talks, China had given priority to its interests as a great power and even reverted to some of the diplomatic traditions of its imperial past. Consequently, it had not given support to all the claims of the Democratic Republic of Vietnam. However, the similarity between the two regimes hid these differences for a while. This was at the time when Pham Van Dong described Mao as "a shining sun", thus seeming to swear formal allegiance to Peking, just as the sovereigns of Annam had once done to the Middle Kingdom.

India made great efforts with regard to the establishment of peace in Indo-China, just as it had done in Korea. On 22 February 1954, Nehru proposed an immediate ceasefire and the Laniel government was then forced by the socialists to state its conditions for accepting such a ceasefire. The conditions were such as to be considered unacceptable by the Viet Minh. Then, on 23 April, Nehru and the rest of the Colombo group[56] proposed that the Geneva conference should begin with a declaration of non-intervention on the part of the four major powers involved, namely China, the USSR, the USA and the United Kingdom, and also with an immediate ceasefire. During the conference, Krishna Menon played the role of an outside conciliator while deploring the fact that India had not been officially invited to the negotiating table. Naturally, as a result, India was asked to preside over the tripartite committee set up to supervise the application of the agreements. Nehru's greatest diplomatic triumph came the following year. He had initiated the pan-Asian meetings held in New Delhi in 1947 and 1949 and in April 1955 and had scored a great success with the first Afro-Asian conference held in Bandung (at which both Vietnams had been represented). Apart from confirming the new China's place in world politics, the Afro-Asian conference demonstrated the political emergence of the Third World in no uncertain terms. The Bandung Conference, coming as it did after France's defeat in the Far East, marked the end of colonization in Asia, and the start of the decolonization of Africa, especially the Maghreb.

7

From One War to Another

THE BALANCE SHEET
IN 1956, General Navarre published *Agonie de l'Indochine*. He was unwilling to bear the burden of defeat and adeptly defended himself by taking the offensive against the politicians.

> They have never dared let the country know that there was a war on in Indo-China. They could neither involve the nation in the war nor make peace.... What is more, they allowed the army to be stabbed in the back. They have tolerated the continuous betrayal by the Communist Party and all its reserves. They have permitted a press confident of its immunity to attack the morale of the soldiers, to sap the nation's morale and to make military secrets public. In the past eight years, there has been too much vacillation, too many mistakes and too much cowardice for it only to be attributable to men, or even governments, successively coming to power. They are the product of the regime. They derive from the very nature of the French political system. A regime which allows the authority of the state to be despised, from which public spiritedness has vanished.... A regime which abolishes the national spirit, which isolates the army from the nation.... A political system which needed only four decades to turn this great and victorious country of 1918 into the sick man of Europe.... If the regime persists as it is, the same reasons which made us lose Indo-China yesterday will inevitably lose us North Africa tomorrow or the day after, and whatever remnants there are of what was the French Empire.

This attack must not be considered as merely the bitterness of a defeated general. It was universally agreed that many in the military subscribed to it (the younger officers adding criticism of the bureaucracy and a senior official whom they deemed to be impotent and politicized). Clemenceau's firmness was contrasted with the betrayal and weakness of the establishment. They also expressed disappointment, and even disbelief, at a country which was so insensitive to the battles which had been fought.[1] They reproached the country for making the expeditionary force conduct an almost shameful war. The quotes of Indo-China veterans since 1948, they recalled, no longer appeared in the *Journal officiel*, and in 1951 a statement was made to the effect that blood collected by the Public Health Department would not be used for those wounded in the Far East. They were angry at having had to abandon loyalists, such as the Meo underground groups, to the enemy. The officers of the expeditionary force departed from the Orient leaving behind their bastards, fond memories—as most of them had loved the life out there—but mostly resentment. The army's discomfiture began to be commonplace. As Minister of Defence in the Laniel government, Pleven was already expressing his fear "that nothing less than military demonstrations were taking place".[2] The army, he added, "may launch a dramatic challenge and the government will have to give in".

"Since a state of peace no longer exists, the government must permanently benefit, at least in part, from the exceptional powers which it has always had during times of war", wrote Commander Hogard in an article in *Revue de défense nationale*,[3] when he was recommending banning the Communist Party. He said: "There is 'one' enemy from Paris to Saigon, from Algiers to Brazzaville." The French soldiers who went to North Africa from the Far East called their first *fellaghas* "Viets". Feeling that they were facing the same enemy and the same combat methods, they had decided to prevent another defeat by any means possible. Some studied the specific nature of revolutionary war and tried to work out how the Viet Minh had scored their successes. With the passion of first-year students, they threw themselves into the study of collective psychology, sociology, Marxism, etc. As a former commander of the air force in Indo-China, General Chassin published the first biography on Mao in French. He wrote, in the October 1954 publication of *La Revue militaire d'information*: "The moment has come for the free world to apply some of the methods used by its enemies, if it does not wish to die a violent death." From the social role that Lyautey had been fond of, officers had now assumed a political role. As the Indo-Chinese conflict had shown, it was no longer essentially a question of fighting for a particular position, it was a fight for control of the masses. Chakotine's *Rape of the Masses through Propaganda*[4] was widely quoted. The February issue of *La Revue militaire d'information*[5] was entirely devoted to the subject of revolutionary war. Colonel Lacheroy, having established himself as a theoretician of this type of fighting from conferences to articles, prefaced it provocatively: "In revolutionary war, the soldier of fortune is a calamity, like the *croix de guerre*."[6] In Algeria, psychological war and action were the order of the day.[7] Rather than leading to the study of social problems and national movements in underdeveloped countries, the Indo-Chinese conflict tended to establish technical solutions, and even practical formulas, against armed subversion.[8] Far from convincing the army of the inevitability of decolonization, the Indo-China war stimulated some of its members, the more imaginative ones, to search for new solutions to face the challenge of a revolutionary war which was seen as linked to the USSR's expansionist strategy. By applying the enemy's methods, as proposed by men like Chassin, Lacheroy, Trinquier,[9] the French army in Algeria attempted to draw on the lessons of the Indo-China experience and tried to vindicate itself. Never again, said the soldiers. Never again the humiliation of retreat, never again dead comrades in vain.

In the aftermath of Geneva, the Minister of Defence stated the balance of the losses suffered by the French Union's troops: 20,000 French,[10] 11,000 legionnaires, 15,000 Africans, 46,000 Indo-Chinese. With regard to the Indo-Chinese, the figures should be treated with caution, particularly because neither the reserves nor the members of the underground were taken into account and because the notion of "missing" is difficult to interpret. The following estimate can be reasonably put forward: the war claimed nearly 100,000 lives in the expeditionary force and the forces fighting alongside it. There was a particularly heavy toll of French officers. Even the highest ranks were affected: two generals (Chanson and Hartemann) died in Indo-China, and several sons of commanders-in-chief were killed (Leclerc, de Lattre, Gambiez). A million francs were spent daily. In total, 1,900 officers fell, the equivalent of a term's intake of Saint-Cyr cadets each year: this is what the conflict cost, people would say towards the end. How many victims did the first Indo-China war claim — 400,000 or 500,000 dead? These estimates were made without anyone being able to provide exact figures.

Until Cao Bang, French prisoners were rare and survivors among the prisoners were even rarer. After October 1950 a system of camps was actually organized. During the hostilities, the Viet Minh allowed small contingents to leave, for propaganda reasons. The convoys were called "peace fighters": Figuères, Raymonde Dien, Henri Martin.... Similarly thousands of guerilla fighters were released during the conflict. Sometimes, the releases took place following talks between the two warring sides. After many difficulties and delays,[11] the French were authorized to airlift those wounded in the RC 4 battle, like those affected after Dien Bien Phu. Men from both sides were also released simultaneously, helping the hostages captured by the revolutionary forces at the beginning of the war.[12] The Geneva agreements provided for the exchange of prisoners in the month following the ceasefire. The command of the expeditionary force released 65,000 men being held in the camps which the Red Cross had been freely able to inspect. On the other side, only 11,000 men were freed out of the 37,000 missing. These figures should however be treated with caution. Again, the case of the Indo-Chinese should be treated separately. Very few of them (9 per cent) were returned to the French military authorities. But all the evidence points to the fact that a large proportion of the 16,000 Vietnamese prisoners were incorporated into the revolutionary forces after re-education. For other categories, the percentage of men released varied between 40 per cent (for troops of European origin) and 50 per cent (for North African soldiers). The survivors looked like skeletons. The statistics, like the pictures of the prisoners, recalled the German concentration camps. Most of the survivors had to be hospitalized. The French officials however preferred not to inform the public. The Viet Minh had not supplied lists and the French were unwilling to jeopardize further additional returns of prisoners by expressing untimely indignation.

It was exceptional for prisoners to be executed. The high mortality rate can be explained by the harsh living conditions imposed on them. The ordeal began, on being captured, with a long march to the camps. The men captured at Dien Bien Phu, depending on the category, covered 600 and 800 kilometres in the jungle in the height of the rainy season. Many were wounded, all showed the signs of the siege. Exhaustion, dysentery, dehydration and rapid infection of their wounds caused the death of half of the contingent. The camps were spread over the mountainsides and could be mistaken for villages. There was no need for barbed wire or for observation posts, the prisoners were "guarded by the forest and the people". The Red Cross never received permission to visit, and the locations of the detention camps were not communicated to the French authorities. Malaria, beri-beri and dysentery ravaged a population almost without medicines or hygiene, badly undernourished, drinking polluted water, submitted to the rigours of the climate and incapacitated with hard labour. The prisoners could not complain: if there was no food and medicine, it was the fault of the colonialists.[13] In any event, as mercenaries and war criminals, the soldiers of the expeditionary force ought to have been executed. They owed their lives only to the clemency of President Ho. They still had to pay. Brainwashing was intended to convert them to the camp of the "peace fighters". It was difficult for physically weakened men cut off from their normal points of reference to resist a system which used tried and tested methods of dialectics and self-criticism, which organized a system of informers, played on the hope of anticipated liberation and doled out humiliation and ill-treatment collectively and individually.

The officers were grouped together in camp number 1. They were made to sign manifestos, denouncing the "dirty war". Lieutenant-Colonel Lepage was used immediately after Cao Bang. Extracts from his interview on the Viet Minh radio were quoted by a Communist deputy after the debate following the defeat. The propaganda was adapted to each category and implemented according to advice of the local communist parties in the soldier's country of origin.[14] Soldiers from Africa had to be turned against French imperialism. It seems that the operation succeeded. After Geneva, Ferrandi accompanied General Salan on a visit to the "Senegalese" and North Africans freed by the Democratic Republic of Vietnam, and found men filled with contempt and surliness whose questions were "insidious". To what extent were the prisoners contaminated by the enemy? This question was sure to embarrass the command. How should the officers who signed compromising documents be treated? The fact that after Dien Bien Phu, Galard's nurse[15] and the Chief Doctor Grauwin wrote an accommodating letter to Ho was not something they could be condemned for: the act was necessary to evacuate the seriously wounded. But other difficult cases could be condemned and a veil of shame was thrown over them. The fact that the French officers had been deeply scarred by their experiences in the camps was a fact. Nevertheless, what many brought back from their detention was not the creed of the Viet Minh but the effectiveness of its methods.

Alongside the exchange of the prisoners, the main work of the mixed military commissions set up by the Geneva agreements consisted of supervising the regrouping of the forces. In Laos, the withdrawal of the Viet Minh regulars was completed in November 1954, but the Pathet Lao set up its administration in the provinces of Phong Saly and Sam Neua. In Cambodia, also evacuated in November, the problem of reunification did not arise. The former members of the underground were re-integrated into national life, or else chose to leave with the APV, like Son Ngoc Minh, the head of the revolutionary government. In the case of Vietnam, the troops' movements had been scheduled in detail by a military conference held in the Viet Minh zone in early July 1954. The French negotiators[16] in Geneva obtained a calendar for evacuation which responded to several needs. As General Ely writes in his *Memoirs*: "We were torn between the desire to use the time necessary so as not to leave the enemy any equipment and the worry of quickly sorting out the arrangements so as to prevent the Viet Minh propaganda having any effect, especially on the Vietnamese troops. It was also desirable that the evacuation of our troops should happen at a rate and in circumstances which allowed us constantly to have balanced forces in Tongking, who would be capable of responding to a Viet Minh breach of the ceasefire agreement."

Despite its complexity, the operation passed off smoothly. The Baodaist troops were the first to reach the South, the command fearing that they would be too receptive to the propaganda of a victorious enemy. On 11 October, as arranged, the expeditionary force abandoned Hanoi to the people's army. The international commission set up shop and later proved itself to be very effective. On 15 May 1955, the last French troops embarked for Haiphong. Cogny, commanding the retreat, took precautions on this occasion against two eventualities: enemy action to force the last colonialists into the sea and action by the French to blow up the port installations before leaving. Attempts at a "scorched earth" policy continuously took place during the Tongking evacuation. As much of the equipment as possible was not destroyed but dismantled. This added to the later difficulties of re-starting the North Vietnamese economy. The Diem government pushed for the transfer of equipment and people to the South.

A tide of refugees accompanied the withdrawal of the French Union's forces. The recent abandonment of the bishoprics by the expeditionary force was followed by the speedy departure of a large part of the population. These people would be amongst the first to want to leave Tongking. The Geneva agreements gave a period of 300 days for the Vietnamese to choose between the two zones. Apart from the movement of some 20,000 regulars, almost no one moved to the North, which, on the other hand, was deserted by almost a million people. Most left out of fear. The sectarianism of the communist cadres (the *canbo*), and the irritations, anxieties and restrictions which they imposed added to the movement south. Townspeople and peasants, Vietnamese as well as members of the ethnic minorities—the exodus carried with it all classes and nationalities. Most of the Nung set sail, as they were too closely involved with the French. The Catholics, however, were the largest group to leave; 65 per cent of them[17] went into exile, often whole villages led by their priest. The two bishops of Phat Diem and Bui Chu[18] plus more than 500 priests supervised the migration of 700,000 of their flock. The cinema news showed the Western public these unfortunates weighed down with their belongings on the bridges of ships or fervently praying at masses. Accompanied by the colourful commentaries of the time, the images were intended to help the anti-communist drive. In Vietnam, as in Germany, they say, people voted with their feet. This massive flight, "a slap in the face for the enemy" (Ely), was also abetted by the French military, as well as by the leaders in Saigon and the American services. For the French military, it was the moral justification for the past fighting, for the others it was preparation for the battle to come.

Through persuasion or force, the revolutionary authorities tried to stem a tide which gave the lie to their propaganda. Numerous incidents took place of which the international commission was informed. There are famous examples. Ten thousand Catholics intending to leave had gathered in the village of Ba Lang; they were scattered by gunfire by the Vietnamese Popular Army. On the north coast of Annam, thousands of refugees had been herded by the Popular Army on to sandbanks which the tide was threatening to submerge; sailors on the French ships cruising at the limits of the territorial waters finally came to their rescue, taking most of them aboard. This time, photos were taken and published.

In addition to the friction it caused with the Vietnamese Democratic Republic, the transfer posed many administrative problems. This mass of refugees had to be assembled, transported, fed, sheltered and finally rehoused. In the North, operations were the responsibility of the French who were mobilizing all their means and obtaining American aid. In the South, the affair was the responsibility of the Saigon government, which was soon overwhelmed by the influx of immigrants arriving at the rate of two boatloads and fifty-odd planeloads every day in the most active period. Paris and Washington gave their help and this was supplemented by private aid. It was a good cause: *Le Figaro* started a fund, the American Catholics mobilized behind Cardinal Spellman, eminent Cochin-Chinese presented gifts.

Once they had fled the catastrophe, abandoning their possessions and land (the Tongking peasant's attachment to his ancestral village is common knowledge), the emigrés from the North faced the difficulties of arrival. Almost all the refugees were resettled in Cochin-China, which had only 6 million inhabitants. This did not go smoothly. The new arrivals, with their different traditions and religions, were not always welcomed. This was to be expected: the twentieth century is full of this type of incident. But this massive migration was useful to both Vietnams. The "unloading" relieved the overpopulated and half-ruined North which was close to famine and removed any potential opponents of the regime. Cochin-China, with its relatively low population density and with the help of international aid, actually profited from the arrival of new blood. The migration, in keeping with the centuries-long movement south-wards of the Vietnamese completed the settlement of the Mekong Delta.

Politically there was a two-fold advantage. The refugees displayed their hostility to the communist system, and because the majority were Catholic, they were naturally associated with the Ngo clan. The minority originating from the North was to become one of Ngo Dinh Diem's most solid power bases.

RELIEF

Integrity and patriotism were the two qualities that the whole world took pleasure in recognizing in Ngo Dinh Diem when, in June 1954, he returned to public life after more than twenty years as an exile at home and abroad. Since 1950, he had lived outside his homeland, mostly in the United States. He had never stopped discussing a subject which pleased those he talked to. It was not enough to be anti-communist to face the Viet Minh, he claimed; colonialism still had to be eradicated for the struggle to be effective. Cardinal Spellman (who had known his brother during his studies in Rome), Senators Mansfield and Kennedy had become his appointed protectors. Born of a mandarin family, but converted to Christianity early in his life, Diem was stamped with the marks of Confucian tradition, and by Spanish Catholicism of the crusading type. From his far-eastern background, he had inherited the feeling for family solidarity. With his return, his family came to assume a position of leadership in the country. His brothers (Thuc, Nhu, Luyen, Can) were his principal lieutenants. The first lady of the country (Diem, like his colleague Salazar, if not actually a monk, remained a bachelor), the infamous Madame Nhu, became the Egeria of the regime. Through her, the Tran clan reached government. Her father Chuong, strong man of the pro-Japanese government of 1945, had the task of representing South Vietnam to the great ally, America. As a letter dated October 1954 from President Eisenhower shows, Chuong gave his "unconditional support" to Diem. Diem, as fierce an anti-communist as he was a stubborn anti-colonialist, was, in America's eyes, the right man in the right place.

Since 1950, the involvement of the United States in Indo-China had continuously been redefined. Paris had succeeded in its efforts at persuasion. The Americans had been convinced that the peninsula had to be defended at all costs against the expansion of communism. They had devised their domino theory. They had to accept the French withdrawal in 1954, resignedly welcoming the Geneva agreements which were cutting their losses. But now, they had to establish a solid *cordon sanitaire* in the region. They had to reinforce Laos and Cambodia, and bind them lastingly to the West. Most importantly, Diemist Vietnam had to become another South Korea. They had to liberate the country from colonialism and its aftermath, strengthen the regime, give economic assistance and train the army, guarantee it militarily and find a pretext to postpone forever the elections of 1956, which everyone already considered as lost because of the balance of the forces.

In Geneva, the Americans solemnly declared that "they took a very grave view of any resumption of aggression, whose nature was seriously to threaten peace and international security". For the whole duration of the conference they continued to envisage a defence pact for the Far East which they would lead. They finally drew up a treaty plan in agreement with the British to be ratified at the Manila conference of September 1954. India, Burma, Ceylon and Indonesia did not take part as they favoured non-alignment. The only participants, other than the western powers, were New Zealand and Australia, who were already members of ANZUS,[19] and Washington's Asian client-states—the Philippines, Thailand and Pakistan.[20] "Each party recognizes that armed aggression in the treaty zone against one of them or against all states or territories which the parties may subsequently designate in unanimous agreement would compromise its own peace and own security, and undertakes in such a case to act, in view of facing the common danger, in accordance with its constitutional rules." The Manila accords were presented as the "Asian NATO", and were signed by eight disparate countries, but they only implied vague undertakings (with the result that Mendès-France did not even deem it opportune to have it ratified by the National Assembly). SEATO,[21] the organization which resulted from the pact, did not understand military integration in the sense that NATO did. In Manila, the French diplomats persuaded their opposite numbers that the inclusion of Laos and Cambodia was contrary to the spirit of Geneva. For Vietnam, the letter of the agreements prohibited any participation. The case of the three countries was therefore settled by an appended protocol. Without being members of the alliance, the "associated states" were covered by the treaty. This last provision was strongly criticized by communist countries, and even by some neutral governments. They spoke of a flagrant violation of the July declarations. The same states would find confirmation of their doubts in Washington's replacement in November 1954 of ambassador Heath by General Collins, former chief of staff of the army.

"There is at least a fifty-fifty chance of saving South Vietnam and that is worth trying" (Collins).[22] The Americans were arriving in greater and greater numbers and attempting to strengthen the Saigon regime whose chances they did not give much for after Dien Bien Phu. Diem had to become the Syngman Rhee of Vietnam. The CIA man, Colonel Lansdale,[23] who had just arrived, confident from his victory in the struggle against the Filipino Huks, set about the task. He would "be the making" of Diem as he had "been the making" of Magsaysay.

When he came to power, Ngo Dinh Diem had been a respected but isolated character, and could just about count on his family, some loyal men and acquaintances of his brother Nhu. With American help, he asserted himself against the opposition and other forces. Dollar diplomacy aided his activities. Expedient gifts contributed to rallying some, to ending the guilty conscience of others, as it was made clear that economic aid was dependent on their support for Diem. The army was the only true leadership and power during this time of semi-anarchy. Its leaders were closely linked by comradeship in arms and even by nationality to France, so they were ill-inclined to submit. A show of force between General Hinh and the Prime Minister turned to the advantage of the Prime Minister. The General allowed himself to go as far as sedition, but not to staging a *coup*. After a series of incredible incidents, Hinh was sent away to Paris. The army had been subjugated, at least for the time being. As for the various sects, Diem was adept at playing on their differences, on corrupting some of their leaders before liquidating the more stubborn of them by force. Bao Dai had finally entrusted to the Binh Xuyen the responsibility of ensuring the public's safety in Saigon, and in the last months of the new government, there was even the possibility of faithful Bai Vien replacing Diem. This sect, which was a mafia that had been turned into a police force, could not be tolerated by the Prime Minister whose authority it defied and whose moralism it clashed with. Its power was broken by force in April 1955. Survivors took to the underground. The energetic and ambiguous Trinh Minh Thé allied himself with the Caodaists (before being mysteriously assassinated), whilst the "Pope" fled abroad. General Hoa Hoa Nam Lua gave in, but Ba Cut became part of a new dissident force — which this time would be fatal for him. The various feudal authorities were at a low ebb or completely destroyed; the men on whom the French presence relied were neutralized and more often than not in exile. All that remained was to settle Bao Dai, now deprived of his local support.

In spite of his traditionalism, Diem could not bear the continuation of the dynasty. The head of state was unworthy because of his corruption, and furthermore he symbolized the French Protectorate, while hindering Diem's progress towards absolute power. The Americans supported this line. Having recently supported the Bao Dai experiment, they believed that, if a person's character was stained, this would risk irremediably compromising the South Vietnamese undertaking. Bao Dai should be forced out smoothly and diplomatically. With Paris's agreement, they prevented the prince returning to his country and a campaign was started based on the escapades of the potentate who preferred the palaces and casinos of Cannes to tackling his people's problems on the spot. On 30 April 1955 an assembly of 200 people met in Saigon, in an allegedly "revolutionary committee" to announce Bao Dai's dethronement (and by its momentum to demand the total departure of the French). The decision had to be ratified "democratically" by referendum in October.[24] Ninety-eight per cent voted in favour; the Americans would have preferred a more discreet and more credible victory. The rulers were to use the same shameless trick in later elections. The electoral sham was staged to satisfy Washington but Washington wanted opposition parties and universal suffrage. But in Saigon, as in Hanoi, only unanimous democracy was appreciated. The regime in the South adopted an official ideology, personalism. This was a fairly loose adaptation which Nhu had made of Mounier's ideas. The same Nhu later created the Personalist Group of Revolutionary Workers, the Can Lao, which was something of a secret society, a clandestine political party and the secret police all rolled into one. A political philosophy was pitched against a political philosophy, one system of rank was pitched against the other; the ideology of personalism was supposed to counter that of Marxist-Leninism.

In 1956, whereas the Diemist dictatorship in the South was well established and seemed to have the country firmly in its grip, the North was passing through a crisis. The lack of equipment and technologists, the need for reconstruction and the change in the economic system, were all contributing to making the beginnings of the Democratic Republic difficult. The brutalities[25] and the arbitrariness of agrarian reform displeased and worried the public. In late 1956, the government was compelled to use force to put down a peasant revolt in Nghê-An, as famous as Ho Chi Minh's province of birth as it was for those prophetic soviets of the 1930s.[26] This parallel development of antagonistic regimes led the odd American expert to believe that the game could be won. The reunification elections provided for in Geneva might be attempted. This view was never accepted by Diem or by Dulles. "The plan is evident everywhere, but never officially admitted because it goes against the very terms of the Geneva armistice, and it is to prevent the reunification of the two sectors of Vietnam", noted Robert Guillain in *Le Monde* on 4 December 1954.

Since the ceasefire, separation at the 17th parallel had been progressively taking shape. The movement of populations was stopped after the French evacuation of Haiphong. The bamboo curtain had fallen. Saigon did not respond to the repeated demands of Hanoi for the re-establishment of normal relations between the two zones, any more than it accepted the opening of discussions (from 20 July 1955) for the arrangement of a vote on reunification provided for by the Geneva conference. In September 1955, the Lien Viet ceded its place to the National Front whose programme was meant to be reassuring since it promised to support two states with different economic and social regimes, linked only federally. The regime in the South considered this juggling with names as pure deceit, at which the communists were known to be very skilled.

In March 1956, by allowing the election of a constituent assembly in the territory it controlled, the Diem government confirmed that it intended to establish a separate state in the South.[27] This policy had the support of the refugees, who had not fled from the communist regime only to fall under its control some months later. The arguments supporting it were many. The Saigon government had not signed the declarations of 1954; it had even denounced them from the start, and was therefore in no way obliged to uphold them. It was stated however that they were in agreement on the principle of general elections but on condition that freedom to vote were truly guaranteed in the North. As Senator John F. Kennedy stated on 1 June 1956: "Neither the United States nor Vietnam will accept a manifestly rigged election which is falsified in advance." The fateful day in July 1956 passed without international opinion being perturbed by the fact that one of the essential provisions of the Indo-Chinese settlement had not been respected. Co-chairing the Geneva conference, in 1957, the USSR even allowed the two Vietnams to be represented at the United Nations, thus seeming to confirm the division.

France was put in a difficult position but it backed this development. The reunification of Vietnam, in the present state of the forces, could only occur, one way or another, under Ho Chi Minh. Should Paris commit itself in this way? Sainteny supported it. After the armistice, he had been appointed in Hanoi as delegate general. In 1953, he published his *Histoire d'une paix manquée*, in which he discussed his negotiations of 1945–6. Now, just as before, he was of the opinion that a solution could and should be reached with the leaders of the Democratic Republic of Vietnam.[28] This strategy, with which the Americans would hopefully

associate themselves, was delicate and only offered very limited pros-
pects for French interests, but it was the only realistic strategy. Sainteny
was received respectfully and treated as if nothing had happened since
1946. He was given the same promises and assurances as had been given
in the letter dated 21 July 1954 from Pham Van Dong to Mendès-
France. The North Vietnamese leaders seemed ready to attempt rap-
prochement. Now the former colonialist could be driven from the Far
East as he was no longer dangerous. As for the French, they had signed
the Geneva agreements and they were expected to apply the policy
clauses. In addition, if they were offered fine words they would refrain
from moving too much equipment out and would contribute to the re-
starting of an exhausted economy.

However, Paris never chose Hanoi in preference to Saigon. The policy drawn up by Sainteny was never really implemented. As commissioner-general and commander-in-chief until June 1955, Ely was particularly against any accommodation with the communist regime. For
him, holding the balance between the two Vietnams amounted to putting friends and enemies on the same footing, dissociating oneself from
the United States and reversing the alliances. Western solidarity took
precedence over anything else. Nor could the important interests
France still had in Cochin-China be compromised. "No double-deal-
ing, an open policy of support for nationalist Vietnam; the economic aid
it needs; indulgence of its government still in shock from the
ceasefire.'[29] These were the general lines of the plan that the General
revealed to Mendès-France on 14 August 1954. Advised by Claude
Cheysson, the Prime Minister was distracted by many other problems
and finally gave his go-ahead to this policy. At the time of the Geneva
conference, he had also told the Saigon government that France considered it to be the only legitimate representative of the Vietnamese
people. Of course, Mendès-France was no neutralist. Through the
"crime of 30 August" he had participated in the winding up of the EDC,
but then had been involved in the Paris treaty[30] and the Manila pact.
American hegemony had to be accepted in South-East Asia. It was up to
the great ally to conduct the policy of containment there. France rede-
ployed her European and African forces. The closure of her last trading
posts in India (in November 1954) accompanied the winding up in
Indo-China.

"Vietnam will fall under communist control, unless the French abandon it totally, one hundred per cent, militarily, economically and politically", declared Representative J. Richards on 13 December 1954 on his
return home to the United States from the Far East. The congressman
was not exaggerating, but his idea was neither new nor original. In

Saigon as in Washington it was understood that the former colonial power had to give way if the Diem regime was to succeed. The withdrawal occurred in a climate which was at times difficult. Campaigns were conducted against the duplicity of the French; they were accused of supposedly supporting local opponents of the regime, and were blamed for declarations by exiled opponents in Paris. The Sainteny mission was quoted as an example of the collusion between communism and colonialism. The American press occasionally repeated these exaggerations.

In fact, the French officials were playing by the rules. Of course, Diem was not the Prime Minister they would have chosen. Paris would have preferred Tran Van Huu or Prince Buu Hoi, both of them advocates of a policy of conciliation with the North.[31] But even though an attempt was made to moderate Washington's man, there was no question of confrontation, even less of bringing him down. Some officers supported the manoeuvres of their friends and traditional clients against Diem. They did so without Ely's approval.[32] The commissioner-general refused to place the power of the expeditionary force behind Hinh[33] or the other factions, thus supporting Diem by his benevolent neutrality. Similarly, if there were some friction with the Americans at a lower level, Ely did everything to facilitate cooperation between the two allies. A dozen working groups were formed to coordinate the policy of the two countries on every matter.

For several months, the United States had been expressing a wish to train the Vietnamese troops. They were given this satisfaction in December 1954 with the signing of the Ely-Collins agreements. Now General O'Daniel, head of the Military Aid and Advisory Group (MAAG), was also in charge of training the national army. In this role, he was theoretically under the orders of "Commander-in-Chief" Ely. This complicated and ineffective system of military cooperation rapidly ensured the relief of French officers by American advisors. This posed problems, as the Geneva agreements forbade any increase in foreign regulars.[34] Vietnam was to be granted full military autonomy in July 1955. The national army, about which there had been much discussion of late, finally took shape as an independent force. At the beginning of the year the French made other transfers of power. After the Paris conference (26 August–29 December 1954), the quadripartite system disappeared. The South Vietnamese government was now totally in control of its financial, customs and monetary policies,[35] and of running the port of Saigon. Since 1 January 1955, it had been receiving American aid directly. The technical services (weather forecasting, lighthouses and beacons, concessions on electricity, etc.) had also been handed over. In June 1955, the government of the South demanded an end to the secretariat of state in the associated states "to remove the remaining ambiguities". Then it recalled the Vietnamese representatives at the French Union assembly. In November, it expelled journalists Max Clos and Lucien Bodard. In February 1956, Radio France-Asie stopped broadcasting, following a campaign denouncing its poisonous influence. On the same theme of returning to their roots, Diem forbade the use of European Christian names.

The final members of the expeditionary force embarked in April 1956. At the Geneva Conference, Mendès-France had promised the Baodaist government that the French troops would be repatriated as soon as the request was made. Since the armistice, the number of regulars had been progressively reduced.[36] In fact, neither of the two parties wanted the continuing support of the French army. Paris needed all its forces to tackle the situation in North Africa. For Diem, the uniforms were far too evocative of colonialism; in addition, it was argued that the expeditionary force would be used against his rule and policy, in particular to force him to accept elections for reunification. The French agreed to pack up and go, but would have preferred to be left at least one base. They had often considered Tourane where installations had been built up since de Lattre's time, or Cape Saint-Jacques. To avoid upsetting the sensitivities of the Saigon leaders, they suggested that the base be mixed. Nothing doing: Diem refused any concessions, declaring that any foreign military presence would infringe on national sovereignty. After 1956, France continued its disengagement. In 1957, the last naval and air force instructors left. In 1960, the last piece of French public property was transferred to the Vietnamese government.

It was believed that once French troops had left the country, the main objective had been achieved. The former colonizer had been removed and the United States was taking over. American experts had drafted the constitutions. The assembly elected in March 1956 did not therefore have to formulate it, only discuss it. The number of American officers was increasing,[37] and they had taken over the training of the troops. Michigan State University reorganized the police force, and reformed the National Institution of Administration which had to be purged of all colonialist traditions. One of its professors, Fishel, became one of Diem's closest advisers. Another professor, W. Ladejinski, developed the plan for agrarian reform. USIS organised the propaganda, the USOM distributed economic aid, and so on. On 13 May 1957, Diem then on a visit to his protector, declared: "The frontier of the United

States extends to the 17th parallel."

"Seven years of war were required for our 'enemies' to chase us out of North Vietnam (where we might still regain some influence); one and half years of 'solidarity' with our allies were sufficient for them to chase us out of South Vietnam", noted Maurice Duverger in *Le Monde* on 21 March 1956, expanding on the theme developed in the same newspaper in December 1955 by Senator Hamon: "In the days following the Geneva agreements, French opinion thought that we had abandoned the North, through the necessity of holding on to the South: it did not know that the South was also abandoned in the following months.'[38] From time to time, parliament got excited. On 21 October 1955, the Council of the Republic at the instigation of Michel Debré voted for a motion emphasizing that "the silence constantly maintained by the government in the face of repeated acts of hostility to France has the gravest consequences for our prestige, interests and future, not only in the Far East, but throughout the world."[39]

These articles and the occasional parliamentary intervention had little effect. At a time when Algeria was becoming a burning issue, French opinion was not interested in these vicissitudes. It barely managed to notice the massive trial held in the spring of 1956. Yet again, the war in Indo-China and the scandals were connected. The Paris court-martial examined the "leaks" from the Committee for National Defence at the end of the conflict. The trial was one of the most tangled, involving leading civil servants (the former Secretary-General of the Committee of National Defence, Jean Mons, was in the dock), journalists of all types, police from various services, double agents, senior officers and politicians. As in the affair of the generals, one revelation succeeded another without any light being thrown on the affair in the end. As in the affair of the generals, the public, despairing of understanding the imbroglio, became convinced that anything connected with the authorities was crooked, that they were rotten to the core. The leaks trial contributed even further to discrediting the regime and cast suspicion on two of the leaders of the left, François Mitterand[40] and Pierre Mendès-France.[41] As the main defence lawyer and a deputy of the far right, Jean-Louis Tixier-Vignancour skilfully aroused suspicions. Discussions linked the war in Algeria with the war in Indo-China. By compromising those who had supported negotiations with Ho Chi Minh, the advocates of the "liberal" solution in North Africa could also be blackened, as well as the leaders of the Republican Front which came to power in early 1956.

A French cabinet dominated by the Socialists aroused vague hopes in Hanoi. On the occasion of the tenth anniversary of the 6 March 1946 agreements, while the Democratic Republic of Vietnam was asking for another conference in Geneva, an open letter was addressed to "Comrade Pineau", the new Minister for Foreign Affairs: "The people and government of the Republic of North Vietnam are always ready to establish and consolidate relationships of friendship with France on the basis of complete equality and reciprocity of interests. We also believe that the French government, led by the Socialist Party, will endeavour to serve the interests of France and the just cause of peace better than previous governments." As a signatory to the Geneva declarations, France was again urged to insist upon general elections. To this, the Mollet government could only respond that as guarantor of the agreements, Paris did not have the means by itself to enforce them. A note dated 16 May 1956 informed the two co-chairmen of the Geneva conference that "From 28 April, France no longer assumes special responsibility for the implementation of the agreements of 1954." The die was cast. France refused the Hanoi regime a full exchange of ambassadors, by agreeing to receive (in April 1956) a mere North Vietnamese commercial attaché.[42]

France had opted for Saigon and a position close to that of the Americans. Consequently, relations between the two capitals continued to deteriorate. The time had returned for Sainteny to be treated as a sort of "senior member of the diplomatic corps". Most of the French in Tongking had left. By late 1954, only a hundred of them remained in Hanoi (of the 6,500 who had resided there before the armistice). Despite fine words, promises and assurances, most of the property owners refused to negotiate with the communist authorities, preferring to abandon their possessions for which they hoped to receive compensation from their government. The country's industries would only be built up with the help of fellow-communist regimes. The few businesses and the few French officers who tried to remain could not prolong the ordeal any longer and were quickly discouraged by the suspicious meanness of a meddlesome bureaucracy.[43] The professors followed. Pierre Huard, who loved the country and was in sympathy with it, stayed at the faculty of medicine until 1959. Financed by Paris, the Lycée Sarraut was an intellectual presence. The ever-diminishing role of the French language and teachers from France caused its closure in 1965.[44]

Despite American involvement, a small colony of 15,000 Frenchmen remained south of the 17th parallel after 1956. Three hundred French teachers still taught, 500 French firms continued their operations, in plantations and in industry—two sectors which they dominated—as well as in commerce and banking. Independence hardly affected anyone apart from the small commercial businesses and the rice-growing sector. The paddy-field owners were dispossessed in accordance with the agrarian reforms. They were compensated by their government, these sums constituting a large part of the aid to the Saigon regime. Although all but gone in the North, the traces of the former colonizer remained in the South. It had been ousted politically, but retained some of its economic and cultural interests.

It was in the kingdoms of the West that French influence was better sustained. In Cambodia, relations actually improved after independence. Laos continued to maintain relations with the French Union[45] and kept its deputies (increased from three to five) at the Versailles assembly until it had been fully organized. But the American presence was becoming more noticeable in the form of economic aid and through the secret services. The two great western allies often collaborated. Their combined support allowed Cambodia to gain access to the sea, through the port of Sihanoukville. But the United States only obtained very moderate success. It could not prevent the Khmer kingdom from sliding into neutrality. In 1955, Sihanouk abdicated (in favour of his father) so as to have room to manoeuvre. The party he created, the Sangkum, won the elections.[46] The prince believed as a result of this that in order to maintain unity and peace in his country, he had to adopt a policy of non-alignment. He secured relations with the states of the Eastern Bloc and arranged economic aid to compensate for the loss of American bounty. In 1957, the national assembly voted in a law to establish the country's neutrality.

The situation in Laos was more complicated. The Pathet Lao did not consider itself as involved in the Geneva declarations, which it had not signed. It retained control of the provinces of Phong Saly and Sam Neua where its forces regrouped. The agreement negotiated by Souvanna Phouma in October 1957 seemed to settle the question. Two communist ministers entered the government: the revolutionary troops were absorbed into the national army and the "rebel" zones passed under the administration of Vientiane. When a right-wing regime came to power in August 1958, supported by the American agencies, doubts were again cast on this delicate balance. In 1959, civil war broke out again, and the country entered a period of turmoil.

The first Americans were killed in Vietnam in 1959 at the time of the "Viet Cong" attack against the Bien Hoa base. For months, the dangers had been growing. Here and there, there were reports of the assassination of a leader, a civil servant or a policeman; the army instituted methodical but futile searches. In 1954, the Democratic Republic of Vietnam machine had not faded away. In the allegedly free zones, the revolutionary committees had turned into defence committees for peace, the tribunals into defence committees for the interests of the peasants. After 1956, the former *canbo*, whose networks[47] the regime's police had only partially dismantled, began to move into action. They managed to exploit the problems of an agrarian policy which took away from the cultivators what the "resistance" had given them. They managed to regroup the many opponents aroused by the all-out repression of a dictatorship which relied almost exclusively on the Catholic minority. In 1960, the South Vietnamese uprising was given a political organization with the birth on 20 December of the FNL. Its president, Nguyen Huu Tho, previously one of the protagonists of the anti-American unrest of March 1950, had led the "peace committee" which in August 1954 had demonstrated for reunification in Saigon. For this, he was imprisoned as a communist. Although international opinion was still ignorant of it, the Vietnamese conflict was under way, and would spread uncontrollably until it became the second Indo-China war.

8

Conclusion

By September 1945, World War II was drawing to a close in Asia. It was during that month that the Vietnamese communists, who had come to represent the nationalist movement, proclaimed independence. The French had been thrown out of Indo-China six months previously but that September they began to take hold there again. Ho Chi Minh's regime was faced with war from the very outset. The situation remained poised between negotiations and hostilities for over a year, but war finally broke out on 19 December 1946. The two sides became locked in struggle throughout the following year, at the very moment when the deep rift occurred between the eastern and western blocs. The struggle between Vietnamese nationalism and the forces of imperialism was affected immediately by the new international climate. In the last quarter of 1947, the French Communist Party launched a massive campaign of strikes, demonstrating that France had entered the cold war stakes. At the same time, the French government began a large-scale military operation aimed at wiping out Viet Minh resistance, rejected any possibility of negotiations with Ho Chi Minh and declared that they would only deal with Bao Dai.

So until 1949 the war in Indo-China remained basically a colonial affair, to be settled within the Union itself. In the course of the next few months, a rapid sequence of events placed the war in Vietnam fully within the context of the cold war. First, Mao's army arrived at the border of Tongking, then France granted sovereignty to the "state of Vietnam". Next came the recognition of North Vietnam by the communist countries and of South Vietnam by the West and finally the outbreak of the Korean war. Just as the victory of the Chinese Communist Party over the Kuomintang caused the centre of gravity of the communist world to shift towards Asia, so the major crises between the two blocs moved from Europe to the Far East. The colonial aspect of the Indo-Chinese war was now only a small part of it, but it did not disappear completely.

The Viet Minh denounced the collusion between the French colonialists and the American imperialists. Meanwhile, as the "foot-soldier
of the free world", the French fought to maintain the French Union of
Indo-China. As time went by, disagreements within the western camp
became stronger and stronger. France urged the United States to step
into the breach to an ever greater extent with military and financial aid,
although there was no intention of allowing them to interfere in the situation. At the same time, official Vietnam was having to haggle for every
ounce of the sovereignty the French begrudged it while being urged to
defend itself against its "rebels". On the other hand, while supporting
the Saigon government, which had to extract its real independence bit
by bit in order to acquire a degree of legitimacy, Washington required
France to continue and even intensify the struggle, yet at the same time
sacrificing the last vestiges of its presence in Vietnam.

The Geneva settlement clarified matters. The former colonizer was
ousted. From 1950 onwards, the Americans took over in South Vietnam
and became ever more deeply involved. They turned it into a bastion of
anti-communism, just as Argenlieu had done when he created the Republic of Cochin-China in 1946. Once again, the Vietnamese revolutionaries declared themselves the champions of national unity and
denounced their enemies as traitors and puppets.

The 1954 agreements did not bring peace to Indo-China as some had
anticipated they would. They simply created a breathing space which
gave the United States time to draw France into the struggle again. The
French defined the war as one of "first resistance", but for Hanoi it was
simply the initial stage of a war that lasted thirty years and during the
course of which its basic aims and methods remained the same. Seen in
the context of the times, the war was one of a series of bloody confrontations that took place throughout South-East Asia. The colonial phase of
the Franco-Vietnamese struggle (1945–9) coincided with the war between the Indonesian republicans and the Dutch, not to mention the
final confrontation between Mao Tse-Tung and Chiang Kai-Shek.
The Maoist revolution, which was also a "revolutionary peasant struggle
led by the proletariat" did not ignore the nationalist factor either. The
communists had proved to be the most effective fighters against the
Japanese and they denounced the men of the Kuomintang as American
puppets.

It would be wrong to think of the Vietnamese revolution as simply an
offshoot of the Chinese revolution, but there were obvious similarities
between these two Asian varieties of Marxist-Leninism. There is an obvious comparison between the second phase of the war in Indo-China

and the Korean war, and it is a comparison that has been made by both sides. Both wars were fought on peninsulas strongly influenced by Chinese culture, whose inhabitants had been under foreign domination since the end of the nineteenth century. Both countries were split in two at the end of World War II and their national governments fought one another from 1950 onwards, supported by the communist bloc on the one side and the West on the other. In both cases, the USSR held back while China intervened actively and took charge of the revolutionary struggle. However, even though the Korean war was a clash between two blocs in which the superpowers were directly involved, no process of decolonization was involved. Although the North Koreans were organizing guerilla bands right behind the United Nations lines, and while the Viet Minh eventually managed to set up an organized, regular army, the Korean struggle was more of a war in the classic sense. In Korea, the opposing forces were separated by a front, the progress of which could be measured daily.

Two other Far-Eastern wars were almost contemporaneous with the war in Indo-China, namely the Huk uprising in the Philippines and the troubles in Malaya. In the case of the latter the communists, who had been behind the anti-Japanese resistance movement, took up arms in 1948 with the intention of destroying colonialism and imposing socialism. Again, this was a war about decolonization which became caught up in the cold war. But the outcome was different from that in Indo-China. Both sides employed identical methods much of the time, but the British had two advantages which enabled them to crush the rebellion. First, the underground fighters were isolated and could not count on massive Maoist backing as the Vietnamese rebels could. Secondly, the insurgents were mainly members of the Chinese community[1] and although it was very large, consisting of 40 per cent of the population, it was none the less a minority. Restricted and localized in this way, the guerillas were only able to mobilize 10,000 or so fighters, and the British forces always had a considerable degree of superiority over them in terms of numbers and equipment.

British decolonization was not always as peaceful as is sometimes claimed. Apart from Malaya, there were Kenya, Palestine, Cyprus, Aden and other trouble spots. However, it is true to say that the rearguard actions fought by the British never had the same scope and consequences as the French colonial conflicts.

The French had to contend with revolutionary struggles in Asia more or less as soon as World War II was over. In 1954, they became involved in one revolutionary struggle after another with scarcely a pause. In

Algeria, they encountered the same techniques at which the Viet Minh were past masters. However, for a number of reasons, the Algerian war had a unique character. First, there was the fact that the North African *départements* were not only closer to France but were actually part of it ("L'Algérie, c'est la France"). Then there was the presence of a million *pieds noirs*, the use of French conscripts in the fighting , and even the fact that there was a large North African community in mainland France. The Algerian war did not turn out to be just an obscure foreign war like the struggle in Indo-China. It became an obsession, the last grand passion of the French. In Algeria, as in Indo-China, the revolutionaries organized themselves into a front, but the FLN in Algeria owed nothing to Marxist-Leninism. Furthermore, it could never declare any one area of the territory a "liberated zone" and set up its own government there. It could never hope to progress to a general counter-offensive. The struggle always remained on the level of guerilla warfare. The French never had to suffer a North African Dien Bien Phu and, in the end, it was not a military defeat but de Gaulle's policy that caused the French withdrawal in 1962.

The era of colonial wars actually began under de Gaulle and it was he who brought it to a close. The Fourth Republic had not got off to an easy start. Threatened by the opposing popular movements of communism and Gaullism, it had had to supervise the reconstruction of France whilst enduring the double trauma of decolonization and a cold war that split the country into two opposing camps. No other western democracy had had to respond to so many difficult challenges. Although severely shaken by the violent, sudden grip of the cold war which coincided with the war in Indo-China, the regime survived. It was precisely the shock of Dien Bien Phu that induced it to allow Mendès-France to try his luck at a negotiated settlement. The success was short-lived. The Algerian crisis caused the downfall of the Fourth Republic. It was too weak to overcome the serious problems it faced. It rose to power at the time of the first colonial war and fell with the second.

Appendixes

NOTE FROM ROOSEVELT TO THE SECRETARY OF STATE CORDELL HULL (2 JANUARY 1944)

I saw Halifax last week and I told him quite frankly it was perfectly true that, for over a year, I had been saying that Indo-China should not fall under French domination again. Instead, it should be placed under the protection of an international committee. France has exercised its control over the country for nearly a hundred years, and its 30 million inhabitants are worse off now than they were before.

You will be interested to know that my opinion has the total support of commander-in-chief Chiang Kai-shek and Marshal Stalin. I see no reason why we should play along with the Foreign Office in all this. The only reason they seem to be opposed to the idea is that they are afraid of the possible consequences for their own possessions and those of the Dutch. They have never liked the idea of an international committee because, in some cases, that prepares the way for independence. This is indeed the aim as far as Indo-China is concerned.

Of course, each case must be judged separately. But that of Indo-China is perfectly clear. France has been bleeding the country for a hundred years. The people of Indo-China deserve a better fate.

MESSAGE FROM THREE INDO-CHINESE OFFICIALS (30 AUGUST 1944)

We felt it was essential to send you a concise statement on the current position of France's interests in the Far East, so that the French government will have a grasp of certain aspects of the problem when it has to define its policy in Asia. Please ask us for further information on any points you feel we have not clarified sufficiently.

Since French interests in Asia consist basically of the block of countries comprising Indo-China, we should like to emphasize first of all that, contrary to the idea which has all too frequently been disseminated, French sovereignty over the colony has been safeguarded. The archives of the Ministries of Foreign Affairs and the Colonies contain numerous despatches showing the outcome of the policy of resistance to Japanese encroachments. The policy has been in operation for three years and the results are as follows. The French administration has remained completely free. No Japanese interference has been tolerated either in technological areas or purely political ones. There has been no pressure aimed at influencing either internal or external policies to the benefit of foreign interests.

French policies in China and Indo-China are interdependent. Thanks to constant concerted efforts in Hanoi, Peking and Tokyo, the basic elements of these policies and of our sovereignty, prestige and civilizing influence have been safeguarded. In our opinion, therefore, it would not be in France's interests to adopt a hostile, still less a warlike stance, with regard to Japan. On the contrary, it is important to maintain France and Indo-China's neutral position so that, hopefully, we can emerge from the war without suffering too much damage. Besides, the continuing loyalty and gratitude of the Indo-Chinese peoples under our protection depends, first and foremost, on the maintenance of peace and they would neither understand nor tolerate any other policy. Any change of rule, even on a temporary basis, might create enormous obstacles to the re-establishment of French sovereignty, particularly in Tongking if the Chinese were to intervene there.

Similarly, it is of the utmost importance that the new French government should realise the dangers of any attack on Indo-China. Such an attack would effectively remove the principle of mutual defence which the Maréchal government agreed to in July 1941 in order to maintain French sovereignty and to safeguard the very existence of our Indo-Chinese armies.

We believe that the situation in our colony may become clear of its own accord when the war in Europe comes to an end and the Japanese, feeling thoroughly threatened, try to reach an agreement. At the moment, we feel justified in being hopeful that the Japanese hold over Indo-China will go away of its own accord, and that the mutual defence agreements will become null and void or else be modified by a process of negotiation. The génésuper Aymé agrees wholeheartedly with these suggestions.

Although the governor-general was prompted to pass a law a year and a half ago granting him extensive powers in the case of a breakdown in communications, it was only to confirm the permanence of French sovereignty and the French position with regard to the Japanese. But when this law came into effect, it was made very clear that the new powers of the governor-general would only apply within the framework of the country's allegiance to France. Therefore, until further notice and until a relationship can be established with the new French government, Admiral Decoux considers himself to be in charge of France's permanent interests here.

All the information that has been circulating recently regarding the autonomy of Indo-China and its subservience to Tokyo is biased or untrue. It will be denied or opposed by the general government, and the French embassy in Tokyo will take up the matter with the Japanese government. It would be a good idea to ensure that the Allies and the French people are also informed of this. For its part, Radio Saigon will make a constant effort to present the situation in Indo-China in its true light.

To summarize: what seems to be needed in order to ensure that French sovereignty in Indo-China and French interests in the Far East remain intact until the end of the war is for the French government to advise the Allies not to make any attacks on Indo-China and for France itself to refrain from any diplomatic or military activity that might give Japan cause for suspicion.

The above suggestions were drawn up with the full agreement of all three signatories for the strictly private information of the French government. We wish to emphasize that it is of the utmost importance that nothing should be divulged or the situation may be irrevocably jeopardised.

Signed: *Margerie, Cosme, Decoux.*

DECLARATION ON INDO-CHINA BY THE GOVERNMENT OF THE FRENCH REPUBLIC DATED 24 MARCH 1945

The government of the French Republic has always felt that Indo-China is destined to occupy a special place within the French community and to enjoy a degree of independence in keeping with its capabilities and stage of development. This promise was made in the declaration of 8 December 1943. Shortly thereafter, the general principles declared in Brazzaville gave more detailed expression to the government's wishes.

Today Indo-China is at war. Indo-Chinese and French troops are fighting side by side. The elite and the ordinary people of Indo-China have not taken advantage of the enemy's manoeuvres. Instead, with unstinting courage, they are resisting so that the cause, one which is shared by the entire French community, will win through. So, once again, Indo-China is earning the right to its destined place.

Events have confirmed the government in its original intentions and it now feels it has a duty to define the status that Indo-China will assume after it has been liberated from the invader.

France, Indo-China and the other members of the community will combine to form a French Union. The foreign interests of this Union will be represented by France. Within it, Indo-China will be free.

Indo-Chinese nationals will be citizens of both Indo-China and the French Union. By virtue of this, they will have access to all federal jobs in Indo-China and in the Union as a whole, regardless of race, religion or origin. Such jobs will be awarded on the basis of equal merit.

The conditions under which the Federation of Indo-China will participate in the federal bodies of the Union will be decided by the national assembly, as will the status of citizen of the French Union.

Indo-China will have its own federal government. The latter will be headed by a governor-general and will consist of ministers responsible to him and chosen by him from among both Indo-Chinese citizens and French citizens resident in Indo-China. A state council composed of the most important persons in the Federation will be authorized to promulgate federal laws and regulations. It will work alongside the governor-general. An elected assembly, chosen by the method most appropriate to each individual country, will be responsible for debating laws and voting on taxes of all kinds as well as the federal budget. French interests will be represented in this assembly, which will also examine all trade agreements and all pacts made with neighbouring countries.

The laws of Indo-China will be based upon religious freedom, freedom of thought, freedom of the press, freedom of association, freedom of assembly, and general democratic freedoms.

The five countries of which the Indo-Chinese Federation consists differ from one another in culture, race and religion. They will each retain their own individual characters within the Federation.

In the common interest, the general government will be the final arbiter in all matters. The local governments will be improved or reformed and government posts in each of these countries will be opened to local people.

With the help of France, the Indo-Chinese Federation will set up its own army, navy and air force within the general defence system of the French Union. There will be equal access to all ranks on the basis of qualification for both Indo-Chinese and French personnel, as well as for individuals from other parts of the French Union.

The aim will be to pursue and hasten the process of political, administrative, social and cultural progress.

The French Union will take the necessary measures to make primary education compulsory and efficient and to develop secondary and higher education. Local language and culture will be taught in close association with French culture.

Trades union activities will be increased and an independent and an effective factory inspectorate of works will be set up in a continuous effort to bring about the social education and emancipation of the Indo-Chinese workers.

Within the framework of the French Union, the Indo-Chinese Federation will enjoy financial autonomy in order to enable it to develop its agriculture, trade and industry to the fullest extent possible and, above all, to enable it to carry out the degree of industrialization necessary in order to be able to deal with the increase in population. Without having recourse to discriminatory legislation Indo-China will use this autonomy to develop trade links with all the other countries, and particularly with China for, like the rest of the French Union, Indo-China intends to enjoy close, friendly relations with China.

The status of Indo-China as described above will come into effect after consultation with the appropriate agencies of free Indo-China.

As a result, the Indo-Chinese Federation will enjoy the necessary freedom and degree of organization to enable it to develop all its resources within the peace-keeping system of the French Union. It will be able to take up its appropriate role in the Pacific region and make the most of the quality of its elites within the French Union.

MESSAGE FROM THE VIET MINH TO SAINTENY (JULY 1945)

We, the Viet Minh League, demand that the following points should be made public by the French and observed in their future policy-making in French Indo-China.

1. The country should be governed by a parliament elected by universal suffrage. A French governor should act as President until such time as we may be sure of independence. This President should choose a cabinet or a group of advisors who are acceptable to parliament. The exact powers of all these officials can be decided in the future.

2. The country should be granted independence within a minimum of five years and a maximum of ten.

3. The country's natural resources should be returned to its inhabitants after fair compensation has been paid to the present owners. France should benefit from economic concessions.

4. All the freedoms laid down by the United Nations should be granted to the Indo-Chinese.

5. The sale of opium should be banned.

We hope these conditions will be acceptable to the French government.

Note: The original text of this document was in English, not French.

DECLARATION OF INDEPENDENCE OF THE REPUBLIC OF VIETNAM (2 SEPTEMBER 1945)

All men are created equal. They are endowed by their creator with certain inalienable rights, that among these are life, liberty and the pursuit of happiness. These immortal words are taken from the American Declaration of Independence of 1776. In its broadest sense, the sentence means, *All nations on earth are born equal and all races have the right to live and be free.*

Furthermore, the Declaration of the Rights of Man and of the Citizen, made at the time of the French Revolution of 1791 states, *Men are born free and equal in rights and they remain so.*

These are undeniable truths.

Yet, for more than eighty years, the French have abused their *liberté, égalité, fraternité* by violating the land of our ancestors and oppressing our compatriots. Their actions are contrary to all ideas of humanity and justice.

Politically speaking, they have deprived us of all freedom.

They have imposed inhuman laws on us. They have set up three different political regimes, in the north, centre and south of Vietnam, in order to destroy our national, historical and ethnic unity.

They have built more prisons than schools. They have dealt mercilessly with our countrymen. They have drowned our revolutions in rivers of blood.

They have suppressed public opinion and practised obscurantism on an extremely wide scale. They have imposed the use of opium and alcohol on us in order to weaken our race.

Economically speaking, they have exploited us shamelessly, reduced our people to extreme poverty and plundered our country mercilessly.

They have plundered our paddy-fields, mines, forests and raw materials. They have reserved for themselves the privilege of issuing banknotes and have kept a monopoly on foreign trade.

They have invented hundreds of unjustifiable taxes and reduced our countrymen, particularly the peasants and small traders, to a state of extreme poverty.

They have prevented our capital from bearing interest and have exploited our workers in an absolutely barbarous fashion.

In the autumn of 1940, when the Japanese fascists invaded Indo-China so that they could set up new war bases from which to fight the Allies, the French imperialists went down on their knees and delivered our country to them.

So then our country was bled literally beneath the double yoke of Japan and France. The result was terrifying. Two million of our countrymen from Quang-Tri in the north died of starvation in the first few months of this year.

On 9 March, the Japanese disarmed the French troops. Once again, the French fled, or at least surrendered unconditionally. They have thus proved themselves absolutely incapable of protecting us. Quite the opposite. They have sold our country to the Japanese twice in the space of five years.

In the period leading up to 9 March, the Viet Minh league invited the French several times to join them in the fight against the Japanese. Instead of responding to the call, the French dealt with the partisans of the Viet Minh as harshly as they could. They even went so far as to murder a number of our political prisoners who had been incarcerated at Yen Bay and Cao Bang after their defeat.

Despite all this, our compatriots continued to take an indulgent and humane attitude towards the French. After the events of 9 March, the Viet Minh League helped a number of French to cross the borders and saved others from Japanese prisons. Furthermore, they protected the lives and possessions of all the French.

In fact, in the autumn of 1940, our country ceased to be a French colony and become a Japanese possession instead.

When the Japanese surrendered, our entire nation arose to reconquer its sovereignty and founded the Democratic Republic of Vietnam.

The truth is that we took our independence back from the Japanese, not from the French.

The French have retreated, the Japanese have surrendered and Bao Dai has abdicated. Our people have broken all the chains that have been dragging them down for nearly a hundred years and turned Vietnam into an independent country. At the same time, the people have overthrown the monarchy, which has been established for over a thousand years, and have founded a republic.

For the above reasons we, the members of the provisional government who represent the entire Vietnamese people, declare that we will no longer have anything to do with the French imperialists. We are terminating all treaties signed by France on behalf of Vietnam and abolishing all the privileges the French have assumed whilst on our territory.

The entire Vietnamese nation is determined, of one accord, to fight all attempts at aggression on the part of the French imperialists to the bitter end.

We are convinced that the Allies, who recognized the principle of equality between nations at the conferences in Teheran and San Francisco, will not fail to recognize the independence of Vietnam.

A nation that has persistently opposed French domination for over eighty years and has fought side by side with the Allies against fascism throughout the last few years is entitled to freedom and independence.

For the above reasons we, the members of the provisional government of the Democratic Republic of Vietnam, solemnly proclaim to the whole world: *Vietnam has the right to be free and independent and, in fact, it has become free and independent. The Vietnamese people are united in their determination to mobilize all possible spiritual and military resources and sacrifice individual life and property in order to preserve the right to freedom and independence.*

THE FINAL GENEVA DECLARATION

1. The conference notes the treaties ending hostilities in Cambodia, Laos and Vietnam and arranging for international control and surveillance over the execution of the terms of these treaties.

2. The conference is pleased to note the end of hostilities in Cambodia, Laos and Vietnam. It is convinced that the implementation of the terms laid down in this declaration and in the agreements on the cessation of hostilities will enable Cambodia, Laos and Vietnam to assume their proper role within the community of Pacific nations from a position of complete independence and sovereignty.

3. The conference notes the declarations made by the governments of Cambodia and Laos to the effect that they wish to adopt measures permitting all citizens to take their place within the national community, particularly with regard to participation in the forthcoming general elections. In accordance with the individual constitutions of these countries, the elections will take place during the year 1955 and will be conducted by secret ballot, with due regard for basic freedoms.

4. The conference notes those clauses of the agreement on the cessation of hostilities in Vietnam forbidding the entry of all foreign troops and military personnel as well as all arms and ammunition. It also notes the declarations made by the governments of Cambodia and Laos to the effect that they resolve not to solicit foreign aid in the form of military equipment, personnel or instructors, except in the interests of effective defence of their territory and, in the case of Laos, within the limits fixed by the agreement on the cessation of hostilities in Laos.

5. The conference also notes those clauses of the agreement on the cessation of hostilities in Vietnam stating that no foreign state may establish military bases in either of the two newly established parts of the country and it will be the responsibility of their respective governments to ensure that the areas allotted to them do not become part of any military alliance and are not used for the resumption of hostilities or for the pursuit of aggressive policies.

It also notes the declarations made by the governments of Cambodia and Laos, according to which they undertake not to enter into any agreement with other states unless such an agreement conforms to the United Nations charter or, in the case of Laos, to the agreement on the cessation of hostilities in Laos. Furthermore, unless their security is threatened, they will not establish bases for the military forces of foreign powers on Cambodian or Laotian territory.

6. The conference notes that the main aim of the agreement in Vietnam is to settle all military affairs in order to bring about an end to hostilities. It also notes that the military demarcation line is a temporary one and may in no way be seen as a political or territorial border. The conference expresses the conviction that the application of the arrangements set out in this declaration and in the agreement on the cessation of hostilities creates the necessary conditions for a rapid political settlement in Vietnam.

7. The conference declares that, as far as Vietnam is concerned, its

political problems will be resolved on the basis of respect for the principles of independence, unity and territorial integrity and the solution adopted must enable the Vietnamese people to enjoy the basic freedoms guaranteed by democratic institutions set up as a result of free elections conducted by secret ballot. In order to allow time for peace to be sufficiently re-established and to ensure that conditions are such as to permit the people to express their will freely, the general elections will take place in July 1956 under the supervision of an international committee composed of representatives of member states of the international committee for surveillance and control of ceasefire agreements. From 20 July 1955 onwards, consultations on the subject will take place between the competent representative authorities of the two regions.

8. Those terms of the ceasefire agreements aimed at protecting persons and property must be strictly applied. In particular, they must ensure that every Vietnamese is free to choose the region in which he or she wishes to live.

9. The competent representative authorities of North and South Vietnam, Laos and Cambodia must make sure that there are no individual or collective reprisals against persons or the families of persons who collaborated with one side or another during the war.

10. The conference notes the declaration made by the government of the Republic of France in which it agrees to withdraw its troops from the territories of Cambodia, Laos and Vietnam when the governments of these countries request them to do so, and within a time agreed by both parties, except in cases where both parties agree that a certain number of troops may be left behind at pre-determined spots and for a fixed length of time.

11. The conference notes the declaration made by the French government, under the terms of which the latter will respect the independence, sovereignty, unity and territorial integrity of Cambodia, Laos and Vietnam when dealing with all problems related to the re-establishment and reinforcement of peace there.

12. All the participants in the Geneva conference undertake to respect the sovereignty, independence, unity and territorial integrity of Cambodia, Laos and Vietnam in all their dealings with them and to refrain from any interference in their internal affairs.

13. The participants of the conference agree to consult one another on all questions referred to them for supervision and inspection by the international committees, so that they can decide what measures are necessary to ensure that the ceasefire agreements relating to Cambodia, Laos and Vietnam are properly observed.

Chronology

1930	Yen Bay uprising. Creation of the Indo-Chinese Communist Party. Nge-Tinh soviets.
1940	
19 June	Japanese ultimatum to Catroux.
26 June	Catroux replaced by Decoux.
30 August	Signing of a Franco-Japanese agreement.
22–26 September	Langson incident.
27 September	Tripartite pact.
1941	
17 January	French naval victory over Siam.
13 April	Soviet-Japanese non-aggression pact.
9 May	Treaty of Tokyo.
18 May	Founding of the Viet Minh.
29 July	Darlan-Kato agreement.
7 December	Pearl Harbor.
9 December	Declaration of war on Japan by the *Comité national français* and appeal to the Indo-Chinese resistance.
1942	
July	Nationalist unrest in Phnom Penh.
1943	
8 December	Declaration on Indo-China by the CFLN.
1944	
30 January	Start of the Brazzaville Conference
3 June	Creation of the French provisional government.
6 June	Operation "Overlord".
23 August	Mordant appointed head of the Indo-Chinese resistance.
30 August	"Telegram from the three".
September	The provisional government set up in Paris.
23 October	The Americans recognize the French provisional government.

October	The Americans land in the Philippines.
1945	
5 February	Capture of Manila.
9 March	Japanese coup.
11 March	Bao Dai proclaims independence in Vietnam.
24 March	The provisional government's statement on Indo-China.
May	Nationalist unrest in Algeria and the Far East.
2 August	End of the Potsdam conference.
6 August	Hiroshima.
8 August	The USSR enters the war against Japan.
9 August	Nagasaki.
13–14 August	Japanese surrender. Beginning of the uprising in Vietnam.
15 August	D'Argenlieu appointed high commissioner in Indo-China.
22 August	Sainteny arrives in Hanoi.
25 August	Abdication of Bao Dai.
2 September	Signing of the Japanese surrender. Declaration of independence by the Republic of Vietnam.
11 September	Arrival of the Chinese in Hanoi.
5 October	Leclerc in Saigon.
21 October	Election of the French constituent assembly.
31 October	D'Argenlieu arrives in Saigon.
26 December	Death of Vinh San.
1946	
7 January	Franco-Cambodian *modus vivendi*.
20 January	De Gaulle steps down.
28 February	Franco-Chinese agreements.
6 March	The French disembark at Haiphong. Ho Chi Minh and Sainteny make a pact.
18 March	Leclerc arrives in Hanoi.
April	Dalat conference.
May	Rejection of the first draft of the constitution.
1 June	Proclamation of the Republic of Cochin-China.
June	Valluy replaces Leclerc. Ho Chi Minh arrives in France. Formation of the Bidault government.
6 July	Opening of the conference in Fontainebleau.
August	Second Dalat conference.
14 September	*Modus vivendi* between Moutet and Ho Chi Minh.
October	Adoption of the constitution of the Fourth Republic.
10 November	Election of the French national assembly.

20 November	Incidents in Haiphong.
16 December	Formation of the Blum government.
19 December	Uprising in Hanoi.

1947

January	Auriol elected President of the Republic. Formation of the Ramadier government. End of Leclerc's and Moutet's mission in Indo-China.
5 March	Bollaert replaced by d'Argenlieu.
22 March	The vote on military supplies for Indo-China
29 March	Revolt in Madagascar.
5 May	Removal of communist ministers.
12 May	Meeting between Ho Chi Minh and Mus.
5 June	Harvard speech.
15 August	India and Pakistan granted independence.
18 September	Bao Dai appeals to the people of Vietnam.
5 October	Creation of the Cominform.
7 October	Beginning of operation "Léa".
November	Formation of the Schumann government. Wave of strikes.
6 December	Talks between Bao Dai and Bollaert.
15 December	Ceylon becomes independent.
23 December	Laos and Cambodia join the French Union. Paris rejects the idea of any talks with Ho Chi Minh.

1948

January	Burma becomes independent.
February	Valluy recalled. Salan deputises.
April	Blaizot replaces Valluy.
20 May	Xuan made president of the Vietnamese government.
5 June	Treaty of Along Bay.
20 October	Bollaert replaced by Pignon.

1949

20 January	Mao's troops enter Peking.
8 March	Agreement reached between Auriol and Bao Dai.
4 April	Signing of the Atlantic pact.
May–June	Revers' mission.
13 June	Bao Dai comes to Saigon.
19 July	Laos becomes an associated state.
September	Carpentier succeeds Blaizot. Beginning of the affair of the generals. Occupation of the "bishoprics".
October	Proclamation of the People's Republic of

	China.
8 November	Cambodia becomes an associated state.
December	General Revers retires. Indonesia gains independence. Franco-Vietnamese settlement. Chinese communist forces arrive at the Tongking border.

1950

January	The national assembly sets up a board of enquiry into the affair of the generals. Recognition of Ho Chi Minh by China, then by the USSR. Ratification of the association agreements of the states of Indo-China by the national assembly.
March	Henri Martin arrested. Passing of the law against sabotage.
20 June	Start of the Korean war.
27 June	Truman's statement on American involvement in the Far East.
30 June	First delivery of American military equipment to Indo-China.
3–8 October	Cao Bang.
18 October	Evacuation of Langson.
19 October	Debate on Indo-China by the national assembly.
26 October	The Pleven plan (EDC).
27 October	Military service extended.
22 November	New debate on Indo-China.
November	Chinese intervention in Korea.
December	Appointment of de Lattre in Indo-China. Signing of the Pau agreements.

1951

13–17 January	Battle of Vinh Yen.
March	Formation of the Lao Dong, or Vietnamese Workers' Party. The Viet Minh becomes part of the Lien Viet. Alliance pact between the three Indo-Chinese revolutionary movements.
March–April	Battle of Dong Trieu.
May–June	Battle of Day.
July	Negotiations begin in Korea.
September	De Lattre goes to the United States.
October	Viet Minh defeated at Nghia Lo.
10 November	Start of the Battle of Hoa Binh.

1952

11 January	Death of de Lattre.

February	Evacuation of Hoa Binh. Lisbon conference.
March	Hinh becomes chief of staff of the Vietnamese army.
April	Salan becomes commander-in-chief.
	Letourneau becomes high commissioner.
June	Sihanouk's "legal *coup d'état*".
October	Vietnamese offensive in Thailand.
November	Operation "Lorraine". Setting up of the Na San base.

1953

January	Sihanouk dissolves the Cambodian assembly.
March	Death of Stalin. Sihanouk begins his "independence crusade". Viet Minh offensive in northern Laos.
12 April	Evacuation of Sam Neua.
27 April	Creation of the post of commissioner-general of France in Indo-China.
May	Ho Chi Minh's government launches agrarian reforms. Salan replaced by Navarre.
	Devaluation of the piastre. Fall of the Mayer government.
28 June	Formation of the Laniel government.
3 July	Memorandum from the Laniel government on political developments in Indo-China. Dejean appointed high commissioner in Indo-China.
27 July	Armistice in Korea.
August	Evacuation of Na San. Signing of the Franco-Laotian treaty "of friendship and fellowship".
October	Saigon congress. Agreement on military sovereignty in Cambodia.
November	Sihanouk wins back his capital. Occupation of Dien Bien Phu. Interview with Ho Chi Minh in the *Expressen*.
4–7 December	Bermuda conference.
17 December	Tam quits the post of President of the government of Saigon.

1954

January	The Buu Loc government takes office.
	Operation "Atlante".
25 January	Opening of the Berlin conference.
18 February	Notification of the Geneva conference.
13 March	Beginning of the battle of Dien Bien Phu.
26 April	Opening of the Geneva conference.
7 May	Surrender of Dien Bien Phu.

3 June	Ely appointed commander-in-chief and commissioner-general.
4 June	Franco-Vietnamese treaties of "independence and fellowship".
12 June	Fall of the Laniel government.
16 June	Diem placed at the head of the Saigon government.
17 June	Investiture of Mendès-France.
24–30 June	Battle of An Khê.
29 June	Withdrawal from Nam Dinh.
20 July	Geneva agreements.
30 August	Rejection of the EDC.
8 September	Manila pact.
9 October	French withdrawal from Hanoi.
27 October	Letter from Eisenhower promising Diem his "unconditional support".
November	Beginning of the Algerian war. The Viet Minh troops complete their withdrawal from Laos and Cambodia.
December	Agreement between Ely and Collins. End of the Paris conference. Signing of the agreements between France, Laos, Cambodia and South Vietnam.

1955

February	Election of Sihanouk.
March	Abdication of Sihanouk and formation of the Sangkum.
March–April	"War of the sects" in Cochin-China.
17–24 April	Bandung conference.
15 May	The last of the French troops leave North Vietnam.
June	Departure of General Ely.
18 July	Geneva East-West summit.
September	Elections in Cambodia. The Lien Viet gives way to the Patriotic Front.
October	Bao Dai deposed.
25 December	Elections in Laos.

1956

February	Twentieth Congress of the Soviet Communist Party.
March	Election of a South Vietnamese constituent assembly.
April	The French troops leave South Vietnam. Dissolution of Cominform.

July	Geneva sets a date for the general elections in Vietnam.
November	Peasant unrest in Nghê-An.
1960	
September	Third Congress of the Lao Dong.
20 December	Creation of the FNL or National Liberation Front in Vietnam.

Notes and References

CHAPTER I: COLONIAL INDO-CHINA (PP. I-28)

1. The Moi languages belong to the Australo-Asiatic group. But some Mois, such as the Sedangs, use Hmong-Khmer-type languages and others, such as the Rhades, Malay-Polynesian-type languages.
2. For example, one Trotskyist pamphlet [90] says, "Thus Vietnam appears to be a typically feudal state."
3. How much this doctrine corresponded to the original Confucianism, i.e. to the teachings of the Chinese leader himself who lived in the fifth century BC, is another matter. However, besides this canonical version there was a non-conformist brand of Confucianism.
4. On 4 May 1919 the students of Peking demonstrated against Japanese imperialism. Action continued in the major cities throughout the weeks that followed. Their slogan was a patriotic one, "Save the country", but political unrest, in which students played a major part, went hand in hand with an upsurge in intellectual activity at the expense of the Confucian past. With hindsight, it can be said that the history of modern China began in 1919.
5. The seventeenth and eighteenth centuries were marked by the struggle between the Trinh and the Nguyen. The former, which served the official Le dynasty, held the North whilst the latter ruled in the South. The Dong Hoi wall (on the 17th parallel) served as a borderline. Bishop Pigneau de Brehaine helped the heir to the Hué dynasties to conquer the country. The victor proclaimed himself Emperor in 1802 under the name of Gia Long.
6. "The South of the Viets", an earlier name in fact, revived by the nationalists in the twentieth century.
7. It was represented in the French parliament by a deputy.
8. Three Annamite sovereigns were deposed by the French. It goes without saying that the mandarins were totally in the hands of the administration. Since they were poorly paid they were naturally drawn to the traditional practice of embezzlement. The competitive system was restored in 1935, bringing about an improvement in quality.
9. International Colonial Exhibition, Paris, 1931, French Indo-China, *Le Laos* by R. Meyer, Imprimerie d'Extrême-Orient, Hanoi 1930.
10. At first, the protectorates came under the jurisdiction of the Minister for Foreign Affairs, as is normally the case for foreign territories (this is how Tunisia and Morocco were treated). The creation of the Union of Indo-China put an end to this situation.

11. Customs tariffs were laid down under the law of 1892, in which Indo-China was made an assimilated colony. French products were exempt, whilst foreign goods were charged at the French rate. However, there was scope for departure from these rates. To quote the words of a Vietnamese interviewed by the journalist Roubaud, "The protectorate is first and foremost protectionism" (*Vietnam*, Paris 1931). In his book *A la barre de l'Indochine* (At the Helm of Indo-China), governor-general Decoux called the colonial pact system as applied to Indo-China "corner-shop politics, selfish and short-sighted". Just before World War II, 3 per cent of France's trade was with Indo-China, 50 per cent of Indo-China's imports came from France and 25 per cent of its exports were sent there.

12. On the other hand, public works were carried out by means of enforced labour and officials and soldiers were paid ridiculously low wages.

13. The *quoc ngu* compiled in the seventeenth century by Alexander of Rhodes.

14. Sarraut managed to abolish traditional learning altogether. In 1939, Indo-China had 500,000 school pupils, 13,000 of whom were taught under the French education system.

15. Figures quoted by P. Devilliers [42] from the *Annuaire statistique de l'Indochine* (Indo-China Statistical Yearbook). In 1938 France had a mortality rate of 15.5 per thousand and an infant mortality rate of 6.5 per cent.

16. Two million tonnes were produced. A whole group of industries was established on the coast of Tongking to exploit this particular source of energy. However, two-thirds of the coal was exported.

17. Meyer, op. cit.

18. The 3,000 other "Europeans and immigrants" included 250 Japanese.

19. One example of the inequality between colonists and natives was the difference in pay between French officials and mandarins. A top-ranking mandarin was paid less than a minor French official such as a *sous-brigadier* customs officer. In business, if a Frenchman and an Annamite both did the same jobs the former would always be better paid and the wages were always in inverse proportion to competence.

20. Owing to war abroad and at home, new groups of immigrants kept arriving until 1949. In 1951, the administration provided the following statistics for the city of Saigon: 998,000 Vietnamese and 583,000 Chinese.

21. It was common for families to be both craft workers and farmers. However, 5 per cent of the population drew their basic livelihood from craft work. The villages of Tongking, in particular, specialized in crafts.

22. *Économie agricole de l'Indochine* (The Agricultural Economy of Indo-China), Hanoi 1932.

23. In 1930–1 a number of regions were hit by famine. In some villages women were seen trying to sell their babies in order to survive.

24. P. Gourou [58] quotes the following example, in the Tongkingese province of Thai Binh, the 253 large landowners were the direct owners of 28,000 mau (5 mau = 1.80 ha) but they had indirect control over 43,000 mau since the former owners had become tenant farmers instead, due to their debts. Given the pressure of population day labourer's wages tended to decrease and farm rents tended to increase. Tenant farmers often owed half their harvests to the owners.

25. Over 57 per cent of families possessed no land. Other features of Cochin-Chinese agrarian particularism were the almost total absence of dikes and

common lands.

26. The Banque d'Indochine was an issuing bank as well as a merchant bank.

27. Big business was dominated by powerful import-export firms such as Dreyfus.

28. The majority of naturalized subjects were half-castes. However, many Eurasians were unable to obtain French citizenship.

29. The abundance and cheapness of labour, the wide range of raw materials, the existence of coal deposits and a tax system that was favourable to businesses all combined to attract investment. To what extent did Indo-China, and particularly the colonies, represent a good deal for France? See J. Marseille's answer in *Empire colonial et Capitalisme français* (The Colonial Empire and French Capitalism), Albin Michel 1984.

30. Initially the colonizers recruited workers from China. After World War I, the number of Chinese workers declined steadily.

31. The Popular Front brought Indo-China an eight-hour day, time off every week, annual holidays and maternity leave. It did away with salary deduction penalties and night work for women and children.

32. Pope Pius XI wrote two encyclicals on the subject of missionaries in 1926. In *Ab ipsis pontificatus exordiis*, he renewed Pope Benedict XV's exhortations originally made in *Rerum Ecclesiae* and insisted on the systematic creation of a native clergy. However, in 1939, the Indo-Chinese Catholic hierarchy was still largely dominated by Europeans (Frenchmen and, to a lesser degree, Spaniards).

33. From *cao dai* meaning divine spirit. The best work on the subject of religion in general is that of a missionary called Father Cadière, *Croyances et Pratiques religieuses des Vietnamiens*, Saigon, EFEO, 1955.

34. Of Hindu origin, Pali was the sacred language of Lesser Vehicle Buddhism.

35. Gallimard 1930

36. Meyer, op. cit.

37 "On the question of colonies and oppressed nations, those parties belonging to countries where the bourgeoisie possess colonies or oppress nations must follow a particularly clear and precise line of conduct. All parties belonging to the Third International have a duty to relentlessly expose 'their' imperialist's feats in the colonies, to support colonial liberation movements with deeds not words, to demand the expulsion of the said imperialists from the colonies, to instill in the workers of their own countries genuine fraternal feelings towards the working classes in the colonies and oppressed nations and to agitate constantly among the troops of the mother country against the oppression of colonial nations." This was the eighth of the twenty-one conditions laid down by Lenin for parties wishing to join the Communist International.

38. L. Roubaud, *Viet Nam*, Librairie Valois 1931. The author went to the country to report on the grave events of 1930. The following year, the Minister for the Colonies, Paul Reynaud, made his inspection. A. Viollis took part in this official journey. His book was re-published in 1949 to assist the Communist Party's struggle against the war in Indo-China.

39. Tran Duc Thao in *Les Temps Modernes* (Modern Times) of 1946.

40. Tran Duc Thao, see above. In 1951, Tran Duc Thau left France and a promising career in philosophy to join the Viet Minh clandestine forces.

41. As governor-general from 1911 to 1914, then from 1917 to 1919, Albert Sarraut was the founder of the Indo-Chinese university. The most conservative

of the colonists protested, saying an educated Annamite was a rival, one less coolie, a thinker. P. Mus observed the following: "Many of our people, and I am talking about well-informed, unprejudiced people, remember having excellent conversations, sometimes of an extremely high quality in human terms, with members of the native population, and their experiences have confirmed them in their conviction that we have destroyed this mutual source of happiness by the untimely imposition of our ideas." [50]

42. Arrested when the French surrendered Shanghai in 1925, Phan Boi Chau was sentenced to death in his absence. He later appeared at the criminal court in Hanoi, where the sentence was confirmed. However, it was never carried out. The new governor-general, Varenne, placed him under house arrest.

43. Exiled in France, he returned in 1925 and his arrival coincided with that of Varenne. His funeral a year later turned into a display of nationalist feeling. Thousands of people attended and many young people wore white arm-bands as a sign of mourning. Phan Chu Trinh, Sun Yat-Sen and Gokhale are three Asian examples of the fascination exercised by western democracy in the early part of this century.

44. The mandarin Dinh took the same view. He translated this policy into a programme of reforms, which appeared in 1936. Patriotism and traditionalism were the values of these men (who also readily quoted Maurras). Later, during the War, they joined forces with the French apologists for the "national revolution". Nguyen Xuan Dinh was one of the last to pass the famous three-yearly competitive examination in Nam Dinh.

45. Viet Nam Quoc Dan Dang.

46. Or "the well-being of the people".

47. Nguyen Ai Quoc means "Nguyen the patriot". Ho Chi Minh means "he who enlightens".

48. From this date onwards, the French Communist Party became more "bol-shevized" and attacked French imperialism ever more virulently, particularly with regard to the Moroccan and Syrian questions. At this 1924 congress, Nguyen Ai Quoc insisted on the revolutionary might of the peasants ("A peasant revolt in the colony is imminent.... The Communist International owes it to itself to organize them").

49. In his pamphlet on the events of 1930 entitled *Les Soviets du Nghe-Tinh* (The Soviets of Nghe-Tinh), Hanoi, ELE. An active participant in the revolution, Tran Huy Lieu was one of Ho Chi Minh's ministers.

50. Being an exporter of raw materials which slumped in price, Indo-China was hit before France. The price of a kilo of rubber fell from 22 francs in 1929 to 4 francs in 1931. Between 1926 and 1933, the Federation's foreign trade went down by two-thirds.

51. The movement was actually situated in the provinces of Nghe-An and Ha Tinh. People refer to the soviets of Nghe-Tinh for short.

52. The other questions came from the Deputies Outrey, Doriot and Moutet. The French national assembly debated the situation in Indo-China at length throughout the month of June.

53. And even foresight, such as Commandant Garnier's report on Ha Tinh. He insisted on the strength and eventual irresistibility of the movement. The lack of complacency in the picture painted by the Board of Enquiry (led by Morché of the Hanoi Court of Appeal) into the events in North Annam could also be

quoted.

54. He spent much of the following period in the USSR. He returned to China in 1938 and installed himself on the Tongkingese border early in 1940, after spending a few months in Maoist Yunan.

55. After the repressive measures of 1930, the Constitutionalist Party tried to lead the nationalist movement from Cochin-China. Its newspaper, *La Tribune Indochinoise*, had several brushes with the administration.

56. The board, headed by J. Godard, did indeed go to Indo-China. But, fearful of unrest, the administration would not allow the Congress to be held.

57. The Democratic Front and the anti-fascist Popular Front that preceded it were not a union of parties and organizations like the French Popular Front. Instead, they were based on a network of committees and ensured the preponderance of Marxist elements. The manipulative skills the communists gained from this proved useful to them and caused them to establish themselves on a firmer footing.

58. However, the crisis left its mark. Take the rubber plantations for example. The crisis put a number of small Vietnamese planters out of business and, in the period leading up to the war, half the area planted with rubber trees was controlled by three French companies. Paris took a whole series of measures to combat the recession throughout the Empire, and particularly in Indo-China. It changed export regulations and customs duties, established fixed import quotas and arranged for systems of compensation etc.

CHAPTER 2: INDO-CHINA UNDER THE JAPANESE (PP. 29-51)

1. A general in the supreme army command. He was not responsible for the navy or air force.

2. End of the Yunan line.

3. At this point the FNEO, already reduced due to the war needs in Europe, was disbanded.

4. Message from Decoux to Vichy: "If we must risk losing Indo-China, it would be better to lose it by defending it than by betraying it".

5. These were territories ceded to France in 1907.

6. It was at this time that Darlan drafted a form of military collaboration with Germany in the Paris protocols.

7. Generally larger than the Japanese troops. After partial demobilization, the French forces numbered between 50,000 and 60,000. In normal times, 25,000 Japanese troops were stationed in the peninsula.

8. Until early 1945 (when the Philippines were captured) an allied attack could only be contemplated from China. The Admiral was constantly humouring Chiang's government and discouraging him from undertaking any operations in Tongking. This policy led Decoux to oppose Vichy's recognition of the pro-Japanese government of Nanking. From January 1942, however, the Chinese Air Force launched sporadic raids on Tongking. The Americans continued them and intensified their bombing raids towards the end of the war.

9. The instigator was Son Ngoc Thanh, a young judge, educated in France and a Cambodian from Cochin-China. He was sent on detachment to the Buddhist Institute, where he started a nationalist periodical called *Nagaravatta* (suspended under the ban of April 1942). Hem Chieu and Son Ngoc Thanh were sentenced to death after the conspiracy of July 1942. The former was pardoned

but died in the Poulo Condore prison, the latter found refuge in Japan. This warning did not prevent the colonial government's enlightened despotism from implementing measures which would offend Khmer traditions, such as replacement of the Buddhist calendar by the Gregorian calendar and the transcription of Cambodian into Latin characters.

10. As the League for the Restoration of Vietnam, the Phuc Quoc played a part in the Langson affair at the end of 1940. The Cao Dao sect was part of it for a while.

11. The final blaze of revolt, but in North Annam. In January 1941, a sergeant in the National Guard led his garrison in an uprising which was immediately quelled.

12. The courts martial passed 106 death sentences. Figures vary on how many victims there were during the fighting, as is normal in this sort of situation. About 100 insurgents were put to death according to the general government, more than 5,000 according to the Communist Party of Indo-China.

13. As the small kingdom of Luang Prabang had just had to give up some territories as a result of the Treaty of Tokyo, Decoux granted it three other provinces, enabling the country to recover the whole of northern French Laos.

14. Decoux had the Emerald Buddha's pagoda restored in the kingdom of Luang Prabang. The task was undertaken by the future prime minister, Souvanna Phouma.

15. Decoux placed him on the throne in 1941. However, it was Prince Monireth, the oldest son of the late king, whom the Third Republic seems to have chosen to receive the long, pointed, golden tiara. In Cambodia, there was no Salic Law, however, and it was the dignitaries who chose the monarch. In fact, they followed the advice of the "protector".

16. To such an extent that the communist historian Nguyen Khac Vien wrote: "The colonial administration wished to take control of the movement to eradicate illiteracy; until that time it had been in the hands of the patriots" [27].

17. A former student at the HEC (Haute École de Commerce, an institute of further education in business management), Trinh Van Binh was appointed Inspector of Customs and Excise; he was to be a member of the Ho Chi Minh government during the Indo-Chinese war.

18. In 1941, it consisted entirely of Indo-Chinese. It was expanded under pressure from the colonists.

19. General Commissioner for Physical Education, Sport and Youth.

20. This was the case with metallurgical, chemical and the pharmaceutical industries.

21. Between March 1939 and March 1945, currency in circulation increased fivefold.

22. In *Ponts de Lianes* (Liana Bridges) (Hachette, 1976) J. Raphaël-Leygues tells the story of a comrade captured by the Viet Minh during the revolution and incarcerated in a prison where he heard the song "Maréchal, nous voilà" ("Marshal, here we are!") sung to new words and bugles playing "La France est notre Mère" ("France is our Mother"). The youth camp had changed from "national revolution" to "national-communist revolution".

23. "Reinstatement of French authority in New Caledonia would be achieved by French forces alone, but it would be essential to provide indirect coverage for their communications with Indo-China via the Japanese navy and if necessary,

given the uncertainty of Australian reaction, direct backup by Japanese Air Force." (Extract from a telegram sent to the Minister for the Colonies.)

24. In 1940, Langlade was living in Malaya where he was director of a rubber-financing company. A supporter of the Free French from the outset, he had already been on an intelligence assignment to Indo-China in the summer of 1941 (at the request of the British).

25. This was known as the tripartite message, since it was signed jointly by Cosme and Margerie, who represented Vichy in Japan and Japanese-held China (see documents in the appendix).

26. See appendix.

27. Before leaving his post, Ambassador Yoshizawa confided to diplomatic adviser Boisanger that "if it lost the Philippines, his country would review its policy in Indo-China".

28. The extent of the American bombings of the peninsula (those of 12 January were particularly heavy) could be interpreted as a sign of an imminent landing.

29. From the beginning of the Japanese presence, the Banque d'Indochine supplied the Japanese with piastres and this matter was a bone of contention between the two authorities. At the end of the period, the yen equivalent was largely fictitious. This tended to link these exchange allowances to the payment by France of the occupation costs. Inflation was fuelled by this supply of Indo-Chinese money to the Japanese troops.

30. They had 60,000 men in Indo-China alone, roughly the same number as the French troops. However, there were another 35,000 men stationed on the Chinese and Thai borders.

31. Some civilians were also killed by the Japanese in 1945, such as the senior resident Haelewyn, who died in the last days of the war.

32. Sabattier commanded the Tongking division.

33. "It is for this reason that the French government requests American intervention in the form of arms, munitions, medical supplies and food and cannot stress enough the importance and urgency of this question" (memo to the State Department dated 12 March). Washington's attitude caused de Gaulle to reprimand the American ambassador severely.

34. General Direction of Studies and Information (formerly the DGSS (General Direction of Special Services) in Algiers.

35. Le Monde of 22 April quoted a communiqué from the Ministry of War on the battle which had just taken place in Dien Bien Phu. The attempt to plant the maquis among the Japanese had failed. There are accounts of these battles of March/April 1945 in Charbonneau and Maigre's Les Pariahs de la Victoire (The Pariahs of Victory), France-Empire 1980.

36. The hostility of the member of the Luang Prabang dynasty explains the one month delay in the case of Laos.

37. The Japanese had considered retaining some Frenchmen in technical posts. The Vietnamese insisted on total exclusion.

38. The social foundations were the same but not the structures. The Chinese Communist Party had to take account of the ruling party.

39. The instrument of this control had to be the Viet Nam Cach Menh Dong Minh Hoi (Revolutionary League of Vietnam) formed in 1942 and managed by an old sinophile nationalist, Nguyen Hai Than. Prudence led the Viet Minh to join the Dong Minh Hoi and for a while Ho Chi Minh was its secretary. But in

Indo-China the communist propaganda slogan was: "All the anti-Japanese nationalist groups have merged under the name of Viet Minh". The French found it very difficult to make sense of the confusion in the midst of these various fronts whose structures varied greatly. The report from the secret services, written just before Ho Chi Minh took control, confused everything and declared that the Viet Minh wanted "the creation of a democratic non-communist state" (quote from A. Ruscio [112]).

40. Office of Strategic Services.

41. See documents in appendix.

42. But Sainteny did have a meeting with the leader of the VNQDD, Nguyen Tuong Tam. The latter made it clear that a restoration of the colonial order, in any form, was unthinkable, since the balance of power was not in France's favour.

43. Anti-colonialist and anti-French, Japanese propaganda over the preceding months had made a special point of emphasising the humiliation suffered by Paris in the Levant.

44. It was on this day that the independent state of Indonesia was declared. The Japanese had decided to grant power, here as well, to nationalists like Sukarno. But, to avoid being compromised in the eyes of the Allies and spurred on by anti-Japanese resistance, the leaders took by force the sovereignty which was about to be given to them.

45. To de Gaulle he wrote: "I ask you to understand that the only way to safeguard French interests and the spiritual influence of France in Indo-China is openly to recognize the independence of Vietnam and reject any idea of re-establishing a French administration here in any form." No mention of these words was made by de Gaulle.

46. Nambo (South) was Cochin-China. Similarly Trungbo (Central Region) corresponded to Annam and Bacbo (North) to the Tongking of the French. For the Vietnamese nationalists, this terminology had the advantage of emphasizing the unity of the country. They were also referred to as Namky, Trungky, Backy. In the following months, the "question of the Three Ky" was often to be raised.

47. Anti-French violence broke out mainly on the night of 19 August in Hanoi and on the evening of 2 September in Saigon.

48. See documents in the appendix.

49. The government formed on 29 August included non-communists. It was more representative than the revolutionary committee, but the main portfolios were given to those who could be trusted.

50. Giap [99].

51. Giap [87].

CHAPTER 3: A PREMONITION (PP. 52–82)

1. The Allies distinguished between three theatres of operation, the Pacific theatre under MacArthur, the South-East Asia theatre under Mountbatten, and the Chinese theatre effectively commanded by the American General, Wedemeyer.

2. A man of the left such as academician Chamson realised this: "The re-establishment of our presence in the Far East seemed to me to be part of the restoration of France, and even of liberty, just as it was for Alsace and Lorraine" (in the preface to the book by J. Raphaël-Leygues, *Ponts de lianes*, Hachette 1976).

The reference is typical of the times: "But soon our flag will be hoisted over Hanoi, Hué and Saigon, as free as Strasbourg and Metz" (Giacobbi, Minister of the Colonies, speaking to the consultative assembly on 12 March 1945).

3. The text is in the appendix. In his memoirs, Bao Dai states that knew of this fundamental text only in 1948. An example of the confusion of the period.

4. "Disposing of all systems of colonization based on the arbitrary, France guarantees all men equal access to public office and the individual or collective discharge of the rights and liberties announced or stated above."

5. The elections would be held on 21 October 1945.

6. The conference is known to have established this preliminary principle: "The aims of the France's civilizing work in the colonies did not permit any idea of independence, nor any possibility for development outside the French Empire bloc." In a note (quoted by P. Isoart [72]), Pignon indicated that Brazzaville only affected Black Africa. The reference made to it in the 24 March Declaration in no way meant that the conference's recommendations applied to Indo-China— it only meant that the same spirit of innovation motivated the two declarations. This comment on the document aimed at dealing with the criticisms made by opponents (Indo-Chinese and others) of the government's declaration.

7. The Avignon congress of December 1944 had mentioned the general delegation of the Indo-Chinese in France. The Marxists (Trotskyists as well as Stalinists) were widely represented in it. The young philosopher, Tran Duc Thao, was one of its activists. The delegation was to send a memorandum to the United Nations.

8. Drafting the 1945 declaration had been a painstaking task. Pignon, a specialist in Indo-Chinese affairs at the Ministry of Colonies, had a decisive role. Despite this, the governor, Laurentie, took responsibility for it, as he gave the text his seal of approval.

9. French Far East Expeditionary Forces.

10. De Gaulle would personally supervise (in detail) the creation of the expeditionary force.

11. The role of the "Europe" section of the State Department should be noted. It used its influence to help France's return to Indo-China.

12. In any event, this was Mountbatten's opinion when he received Leclerc on 22 August: "If Roosevelt were still alive, you would not be able to re-enter Indo-China."

13. He arrived on the same plane as Patti. Sainteny was the only Frenchman sent to Indo-China at the end of August who was not killed or arrested.

14. See A. Patti, *Why Vietnam?*, Berkeley, University of California Press 1980. The desire of the Viet Minh to play upon the Allies', and particularly the Americans', anti-colonialism at that time was manifested in the towns by streamers and inscriptions in English, sometimes stating "*Independence or death.*"

15. The Imfeld group held Luang Prabang in the first days of September.

16. For a time, they forced the communists to become a minority on the executive committee.

17. "Sole mission: to disarm the Japanese. Do not become involved in peacekeeping." These were Mountbatten's instructions on 18 September.

18. In his "proposal for the Japanese surrender", the General Chief of Staff of National Defence made this demand on 11 August: "The French (European) military personnel, now prisoners, in Indo-China will immediately be re-armed

with the equipment of the Japanese troops present in the territory. These re-mobilized troops will be placed under the orders of the designated French command." But the Japanese were in no rush to release their prisoners. For several weeks after the declaration of surrender, one could witness the strange spectacle of armed, defeated men detaining the supposed victors. It should be said that the attitude of the Allies was at the very least ambiguous. P. Mus [50] relates the story of an American officer greeted as a liberator by the French in one camp which the Viet Minh had taken over after the Japanese. He replied to the administrator Ramadier (the younger): "These people must have their reasons for having put you there. Stay where you are."

19. "The war of reconquest was beginning" (Nguyen Khac Vien [27]).

20. Dewey, Chief of the OSS for the south of Indo-China and nephew of the American politician, was assassinated during this troubled period.

21. Sometimes the press confused the words Vietnam and Viet Minh. It butchered most of the names. It mixed facts and allegations. Thus, while speaking of the retaking of Saigon, on 25 September *Combat* stated: "The Annamese 'government' was arrested." No better informed than the other newspapers, *L'Humanité* was particularly circumspect at first. 22. Letter to Leclerc on 27 October 1945. It is clear that for de Gaulle the Indo-China problem was basically caused by the attitude of the great powers. Similarly, only 5 per cent of French considered that "responsibility for the troubles in Indo-China" rested with the Indo-Chinese (poll of September 1945).

23. In theory, fighting had ceased on 2 October following a truce negotiated by Gracey. The truce was destined to be short-lived.

24. On 12 November, Andrée Viollis chaired a meeting on the theme of "Friendship between the peoples of France and Indo-China" in the Salon de Wagram. This was the first Communist meeting for "peace in Indo-China". When Liberation came, the Communist Party had strongly recommended the nationalization of the Banque d'Indochine.

25. The 9th DIC was "whitewashed"; many FFI were integrated into it. Officially, these young solders were told that their responsibility was to disarm the Japanese and stamp out acts of piracy.

26. General Nyo did not have enough men to occupy the region and would attempt moving units from one sector to another. This "revolving appeasement" was not very effective. When the troops withdrew, the Viet Minh re-installed themselves, slaughtering the inhabitants who had revealed their sympathies by helping the French.

27. The "veterans" had readily spread the story of the "French of the class of '45", desperately looking for an Indo-Chinese dictionary. "The officers of the former Indo-China army were slightly amazed by the methods used to pacify the country which they knew as well as its inhabitants; the new men were generally incredibly pretentious, and listened to them disdainfully, smiling sardonically", wrote General Sabattier [79], bitter at having been removed from the administration of Indo-China by de Gaulle. Many statements express the resentment of those in charge during the Japanese period.

28. Son Ngoc Thanh had returned from Tokyo after the operation to become Minister for Foreign Affairs. Having been a leading member of the Cambodian government under Japanese rule, he finally become its leader on 14 August.

29. Vinh San wanted to see his family in Reunion before returning to Indo-

China. It was during this trip that his plane crashed near Bangui. Vinh San was also known by the name of Duy Tan, which he had had as Emperor.

30. During the Indo-China war, two other effective literacy campaigns were conducted. "Everyone was talking about the red disks on house fronts. The number of the disks indicated how many people in the household were still illiterate. People were therefore encouraged to end illiteracy as soon as possible." This statement by Figuères [97] exemplifies the practical methods used during the campaigns.

31. The Chinese also circulated their national currency. It was arbitrarily overvalued in relation to the piastre. This method of plunder has been used by other armies of occupation.

32. The Communist Party in theory no longer existed after 11 November. This did not prevent Nguyen Khac Vien, historian of the regime, from writing that, "on 25 November, the central committee of the Communist Party was elaborating its guidelines for resistance" [27]. This is just one example of the phenomenon.

33. This was the first curious occurrence. After the agreement with the Viet Minh, the VNQDD and DMH parties did not take part in the election. However, a number of seats were automatically assigned to them. The Viet Minh controlled the police, the army and the radio. Its candidates often stood unopposed. Despite this, there was hardly any doubt of Ho Chi Minh's mandate.

34. J. Lacouture and P. Devilliers, in his press service, should also be mentioned as belonging to the Leclerc's liberal team. In 1946, both of them worked on the *Paris-Saigon* newspaper, whose objective would be the entente between the French and Vietnamese.

35. On 9 January Baylin, director of the Banque d'Indochine in Hanoi, was assassinated. Baylin had participated one month previously in the "inter-Allied conference" which settled the matter of the 500-piastre notes. In the summer of 1945, the Japanese had printed millions of high denomination notes. Taking the orthodox financial position, Saigon had decided that the denominations of 500 piastres, issued between 9 March and 23 September, were worthless. The Chinese subsequently protested because they held most of these notes in the North (military and civilians). The conference of 10 December set the exchange rate level with the denominations held by the Luhan army. This is an example of Chinese pressuring and dealing.

36. France abandoned its concessions in China. France granted China privileges in Haiphong. This caused people to say that China was installing France in Tongking while it was eliminating the system of concessions from its own territory.

37. But *doc lap* can also be translated as "liberty" or "autonomy"...

38. A telegram from Leclerc on 14 February read thus: "You should not hesitate to use the word *independence* for the success of the negotiations."

39. It should be said that the February Sino-French agreement totally ignored Ho Chi Minh's government.

40. This was the first of the Admiral's trips to Paris. The high commissioner saw a number of important people on this occasion, including Deputy Prime Minister Thorez. According to d'Argenlieu [82] he told him: "In view of the party to which I belong, I naturally wish that everything is settled for the best with the Viet Minh, but our flag comes first and foremost! So, if you have to hit them, hit

them hard."

41. A member of the DMH, Nguyen Hai Than, became president; a member of the VNQDD, Nguyen Tuong Tam, was in Foreign Affairs. A "non-party" man held Defence. He was Phan Anh, who, as a minister in Kim's cabinet, had been good at rallying the youth organizations set up by the Decoux administration. This is not the only case of an important member of the Japanese period having been reinstated. Bao Dai's former delegate in Tongking in 1945, the Viceroy Phan Ke Toai, would later become minister of the Interior in Ho Chi Minh's government.

42. Sainteny recalled "the admirable attitude of the French sailors and soldiers who without a moment's hesitation stoically waited for the order to respond" [86].

43. Ho Chi Minh's strategy caused him to be severely criticised by the Trotskyists. C. Lefot in *Les Temps modernes* in March 1947 wrote: "It is no surprise that one of Ho Chi Minh's first acts in November 1945 was to dissolve the Communist Party in the name of national and "racial" [*sic*] unity.... Dissolving the party was political suicide. But for us it was only a symbolic counter-revolutionary gesture. For Ho Chi Minh, it meant playing the trump card of feudal bourgeoisie.... It was the Communist Party which took over the historic mission of nationalism. It was the Communist Party alone which filled the role of counter-revolution." And it categorized the agreement of 6 March as "the lamentable surrender of all our ideological and political plans."

44. It should be noted that the text also provided for "units responsible for the defence of the naval and air bases." It added: "The duration of the mission entrusted to these units will be defined in subsequent conferences." The reunion of 3 April would end in an agreement between Salan and Giap specifying certain methods of applying the military accord of 6 March.

45. The Sainteny-Ho Chi Minh compromise also influenced other parts of the Empire. On 21 March, the Madagascan deputies in the constituent assembly proposed a bill asking that the island become a free state as defined in the agreement of 6 March.

46. The Admiral commented that "a commissioner of the Tongking Republic is signing with President Ho, in keeping with its rank as a federated state." On the other hand, "the Emperor of Annam Bao Dai has just abdicated, on the authoritative invitation of the adventurer Ho Chi Minh. After he left Hué and went over to the DRV, in the capital Hanoi, the legitimacy of the government in Annam and Tongking was lost. The origin of this is obtained by the provisional government of new France for Indo-China" [82].

47. The French Union was briefly mentioned within the outline for the constitution which he presented: "The future of the 110 million men and women living under our flag is to be organized as a federation which time will gradually clarify, but the new constitution has to mark its beginning and control its development."

48. Max André met Ho Chi Minh in Hanoi in January 1946. He had already led the French delegation in Dalat.

49. The French Communist Party was represented by Lozeray, an expert in colonial matters who would prove himself to be very discreet.

50. The key man in these contacts was R. Aubrac, who had been regional commissioner of the Republic in Marseilles at the time of the liberation. Aubrac was dismissed in January 1945 by de Gaulle who accused him of serving the

"anonymous dictatorship of the Communists". Aubrac remained a friend of Ho Chi Minh and continued to play a discreet role in the two Indo-China wars.
51. "We want our independence, and Franco-Vietnamese collaboration", Ho Chi Minh repeats again and again in his public statements.
52. In a memorandum dated 26 April 1946, the Admiral wrote: "The reunion of the three *kys* cannot be imposed geographically, historically, or economically— quite the contrary. Geographically it is impossible, because the Mekong basin firmly unites Laos, Cambodia and Cochin-China. The Annamite mountain range isolates it from Annam. Historically, it is impossible because the settlement of the Annamese from the North was replaced by centuries of occupation of these lands by the ancient Khmers. This settlement was accidental and brief. France's occupation has lasted for almost a century.... As for the argument of the commonality of the language, it is puerile or invalidated by its racist tone. The argument of linguistic unity was that of the Fuhrer to force the German minorities to become assimilated by the great Reich."
53. South Annam and the mountain people were also represented.
54. Allusion to an episode in Ho Chi Minh's campaign of seduction. On 25 June at a reception at the Royal-Monceau, he offered each woman a flower.
55. *Le Monde* on 2 August under the name of R. Roore.
56. During the height of the Vietnamese revolution and when the colonial system had been done away with six months previously, 65 per cent of the French (as opposed to 12 per cent) thought that Indo-China would be "left to France" (IFOP poll of September 1945). Another illusion was that a poll conducted immediately after the German surrender showed that for 80 per cent of its population (10 per cent disagreed) France would remain a great power. Maintaining the Empire and power are linked in the public's mind. The country had a world role because of the extent of its overseas territories.
57. In [113].
58. The Communists dominated (in July 1945) the *états généraux de la renaissance française*, the last great rally of the Resistance. The following resolution was passed: "The overseas peoples can improve their lot and achieve a life of freedom and happiness, not in a false independence—which in the present state of the world would only be misleading—but in a brotherly union with the people of France." At the June 1947 congress, Fajon would again rebuke the people of the former Empire: "Breaking with the French Union can only bring you a semblance of independence, a prelude to intolerable domination by powers where the bankers are your masters, where racist bigotry rules, where the lynching of blacks holds sway."
59. The National Council's resolution of 19–20 March 1947 would state: "The present task of the Socialist Party is to show the overseas peoples that their true freedom depends on a freely agreed association."
60. Two Indo-China experts acting behind the scenes can be mentioned as defenders of the colonial tradition: Varenne and Baffeleuf. The former governor-general, then Bidault's Minister of State (UDSR) was head of the National Association for French Indo-China. As Chairman of the Chamber of Commerce in Hanoi, Baffeleuf headed the Action Committee for the French Union, a French colonization organization created by the *états généraux*. In August 1946, reuniting some of the colonial representatives, the *états généraux* reaffirmed "the sacred principle of French sovereignty" overseas.

61. "When we learnt of the defeat in my country, when we knew that Paris had fallen, I cannot describe to you the scenes which took place, the feelings of grief of the factory worker, of men who live in the most complete destitution, nor can I accurately describe the sadness and sorrow of the peasants." (Saravane Lambert, deputy from India, meeting of the constituent assembly, 18 September 1946).

62. The Communists, on the contrary, recognized in the text the merit of "abstention in establishing the permanent bodies of the French Union". "We think, in fact, that we no longer belong to the times of the 'granting of charters to countries' and that both for the future of the relations of France with the people of the overseas territories and through respect of the right of people to manage their own affairs, the bodies could only be created by an assembly which unites the representatives of the different parties in the Union to this end on the basis of free consent and in equal numbers" (Fajon, during the meeting of 20 August).

63. The associated states did not participate in the election of the president of the Union. "In this Union, France benefits from a 'splitting of offices', because it is both one of the federated states and also, primarily, the federal state. Because of this fact, all the states of the Union were not associated as they might be as friends, but only connected individually and each for its own account to France by a link of federated state to federating and federal state" (Nguyen Dac Khe, conference at the Polytechnique on 19 June 1953).

64. Progress was made on the status of Indo-China during the Fontainebleau conference. The remit of the Federation would essentially be the economy.

65. Union for the defence of the French operations in Indo-China.

66. Inspirer of "separatist" policy, J. Cédile had just left the position to Torel who dreamed of another solution—the restoration of the monarchy.

67. The Chinese killed eleven French soldiers in Hanoi on Easter day.

68. In October 1945, a meeting was held to prepare the way for a trades union congress. It was held in March 1946 and decided on the creation of a single union. In May, the General Vietnamese Confederation of Labour (Tong Lien Doan Lao Dong or TLD) was born. An early communist would lead the TLD during the Indo-China war. Hoang Quoc Viet was one of the rare Viet Minh leaders to have belonged to the working class.

69. On 3 August, a French convoy was attacked on the way to Langson; there were eighteen killed and thirty-nine wounded.

70. This struck A. Blanchet so much that he entitled his record *In the land of the yellow Balillas* (Ed. Dorian, 1947).

71. It is generally believed that the intervention of the navy's artillery resulted in the death of 6,000 civilians. General Fonde contested these numbers, considering them to be very exaggerated. Commander Fonde was then chief of the French delegation at the mixed liaison commission.

72. The election disappointed at least one person. The Admiral was hoping for a negative vote and the return of de Gaulle. He was a conservative and his policy is in part explained by his desire to wait for the General, who had returned to politics, to impose his views. After 20 January 1946, the high commissioner had continued to report to the former head of Free France. He wrote to him on 10 August 1946: "I am writing to tell you that in spite of everything, we must hold on and act. If things finally became cowardly and and we abandon, then of course you could not be the means of execution."

73. The Indo-China war began under Blum, the Algerian war under Mendès-France. Is it coincidence that each of the colonial wars began when the French government was led by a man known for his liberalism in colonial matters? Didn't the Viet Minh, and the FLN, play on the embarrassment of the left's team (Moutet-Blum in 1946, Mitterrand-Mendès in 1954) when faced with the rebellion?

74. Following the 20 November incident, the French took control of Langson. With Haiphong and Langson, they gained control of both the main gateways to Tongking.

75. They included H. Morché, the former presiding judge (known for his liberalism) of the Court of Appeal of Hanoi. He would die during captivity. A few hostages remained imprisoned for the duration of the war. This happened to René Moreau, captured in Vinh, where he was fulfilling his consular duties. See his statement [132]. As at the time of the massacre in the city of Heyraud, the killings—of which the Eurasians were the main victims—often went hand in hand with mutilation. "At the Sûreté I saw the atrocious photographic records of these tragic days: sexual mutilation, a liver rammed into a mouth, a bamboo bag filled with women's breasts, daggers stuck into eyes", recalled R. Guillain (*Orient extrême*, Arléa/Le Seuil 1986)

CHAPTER 4: A FORGOTTEN COLONIAL WAR (PP. 83–115)

1. In fact, on the Communist side, explanations for the events of 19 December varied. At first, the aggression of the French troops was denounced, then it was explained that it was necessary to resume the armed struggle. Tran Duc Thao wrote, in March 1947, in *Les Temps Modernes* that "on the 19 December, at the end of a day of confusion during which an attack was launched on the residence of President Ho Chi Minh, the Vietnamese moved to counter-attack." French writers, such as Viollis or Figuères, remained vague when they were not avoiding the issue entirely. The present version from Hanoi states that the leaders at the time knew that any conciliation with "French Colonialism" would be impossible and that war was inevitable. This explanation after the event thus seems to coincide with the explanation that the high commission was giving in December 1946.

2. The prefect Bollaert had been one of De Gaulle's delegates in occupied France. He was arrested and deported to Germany. Leclerc had been considered as a replacement for D'Argenlieu. The offer was put to the General on his return from a fact-finding mission in Indo-China and he refused it twice on the advice of de Gaulle. Another change in the political situation in the Far East was the dissolution in January of the Interministerial Committee on Indo-China at the instigation of Moutet, who, as Minister for French Possessions Overseas, insisting on being completely responsible for the matter.

3. "In Indo-China, we have attempted to follow the policies of consensus. They met with agression. A conflict organized in secret suddenly led to the atrocities in Hanoi.... One day soon, [France] will no doubt find representatives of the Annamite people with whom one can reason. She will then not fear the creation, if such is the wish of the people, of the union of the three Annamitic countries, any more than she refuses to accept the independence of Vietnam within the framework of the French Union and the Indo-Chinese Federation."

4. Votes cast: 411. For, 411, Against, 0. At the session on 22 March, Castellani

warned: "I have just returned from Madagascar where, it has to be said, the events in Indo-China are being followed with great interest. A real party, formed along the same lines as the Viet Minh, is being created in the country at present, and its one ambition is to remove the French from their position of power on the island." One week later, the insurrection broke out, in which the parties were divided along similar lines to those in Indo-China.

5. This view was repeated in a book by General Sabatier, *The Destiny of Indo-China*, 1952. It was also explored by several right-wing Vietnamese nationalists.

6. Which did not prevent it from making further contact. On 11 August 1947, the French representative in Bangkok, P.-E. Gilbert, met a Viet Minh emissary who outlined the terms of an agreement to him.

7. On this occasion, the left wing of the party once more opposed Ramadier. In spite of Guy Mollet, the national council of the SFIO ratified the decision by a small majority.

8. "Yes, we must deal with the truly qualified representatives of the Vietnamese people whoever they may be, without making any exceptions either on political or personal grounds. Yes, Ho Chi Minh, who is not dead whatever might have been said, who is quite alive, and with whom M. Paul Mus had a meeting, from whom I received a personal message a few days ago through entirely official channels, remains the genuine and qualified representative of the Vietnamese people."

9. Giap was replaced at the head of the Ministry of Defence by an "independent", who commanded the Army.... In theory, the reshuffle theoretically caused the "Marxists" to be in a very small minority within the government. This was also a way of proving that the government had the unanimous support of the country and that there was no other representative force.

10. It may be recalled that de Gaulle had declared a unilateral truce in Algeria on the eve of the Evian negotiations in 1961 so as to show goodwill on the part of the French.

11. As well as being under pressure from the French and from right-wing Vietnamese nationalists, Bao Dai was also receiving advice from the Americans. On 22 September, he had a long meeting with William Bulitt, former ambassador to Paris and a prominent member of the Republican Party.

12. "The government has decided to grant a full mandate to the French high commissioner in Indo-China so as to pursue, without dealing with Ho Chi Minh's government, any actions and negotiations necessary to establish peace and freedom in the Vietnamese countries" (23 December). Bollaert repeatedly stated that he would never again deal with the Viet Minh. Tran Ngoc Danh, the Viet Minh's representative in Paris, was in fact arrested in January 1948 (he was released a month later for reasons of ill health).

13. Xuan thus abandoned the term "government of the Republic of Cochin-China" in favour of "provisional government of South Vietnam". At the same time, Bao Dai asked for the high commissioner for the Saigon government to be replaced by an administrative committee (as in Hué or Hanoi).

14. The persistence of the desire for autonomy amongst Cochin-Chinese notables can be explained mainly for political reasons (many of them having compromised themselves in the separatist experience) or economic reasons (it not being advisable for wealthy Cochin-China to be absorbed into Vietnam). Governor Tran Van Huu supported this desire for a separate identity. He was

applauded by the Cochin-Chinese assembly when he declared that he did not have to obey the orders of the central government as long as the French assembly had failed to make a pronouncement on the status of the colony.

15. One only needs to read *Le Journal du septennat* to see how much Auriol held on to the prerogatives of this post, which at the time did not stop a certain amount of friction with ministers.

16. The attachment of the colony to Vietnam being considered as a cession of French territory, it was necessary, under Article 27 of the 1946 constitution, to proceed to the "consultation of the peoples concerned" and for a resolution to be passed by the national assembly. The assembly ratified the operation in June. On this occasion, the Communists and a small proportion of the right voted against the government.

17. Where he was given two guardian angels, Cousseau, the man with the Hong Kong contacts, and Faugère, a Eurasian who was head of Security in Hanoi and who was severely tortured by the Japanese after the coup on 9 March.

18. Quoted by Devillers [42].

19. The Prince wrote, with Senghor and Lemaigne, "The French Imperial Community" (Alsatia 1945). Written during the war, the work consisted of reflections on the future of the Empire.

20. The French were reproached not only for their ubiquitous presence in national life, but also for doing little to defend the interests of the kingdom. Until November 1946, they were criticized for not yet having obtained the return of the provinces taken by Thailand, then worry was expressed over their policies in Cochin-China. Any prospect of annexing the province to Vietnam was a further irritant. The 1949 agreements were therefore very badly received. Not only was the territory over which Cambodia had historic rights being integrated into Vietnam, but no special provision had been made for the Khmer minority, and no adjustment of the contested border had been made. This was yet another aspect of the Indo-Chinese question.

21. The Pathet Lao government was thus led by members of the ancient ruling family of Vientiane. The rivalries between the princes of Luang Prabang and the princes of Vientiane therefore became an issue. The Province of Vientiane had been made part of the kingdom of Luang Prabang in 1941. At that time, Pethsarath had renounced his hereditary rights over the ancient kingdom while retaining the title of Prime Minister to the Luang Prabang sovereign.

22. Pethsarath chose neither allegiance to the French or collaboration with members of the underground. He remained in exile in Thailand.

23. "We will have to negotiate and the sooner the better", wrote the General in a long report dated 10 January 1947, which contradicted the version of events produced by his superiors Valluy and d'Argenlieu. But Morlière was one of a very small minority amongst the army commanders in Indo-China to hold this view.

24. Valluy stated the objectives of the operation in his directive of 19 July 1947. The aim was definitely to end the war: "We have set a time limit of only a few months. Suffice it to say that we are fighting the last round and that we have to win within the time allotted."

25. This was an expression of the economic and financial problems the country facing. For the French section of the population, the year 1947 was especially difficult. Inflation was at a peak, bread rations were lower than during the war.

The great strikes towards the end of the year took place against this background of poverty. The Marshall Plan, which was to help France greatly, and was already doing so by the winter of 1947–8, was particularly welcome. This help given by the United States to ailing imperial powers was to be considered by certain leaders of the colonized world as specifically American aid to colonialism.

26. During the first few hours of operation "Léa", it was thought that the government had been captured by the parachutists who had just landed on Bac Kan. The broadcasting of this false piece of information over the radio of the *Catalina*, which was flying over the operation zone, subsequently led to an enquiry on naval security. On the other hand, the Dutch capture in 1948 of the entire republican cabinet in Indonesia, and the capture by the French in 1956 of the leaders of the FLN in Algeria, had no significant effect on the progress of the wars of independence in the two colonies.

27. The word is Wingate's, the British officer who organized the fighting in the Burmese jungle during World War II.

28. Chailley, *Tropiques*, No. 358, 1954.

29. Thus, soldiers searching for hideouts could have their feet pierced by traps hidden underwater in paddy-fields.

30. Giap [99].

31. "At the end of the year, it was the rebels who went on the offensive with the 'Le Loi' campaign, directed mainly at 'Muong' country. The rebels won a fair number of victories which were a sign of their leaders' improved ability to control large numbers of men over relatively extended fronts" (from a combined report by the Saigon office of the Deuxième Bureau for General de Lattre, quoted by Ferrandi [43]).

32. Giap [98].

33. The system was neither watertight nor irreversible. For example, officers of the regular army could be used as temporary reinforcements for the regional forces or militias.

34. The Viet Minh had a purchasing office in Bangkok which ran a prosperous business until 1954.

35. A distinction must be made between the Security Force (Cong An), the Deuxième Bureau (Trinh Sat), and the Army Propaganda unit called the Dich Van (literally, "moral intervention"). In general, a Dich Van unit included three commissars (one for "educational propaganda", one for "patriotic emulation", and one for "current affairs"), two secretaries and some twenty armed men. Dich Van methods ranged from persuasion to murder, ensuring that the population was put in the right frame of mind and paving the way for the transfer of villages to the Viet Minh.

36. Example quoted by B. Fall (95) from the newspaper *Tin Duc* dated 20 June 1952.

37. Hogard, in *Revue de Défense nationale*, December 1956.

38. *Le Monde*, 4 August 1954. Although this article on the revolutionary war appeared anonymously, it was in fact written by Colonel Lacheroy.

39. At first, some refused to use the term "war". "In spite of what may have been said, this is not an expedition, a conquest or a war, but a police operation", as Burdoux stated to the national assembly on 21 March 1947.

40. Many French people did not even know how Vietnam stood in relation to Indo-China. In July 1948, somebody as well informed as Paul Reynaud again

repeated the old colonial distinction between the five countries of which Indo-China consisted: "We would be committing a grave error if we did not make the greatest effort to maintain and develop the Federation which unites the five countries, and which has contributed greatly to increasing its economic power and widening its horizons" (from a speech made at a luncheon of the French Association in Indo-China).

41. The officer corps was altered by discharging all the officers of 1946 in one go, rather than by weeding them out gradually. On this occasion, more than half of those who had graduated from a major military academy (Polytechnique or Saint-Cyr) left the army.

42. There were 50,000 for the rest of the French Union.

43. Thus, in March 1948, an attempt failed on the life of Bollaert, the high commissioner, in Nha Trang, Annam.

44. Companies whose premises had been damaged or could no longer be used because of the war, received compensation. They nearly always transferred the sum of the damages to other territories within the French Union. One example of the diversification of geographical risks is the case of the bars and ice cream parlours of Indo-China. In 1949, they formed an association called the Société des Brasseries de Côte-d'Ivoire. At the 1950 assembly, the Chairman of the Banque d'Indochine declared that "the total investment of the company in China, Indo-China and South-East Asia only represents an eighth of our portfolio of securities."

45. A flexible system of customs posts was established by the Viet Minh at points of contact with French regions. Taxes were sometimes even collected inside these zones. The tariffs set by the RDV government obviously gave top priority to the war effort: so-called luxury products were heavily penalized, those which were necessary for the armed struggle were exempt.

46. Letter published in *Témoignage Chrétien* on 2 September 1949.

47. Here are two eye-witness accounts amongst many others. "One day, he told me, a junk was spotted in the forbidden zone. We circled it, which didn't seem to bother them. We shot at it, and, of course, the junk sank. The Viets jumped into the water, gesticulating wildly. The plane continued on its way when the navigator cried out, 'I made a mistake, we're not in the forbidden zone. We're for the high jump.' And, sure enough, there were many mistakes of this kind and calls to order from Admiral FMEO. So we had to turn around and mow down all the Viets one by one with machine guns to stop them going and kicking up a fuss." (*Télégramme de Brest*, 26 March 1985) "I also had occasion to hear the 'notables' of a village complain to me thus: 'We know, from experience over the centuries, what war is, we know its customs. We agree to your soldiers seizing our livestock, our jewels, our buddhas, that is normal. We are less happy when they rape our women and girls, but we are resigned to it, it has always been so. But we protest when they treat us, the elders and dignitaries, and our sons with the same lack of respect.'"

48. "This is the oil slick method. Terrain is only gained in front after having thoroughly organized that which is behind. The unsubjugated natives of the day before were used to help us defeat those who had to be quelled on the following day." (Gallieni, *Principles of Pacification and Organization*).

49. Quoted in *Le Monde* on 16 July 1948. The Plain of Reeds was the setting for numerous operations. Because of the nature of the terrain, the navy played an

important role. During the war, many amphibian manoeuvres were organized, in which the "dinassaults" (naval assault divisions) were used. They generally consisted of eight vessels.

50. In colonial slang, "bep" meant a cook.

51. Traitor.

52. G. de Chaumont-Guitry [105].

53. Pejorative term used by the men of the expeditionary force as an alternative to "Viets". The word is a distortion of *nha qué*.

54. The Vietnamese governor of Cochin-China was also killed in the Sadec attack. A graduate of the Ecole Polytechnique, Chanson had, for two years, carried out the process of pacification in a most methodical way.

55. Fighting frequently broke out between the Hoa Hao and the Viet Minh. In September 1945, a massacre of Hoa Hao took place in Cantho (the principal town in the region in which they were established).

56. The attitude of the church in the United States also deserves to be mentioned. In May 1948, the outspoken Cardinal Spellman arrived in Saigon with a retinue of American priests. During a mass, one of them, Monsignor Fulton Sheen, stated, "We are bringing to the populations of Indo-China the salvation of the Roman Catholic Church. Old Europe is politically finished. The church is greatly counting on the Far East which will become a solid pillar of faith in Christ. The Cardinal's visit is the best proof of the confidence which the Church has in you."

57. Evidence in J. Leroy's *Un homme dans la rizière* (A Man in the Paddy-fields). Paris, 1955. After the Geneva agreements, the colonel was to plot against Diem, continuing his career in the French army.

58. The White Thais were distinguished from the Black Thais by the colour of their robes.

59. Similarly, the autonomous *muong* territories (around Hoa Binh) and the *nung* territories (around Hai Ninh) were created in 1948. To run the latter, the French used a minor warlord, Vong A Song, who had been part of Alessandri's backup. This policy of granting autonomy to the minorities was denounced by the Viet Minh as being part of the old colonial divide and rule strategy, yet it was continued and completed by the North Vietnamese government after 1954. The Diem regime, on the other hand, advocated assimilation, which caused it several serious difficulties.

60. They finally embarked direct for Formosa in 1953.

61. There is a parallel in the 1946 French plan for a Vietnamese Free State, as a member of the Indo-Chinese Federation and the French Union with the Linggadjati Agreement (November, 1946). The republic born in August, 1945 was to become a member of the United States of Indonesia, which would become part of a Dutch-Indonesian Union to be created. In both cases, the multi-level structure imposed a dual limitation on the sovereignty of the revolutionary state.

62. The second New Delhi conference (January 1949) created an Asiatic group. The first conference (23 March–23 April 1947) had been convened at the instigation of Nehru, a few weeks from the declaration of independence. It was an assembly of delegates from almost the whole of Asia (including the USSR and Vietnam) and it strongly denounced colonialism. The second conference was held at governmental level and did not have the same geographical composition

(thus, Soviet Asia was not represented). It favoured Indonesian independence. This was the birth of the Afro-Asian independence movement which at the time was led by India.

63. From *Le journal du septennat* by Vincent Auriol. In this interview of 4 February 1949, General Aumeran protested at the transfer of Cochin-China to Vietnam.

64. The *Hukbalahap* resistance was born in 1942. It was run by socialists and communists and, with allied help, conducted guerilla warfare against the Japanese. This fight was both "anti-feudal" and nationalist and continued after the Japanese surrender. The Americans supported the Filipino forces (both public and private) who were fighting a limited movement in the province of Centre-Luçon. The June 1948 agreement, which was not adhered to, merely created a pause in the conflict. By 1954, the "Huk rebellion" was considered to have been quashed.

65. Malaya (from which Singapore had been detached) had not been promised immediate independence like the other large, neighbouring British colonies. The British hesitated over how to organize the peninsula and only granted it relative autonomy.

66. In [99].

CHAPTER 5: FRONT LINE IN THE COLD WAR (PP. 116–148)

1. Organisation of army resistance. G. Revers, a postman, was "activated" at the end of the 1914–18 war. He had been head of the military office of Admiral Darlan at the beginning of the Occupation, but had cleared his name by replacing General Verneau at the head of the ORA during 1943.

2. "Les mains sales", the recent play by Sartre, gave him the title of a series of articles for *L'Humanité*. Because the affair went on for several months, "Les mains sales" ("Dirty Hands") was serialized.

3. The Technical Bureau for Liaison and Coordination was a small information service of the Ministry of French Possessions Overseas. The DST belonged to the Interior Ministry, and the SDECE (ex-DGER, future DGSE) to the Ministry of Defence.

4. "The piastres deposited in an account at the Bank of Communications are legally paid to a Parisian representative who cashes their value in francs on the basis of one piastre for 17 francs. The correspondent pays the funds into Switzerland into a bank which first converts the funds into local currency, then dollars and the bank then credits the Bank of Communications in Hong Kong. Another channel goes through the Banque Commerciale pour l'Europe du Nord which makes the conversions in the Netherlands" (Brau, *Les Armes de guérilla*, Balland, 1972).

5. A former civil servant at the Exchange Office in Saigon, J. Despuech, played a major role in the campaign. His book (*Le Trafic des piastres*, Deux Rives, 1953) is the reference work on the issue. See also (A. Laurent, *La Banque de l'Indochine et la Piastre*, Deux Rives, 1955)

6. Head of the CGT in Tunisia (where Mast was resident-general from 1943 to 1947). Bouzanquet helped to "make" Peyré. It was he in particular who introduced him to Revers.

7. An article by Beuve-Méry in *Une semaine dans le monde*, 17 January 1948. An article by Cachin in *L'Humanité*, 21 January 1948.

8. "The Republic ... will never use its forces against the freedom of any people", stipulated the text of the statement of intent.

9. At the Genevilliers Congress in April 1950.

10. Dussart, a specialist in this condemnation, had produced his most in-depth article in *Les Lettres Françaises* of 9 August 1946 (a description of a search in the Plain of Reeds). The accusations of December 1945 (which Dussart also contributed to) were not confined to the French communist press. English-language newspapers also made something of the same facts.

11. In 1945, Minister Diethelm had been attacked on this subject. Former SS members and collaborators were being used, but the FTP parties were not trusted. The day after Dien Bien Phu, a Communist deputy said of this battle: "A third of the active men were former SS prisoners, Germans freed on condition that they join the Foreign Legion and be sent 'to break the Viets' so that they would be pardoned for having broken the French" (Pronteau, National Assembly, 1 June 1954).

12. In May 1951, the Communist Party consequently alerted public opinion to an act of reprisal. In response to the murder of a Sûreté inspector, Haasz, 20 internees were shot on the order of the deputy chief of the Sûreté, Jumaeu, with agreement with the mayor of Dalat.

13. When five soldiers had been condemned to death by the military tribunal in Hanoi, Pleven told the assembly during the Indo-China debate of January 1950 that during 1948 forty-one Frenchmen had been charged with homicide.

14. The note which Colonel Gambiez had read out on 30 September 1950 at the beginning of operation "Phoque": "As a signatory to the recent Geneva Convention of 8 December 1949, by dispelling in some way the notion of 'guerillas' and extending to the rebels the benefit of the treatment due to regular soldiers, France is honoured to have always been in the forefront of movements to ensure the maximum respect for the person, and has the obligation, despite the treacherous nature of this struggle she has assumed, to show that once again she is equal to the civilizing mission which is the justification for her presence in the overseas territories.... As a repository of an ancient civilization, as harbinger of a tradition born of the great civilizations of antiquity, rekindled by Christianity, France has the obligation, in this respect too, to show those who are in her care that she has not forgotten the legacy of which she is proud: respect for the individual, pity for the weak fleeing fearfully before the troops at our first appearance, respect for property and perhaps especially by resisting the pillage of those thousand things which are the most treasured possessions of families in all parts of the world; also respect for holy places and places of worship.

15. This intensification of action against the war followed the meeting of the Central Committee on 9 and 10 December. Some days before at the Cominform Conference (held in Hungary), Suslov had indicated that the conflict between the two camps was increasing and that consequently the fight for peace had to be escalated.

16. Cherbourg was an exception.

17. In July the correctional tribunal at Versailles convicted Linet, the CGT shop steward at the Renault factory and a member of the Central Committee. He was accused of having overturned cars destined for Indo-China. In June, the Cail de Denain works dismissed three CGT militants who were considered to have been responsible for an act of sabotage. A piece of steel intended for national

defence had been thrown into the canal. And so on.

18. Jeannette Vermeersch railed for two hours against the French action in Indo-China. The violence of the charge led the elderly chairman Herriot to remark: "I would never have believed a woman capable of so much hate."

19. This was the case with the officers serving on the *Rafale*, the Saigon-Nha Trang train.

20. Y. Roucaute in *Le PCF and l'Armée* (PUF) even mentions names.

21. In another case, there was a certain captain who played a role on the Viet Minh side during Dien Bien Phu. The extraordinary adventure of the deserter Frey was told by P. Sergent in *Un étrange M. Frey*, Fayard 1982.

22. Officially, 288 Frenchmen, 338 North Africans, 78 Africans and 1,373 legionnaires deserted. On this subject, see the work by J. Doyon, *Les Soldats Blancs d'Ho Chi Minh*, Fayard 1973.

23. Some French managed to contact the Viet Minh through the GCM, beginning with Cédile in 1945. The historians, Boudarel and Chesnaux, belonged to this group.

24. In the parliamentary debate on 19 October 1950, Frédéric-Dupont estimated that 60 per cent of the weaponry arriving in Indo-China was wilfully damaged. The figures were disputed by Pleven, for whom the sabotage was marginal.

25. After the extremely violent demonstration in May against General Ridgway, the Minister of the Interior issued search warrants and arrested people. Duclos, number one in the Party in the absence of Thorez who was receiving treatment in the USSR, was arrested for conspiracy. In October 1952, following new searches in the Communist organizations, search warrants were issued for "actions to demoralise the army". The leaders of the UJRF (like Ducoloné and Laurent) and the CGT leader Le Léap were arrested.

26. Sartre, ed., *L'Affaire Henri Martin*, Gallimard 1953.

27. Mus and another sixty or so personalities (including Gide) signed a letter to Auriol in December 1949 which suggested a meeting with Ho Chi Minh to propose a peaceful settlement of the conflict on the basis of a ceasefire followed by elections under the control of the UN.

28. Speech to the assembly on 19 October 1950. However, in his preface of February 1950 to a collection of letters [105] by a sergeant in Indo-China, G. Thibon—who was by no means a left-winger—explained that there had been allusions to reprisals and torture because "similar facts have largely been spread by the French and foreign press."

29. Recommended by Revers, the evacuation of Bac Kan took place in August 1949.

30. Colonel Constans used the services of a slightly unusual butler for his socialising, in the person of the legionnaire Burgens, alias de Broca, who had been a leading member of the Vichy regime.

31. With the end of the rainy season, military activity was resumed throughout the territory.

32. It is estimated that 30 per cent of the stocks might have been destroyed.

33. "Because of the effort which we have to make in Europe, we had foreseen, for 1951, a determined reduction in the number of regular soldiers and non-commissioned officers to be sent to Indo-China" (Pleven, to the national assembly on 19 October 1950).

34. Recognition was made at the instigation of the DRV which wanted its legitimacy to be recognized several days after the transfer of sovereignty to the "state of Vietnam".

35. The hypothesis was then advanced that, in the Far East, Stalin was manoeuvering to isolate China because it feared a "new Titoism".

36. In the Far East, South Korea and Thailand were the first countries to recognise the Bao Dai regime. In Thailand, recognition caused a government crisis. This recognition was one of the first demonstrations of the pro-Western allegiance of the country, an alignment which would be confirmed during the Korean War.

37. The same idea was expressed in a letter by ambassador Chauvel to the head of government, Bidault: "I suggested to the Americans that we were no longer able to continue our national effort beyond a specified date: that it was appropriate to consider the international interest in the affair; that if the interest were recognized it would be Washington's duty to take it over, it being agreed that we would continue to contribute to the common effort" [127]. In his article, Duverger proposed another solution: negotiations should be started with China.

38. Until then, the Americans had asked that airplane propellers made in the USA be removed from British planes sent to Indo-China. They did not want to accused of supporting colonialism.

39. A conversation on 20 February between J. Chauvel, then ambassador at the United Nations, and MacArthur, deputy director of the Office of European Regional Affairs [144].

40. Auriol noted in his *Journal* on 18 January 1950 "It is all right for them to make comments when we are alone: we can tell them they had misunderstood the idea of the French Union. We can have discussions, but what they have said to encourage Bao Dai cannot be permitted."

41. As a member of the Cultural Marxist Group, the Frenchman Palisse was one of the organizers of what happened on 19 March. He was later expelled from Indo-China.

42. On the role of the Chinese (communist and non-communist) in the Indo-China war see Chen King, *Vietnam and China*, 1938–1954, Princeton, Princeton University Press 1969.

43. A. Fontaine wrote in *Le Monde* on 18 October 1950: "It would seem normal that, as a soldier of the Western camp, the French fighter in the Far East would no longer have the feeling of being shoeless, abandoned, a pariah." Since the beginning of the conflict, the cadres of the expeditionary force had complained about needing equipment, about having to indulge in do-it-yourself. It was completely different from the American war in the sixties.

44. Two debates on Indo-China, one on the extension of military service to eighteen months, and one on the EDC.

45. The same theme was developed by another famous Progressiste, P. Rivet, who had left the SFIO in 1948 because he disagreed with the Indo-Chinese policy adopted by the party.

46. He represented France in the Economic and Social Council of the United Nations. He opposed the Soviet demand to admit the DRV to the body in 1948. "No Vietnamese Republic exists, nor", he explained, "has it ever existed. If there were a Vietnamese state, it would have a capital, borders, a government, an administration and diplomatic representatives." Mendès later confessed that his

visit to international borders, and particularly his contact with the representatives of the newer states, had made him very critical of the war in Indo-China.

47. Another argument of the same type as Mendès's would develop: the war in Indo-China hindered economic expansion, the best way of fighting communism was in France itself, because of its effects on society.

48. In January 1950, in the name of his party, Gaston Defferre suggested a document to the assembly (which only the socialists approved) recalling "the overpowering need not to neglect any effort or process, either through armistice or recourse to the international courts, aiming to bring peace and union to Vietnam". At the May 1950 Congress, the following resolution was passed: "The Congress asks the French government to use the Security Council in the Indo-China problem and, from now on, to promise, vis-à-vis the UN, to recognise the real independence of Vietnam, when peace has come, in the freely accepted context of the French Union and to withdraw its troops at the request of a Vietnamese government resulting from free elections." It should be recalled that at the time the SFIO for once was not in the government and that the USSR was boycotting the Security Council in protest against continued nationalist Chinese representation at the UN.

49. Varenne and Viollette, liberal governors-general between the two wars, proved themselves eager defenders of the Empire after Liberation. On the one hand, French opinion was massively in favour of the Empire. A poll in February 1950 asked the question: "Do you think that it is in France's interests to have overseas territories?" 81 per cent of the people questioned replied "yes", 5 per cent "no". "Do you think that, all in all, France has worked well in the overseas territories?" asked the same poll and 62 per cent of the people agreed. The public's "colonialism" went hand in hand with a certain scepticism about the durability of the French Union. From April 1947 (it is true that the Madagascan revolt had just been added to the Indo-China affair), "yes" and "no" were equal on the following question: "Do you think that all the people in the French Union will finally sever all the links that unite them to France?"

50. Mendès-France voted neither for the government nor the Communists' agenda. He preferred the agenda of the Progressiste Serre, calling on the "government to take the action necessary to put an end to hostilities without delay on the diplomatic level" (190 for, 398 against).

51. Aumeran was a nationalist. His criticism had nothing to do with Mendès's.

52. Strangely enough, the Prime Minister allowed several doubts to show through, in the form of an opening: "Is the Viet Minh a movement of patriots, convinced that they are struggling for their independence, or is the Viet Minh a movement somewhere between us and other countries or other forces which, to accomplish a great plan, need to establish in Indo-China, as in other parts of Asia, the maximum number of forces? That is the question. I say that no one as yet can give a complete answer and I will say that the answer can only be given by the Viet Minh" (Pleven, 22 November).

53. Along with Rous and Déchézelles, Doctor Boutbien was one of those most forcefully against Moutet in 1947. At the time of the national council on 20 March, he fervently defended the idea that the only solution in Indo-China was negotiation with Ho Chi Minh.

54. Of course, the SFIO was as monolithic as usual. Discipline in voting played a part. But a minority showed its hostility. Depreux wrote in L'Observateur of 2

November: "Recourse to the UN, behind a nation not integrated in one of the blocks, like Switzerland, Sweden, India, official or officious negotiations, even the devil, or with those who pull the strings", what did it matter as long as the war ceased.

55. The Indo-Chinese states ceased being a part of Overseas France after the formation of the second Queuille cabinet (2 July 1950). In this stillborn government, Reynaud was Minister of State responsible for relations with the Associated States and Far East Affairs.

56. Approached by Ramadier, he had already refused to succeed d'Argenlieu in February 1947.

57. On the same day as de Lattre was nominated, Peking protested against aerial bombardments, attacks by Nationalists protected by the French, and the burning and pillaging of many border villages. Despite the fact that protests did not increase, they were not new. Therefore despite their recognition of the DRV government, Peking resented the "atrocities" of the expeditionary force against the Chinese in Indo-China: "The atrocities committed by the French armed forces against Chinese nationals in Vietnam cannot be tolerated by the Chinese people." Since April 1950, Mao's army had occupied the island of Hainan, opposite the Red River Delta, blocking the Gulf of Tongking.

58. Note that the two last battles were less "classical" than Vinh Yen. At Dong Trieu, as at the battle of Day, "the Viet Minh divisions had used guerilla tactics in their mobile warfare. They only attacked by night from rocks which by day gave excellent cover against the air force. The enemy only attacked outposts or isolated groups" (General Gras [46]).

59. The agreed 15,000 soldiers would be obliged to leave Indo-China before 1 July 1952.

60. When asked, the Tunisian and Moroccan governments refused to take part, showing once again that, strictly speaking, the two countries were not part of the French Union.

61. "The only solution to the problem is the creation of an inter-allied theatre of operations in South East Asia", said Gaullist Palewski to the national assembly (28 December 1951). This statement resulted in his being treated as a hysterical madman by the Communist R. Guyot, who spoke of provocation in the war.

62. The connection was not only military. The birth of the EDC implied the construction of a federal Europe. How could this integration be reconciled with participation in the French Union? The question was asked from time to time, for example during the great debate on foreign policy in November 1953 (in which Senghor pleaded for the entry of the French Union into Europe).

63. During the December 1952 debate on the budget of the associated states, the report of the finance committee of the national assembly set the expenditure for 1953 (in millions of francs: French expenditure, 285: expenditure by the associated states, 35: American military aid, 119: American financial aid, 150. In the last part of the war, the United States would cover 80 per cent of financing.

64. Promise made by Bidault in a letter to ambassador Dillon (in exchange for an increase in aid).

65. Among the military, two men would be in Saigon after the war: General Collins, then army chief of staff and General O'Daniel who trained the South Korean army. Vice-president Nixon would come in October 1953, a few days after the head of the Senate Republican majority, Knowland. The visits of these two

"hawks" showed that the Americans were troubled by the exhaustion of the French.

66. In the parliamentary debate of 19 October 1950, Daniel Mayer had been able to quote the "Voice of Vietnam" to show the ideological transformation of the DRV. A campaign had been launched in the Viet Minh zone in the second half of 1950, for the study of the great texts of the Chinese revolution.

67. The Lien Viet had been created at the instigation of Ho Chi Minh in May 1946, as a sort of national super-front, of which the Viet Minh was the main component. The Viet Minh disappeared in February 1951, after amalgamating with the Lien Viet. But the French kept referring to the Vietnamese enemy as the Viet Minh. We have kept to this convention. The Lien Viet democrats should not be confused with Doctor Thinh's. "It is under the influence of our party that intellectuals and students founded the Vietnamese Democratic Party in June 1944.... It was a creative application of Marxist-Leninist principles to the concrete conditions of our country on the 'search for allies'" *Histoire de la révolution d'août*, Hanoi, ELE 1972).

68. On several occasions, the French services (and the Baodaists) tried to establish contact with this non-communist nationalist either to get him on their side, or to confuse the enemy.

69. For some, Hoa Binh had routed the enemy battle force from the Delta. For others, Hoa Binh had allowed significant infiltration, by mobilizing the most important French equipment. The Delta had not been frontally attacked but its "decay" had been helped.

70. A technical term used by the Wehrmacht during its retreat at the end of World War II.

71. Colonel Trinquier, who was one of the organizers of the counter-guerilla action, described his activities in *Les Maquis d'Indochine*, Albatros 1976. As a fervent exponent of this tactic, Trinquier vainly proposed the creation of an underground in Tunisian territory during the Algerian war.

CHAPTER 6: LIQUIDATIONS (PP. 149–182)

1. During the time of de Lattre, Nguyen Huu Tri was dismissed and Tam was charged with the task of combatting the formation of Dai Viet cells. However, Nguyen Huu Tri had just resumed his post as governor of Tongking.

2. His father, who was killed in 1936, had headed a *kha* uprising at the beginning of the century. In the language of the Thais, *kha* means slave. These primitive tribes belonged to the same group as the Mois of Vietnam.

3. Another person who came back in 1953 was Saloth Sar, alias Pol Pot. He rejoined the communist guerillas. He had gone to Paris in 1949, where he had been one of the group of Cambodian students (including Ieng Sary and Khieu Samphan) that had liaised with the French Communist Party via Maître Vergès.

4. The *Livre noir*, published in 1978 by the Khmer Rouge, wrote the following about the Cambodian revolutionary leaders of the time, "These men were under the thumb of the Vietnamese and relied upon them totally. They were capable of nothing and understood nothing. The Vietnamese made all the decisions."

5. That same month, a provincial governor was killed by the rebels and a bomb went off in a *lycée* in the capital.

6. In a lecture he gave at the École Polytechnique on 19 June, the lawyer Nguyen Dac Khê produced the following analysis: "We started out on 8 March 1949

with the idea of establishing independence and now, five years on, we have managed to achieve co-sovereignty. On both a national and an international level, there are now two rulers in Vietnam. They share the reins of power and nothing much can be achieved without the agreement of both. In principle, that is, because what happens in reality is that they ignore one another. When this leads to an event such as the devaluation of the piastre, I think you will agree it is disgraceful." He made the proposal that the country should move on from co-sovereignty to Vietnamese sovereignty.

7. The quadripartite system seemed ill-conceived. In devaluing the piastre, France had ignored it to a large extent. Cambodia reacted by applying its own measures with regard to customs duties, and this was contrary to the Pau agreements.

8. In April 1953, the Mayer government altered the nature of the French presence in Indo-China. Until then, there had been a high commissioner in Saigon plus five other commissioners. The high commissioner looked after the general government of Indo-China and the five others were each in charge of one of the five regions. The change came about for theoretical reasons (and it was not the only example of this). From now on, there was one commissioner per state and a commissioner-general in Saigon. However, the change of structure did not lead to the appointment of new men in this case.

9. This confusion about responsibility was not new. It was not until 11 March 1954 that a council of war was set up in order to lend coherence to the proceedings.

10. Article 2 of the treaty stated that the general running of the French Union and the coordination of its joint means of defence would be the responsibility of the Supreme Council. At a meeting held in 1952, they had asked for and obtained the creation of a permanent general secretariat to the leaders and supreme council of the French Union. It was set up in 1953 and headed by the prefect of police, Chérif Mecheri. In pretending to hand over the running of the Union to the Supreme Council, the Franco-Laotian treaty gave formal satisfaction to a long-standing claim on the part of the associated states. The new institution was given greater power, in theory, just before it was abolished.

11. See Marshal Juin's report of March 1953.

12. The subject of the decree of May 1953 was taken up again and brought to a proper conclusion by the law on agrarian reform passed in December 1953 by the central committee of the Lao Dong and by a special sitting of the national assembly. The latter had not met since November 1946. In the meantime, it had exercised its powers through a permanent committee consisting of 15 members. The latter was chaired by the veteran communist, Ton Duc Thang, who had taken part in the Black Sea mutiny and spent long years in the Poulo Condore prison.

13. 125,000 regular troops, 75,000 regional troops and 200,000 local troops.

14. In Africa, recruitment propaganda dwelt almost entirely on the financial benefits. Consequently, it was usually necessity that prompted men to go to Indo-China. In Algeria, most of those who joined up were day labourers, so it was easier to recruit in winter because once autumn was over work became scarce.

15. This does not mean that ethnic minorities were not represented at all. There were many Thos in the People's Army of Vietnam. They were particularly suited to the kind of operations that took place in highlands, and large numbers of

them fought at the battle of Dien Bien Phu. General Chu Van Tan presided over a meeting of ethnic minorities in September 1953.

16. Nine if you add the 18,000 regulars of South Annam.

17. The mobile unit was the largest type of unit in Indo-China. It corresponded to a third of a division.

18. "Information of our approach flowed freely, even though it had been kept a secret until then. As a rule, though, the Viet Minh are always aware of our man-oeuvres in advance. Even before the troops have been ordered to carry them out, they have worked out which direction we are heading in and evaluated our strength.... They are thus safe to attack. They know exactly what they are facing and they take up their machine-guns and destroy convoys and wipe out patrols" [105].

19. Not the best ones if we are to believe the expression "Dans le béton, les plus cons" ("The stupidest are behind the concrete").

20. It was almost impossible to evacuate the position by night. At the same time an ambush was being prepared for the relief troops. Either way, it was impossible to move to and fro safely.

21. It was evacuated hurriedly by air. The Thai auxiliaries were "forgotten".

22. The French offered to put Bao Dai in charge of the operation. He declined and appointed Giao, a loyal follower of his who had served for a long time as gov-ernor of Annam. Another example of this handing over of operations to the Viet-namese was the GAMO (operational mobile administrative groups) which came into being at the time of the Tam government. They consisted entirely of native Indo-Chinese. They followed troop movements closely, moving in and taking charge of administration as soon as any given area had been cleared. Amongst other things, they were responsible for policing, propaganda and social prob-lems.

23. In 1948, 52 per cent of those surveyed wanted to carry on with the war in Indo-China until it was won. The figure had dropped to 15 per cent by May 1953. The war had become a tiresome affair and little was actually known about it in France. Only 30 per cent of newspaper readers regularly read the news on Indo-China (only 17 per cent of women and 20 per cent of those who had only received primary education).

24. Reynaud, Mendès, Bidault, Marie and Laniel. May 1953 was not only marked by the longest government crisis since the war, it also marked the end of the RPF. The Gaullists were now free to participate in Laniel's cabinet, as did Marc Jacquet.

25. An account of the mission was given in a note from J. Raphael-Leygues to President Auriol. The text of this note is in Leygues' book *Ponts de lianes* pub-lished by Hachette in 1976.

26. He expressed his concerns to the SFIO, to the assembly of the French Union and then, from 1951 onwards, to the French national assembly. He first went to Indo-China in 1949, in the capacity of advisor and submitted a report of his findings to President Auriol. The visit confirmed him in the belief that it was necessary to seek an immediate solution by talking directly to the Viet Minh. While he was there, he spent much time in the Plain of Reeds talking to Nguyen Binh. After his return home, he received a letter from the leaders of the Viet Minh approving the idea of direct contact with the Ho Chi Minh government.

27. He took up these arguments again in the book *Aux frontières de l'Union*

française which was published in 1953 with a preface by Mendès. As early as 1904, O. Reclus uttered the famous words, "Let us leave Asia and take Africa". In the period between the two wars, Admiral Castex, remarkable military strategist that he was, also advocated withdrawal from Indo-China. At the UDSR conference in the autumn of 1953, François Mitterand (who had just resigned from the Laniel government) pushed through a motion demanding immediate and direct negotiation, beating René Pleven by a few votes.

28. The assembly asked the government to "put into effect a policy aimed above all at: a) Strengthening the armed forces of the associated states so that the French military effort could be gradually decreased; b) pulling out all the stops in order to achieve negotiated peace in Asia; c) ensuring a fair distribution of effort and sacrifice among the free nations in all parts of the globe where they must exercise their solidarity. "And also intervene with the French government to ensure that the defence and independence of the associated states should be taken care of within the framework of the French Union."

29. *Esprit*, March 1954.

30. *Esprit*, May 1954. In the debate on Indo-China, Mendès put forward the argument that neither China nor the USSR had any interest in ending the war and, even if Ho Chi Minh were to be abandoned by his allies, the Viet Minh would carry on the struggle. In his own words, the international solution "is the use of skilful diplomacy to change a policy which will lead to the prolongation of the war."

31. This mission resulted in a Franco-Chinese trade agreement. Having been placed under a strict embargo by the United States, the People's Republic of China now showed a greater desire to improve its trade relations with Europe.

32. The Bermuda conference had been on the cards since the time of the Mayer government. During the government crisis of May–June 1953, the presidential candidates undertook to get together with allied nations and seek a solution to the Indo-Chinese question. The meeting was postponed because of Churchill's ill health. When it did take place, Laniel fell ill right at the beginning and so Bidault was the French representative. Edgar Faure wrote the following in his memoirs, "I supposed that Laniel had been struck down by a psychosomatic illness on account of his mental block about entering into conflict with his minister and embarking on such delicate negotiations from an opposing viewpoint."

33. There had been a possibility of mediation on the part of New Delhi since 1950. The French could pay Nehru for his services by coming to an amicable agreement over the question of French banks in India. At the end of 1953, the government came up with the idea that Nehru could act as go-between and arrange a Franco-Chinese conference in India.

34. The coolie cyclists travelled about 25 kilometres a day carrying loads weighing 200 kg. To give an example of the transport problems the Viet Minh were up against, when a Viet Minh division was on the road it had to take at least twice as many helpers as there were soldiers just to carry the supplies. Any civilians were liable to be asked to carry out these auxiliary services, which were organized by the Viet Minh. Even political commissars took part in some cases.

35. Nixon's attitude was consistently belligerent. He even suggested sending American soldiers to China. Johnson's reply was, "I am opposed to sending GIs into the mire of Indo-China for the sake of a bloody escapade that will only perpetuate colonialism and the exploitation of man by man. We must base our

policy upon the Monroe Doctrine and upon the idea of 'Asia for the Asians'."
Dien Bien Phu sent a shock wave through American public opinion. Despite everything, surveys carried out in the spring of 1954 showed that a majority of
about 60 per cent was opposed to any kind of direct intervention on the part of
the United States.

36. It is known for certain that there were Chinese engineers and advisers at
Dien Bien Phu, although it is impossible to say exactly how many.

37. General Navarre wondered whether it would be possible to disrupt the Viet
Minh's movements by making it rain over the areas in which its convoys travelled. The scientists he consulted said not.

38. Even the main route between Hanoi and Haiphong was becoming more and
more dangerous. At the time of the battle of Dien Bien Phu, the road was only
passable from 11.00 am to 4.00 pm. Every morning it had to be cleared of mines
and repaired.

39. There had just been an alarming incident. On 12 April, guerillas attacked
the train from Phnom Penh to Battambang and killed about a hundred of the
passengers. The French chief-of-staff estimated that there were between 4,000
and 5,000 regular "rebel" forces in Cambodia at that time.

40. The Viet Minh's proposal to join the French Union seemed absurd at a time
when nationalists on the opposing side would no longer hear of it. A French
commentator explained that it would have been like the USSR wanting to join
NATO.

41. On 12 June, Benouville said, "It has become a habit with this assembly to
bring up the question of Indo-China every single week". The same arguments
were repeated over and over again from one sitting to the next. But confidence
was waning and the government was beaten by 263 votes to 322 on 9 May when
it asked for priority to be given to the agenda it had just accepted. It asked for a
vote of confidence on the question of rejecting other agendas and lost again by
293 votes to 306. Laniel had failed to reverse the trend. However, the constitutional majority of 314 votes had not been reached, and so it was not a real crisis.
It was not possible to dissolve the assembly in accordance with the wishes of the
MRP.

42. This prospect loomed larger and larger. In their agenda of 9 June, the
Socialists stood firm against "any measure, such as sending in more troops,
which would be liable to cause an escalation of the war".

43. Washington had been blowing hot and cold for weeks. But, for the time
being, it seemed to give up any idea of intervention. On 11 June Dulles said,
"Peace will not be brought about in Indo-China by means of a unilateral military
intervention".

44. There were even more violent criticisms than this "fighting talk which reminded one at times of a Red Indian war-dance" (Le Monde). Vallon was particularly aggressive. On 4 May he said, "You have to have more than blood on
your hands if you want to try and be Richelieu or Talleyrand."

45. During the discussion that followed the reading of his statement he said,
"Tomorrow we shall be negotiating with men who have been our enemies for
years. When I sit opposite them, I have no intention of allowing them to think
that France is now represented by a government that owes its existence to the
Communist Party, which has so often shown them not only sympathy, but even
solidarity."

46. *L'Express* of 29 May gave an account of General Ely's recent report. As a result, its premises were searched and all copies were seized. Jacquet, who had friends on the staff of this pro-Mendès newspaper, was implicated in the leak. Consequently, he was forced to resign. The Gaullist, Schmittlein, was to succeed him but his political allies dissuaded him from accepting. So, Frederic-Dupont became Secretary of State for the Associated States for a few days. He had often reproached past governments for not conducting the war with a firm enough hand. Consequently, his nomination gave fuel to the arguments of Bidault's opponents. The press protested vigorously over the *L'Express* affair, a conflict which was a foretaste of the stormy relationship that was to exist between the government and the press during the Algerian war.

47. However, Buron and Monteil refused to toe the party line and agreed to be part of the cabinet. From the moment the government took office, the majority of the abstentions came from the MRP. However, Christian writers such as Mauriac (who moved from *Le Figaro* to *L'Express* in 1953) supported Mendès-France. At the beginning of June, a number of Catholic intellectuals, including Bédarida and Latreille, put their signatures to a document calling for opposition to "all the over-simplified arguments that try to represent the war in South-East Asia as a crusade on behalf of Christian civilization."

48. At first, however, the French side did not envisage granting all of the north to the Viet Minh. They talked about neutralising the bishoprics and keeping hold of Haiphong.

49. There is a considerable distance between the 16th and 17th parallels and the area concerned includes Hué, Tourane and the road to Laos. The division at the 17th parallel was a historical rather than a geographical one. It almost touched the Dong Hoi wall, which had separated the Trinh area of Annam from that of the Nguyens until the reunification brought about by Gia Long early in the nineteenth century.

50. Thanks to its last-minute demands, Cambodia retained the right to allow foreign military bases on its soil and to form military alliances. Items of note in the agreement on Laos were provision for the retention of two French bases and for French military instructors for the royal army. Laos was granted the right to bring in arms and troops if necessary for reasons of security.

51. See Appendixes.

52. It must be said that, from the point of view of principle, the situation was rather confused. France signed the ceasefire agreements on Vietnam and Laos as the leader of the French Union. But, at the same time, under article 10 of the final declaration, the French government agreed to withdraw its troops from the three countries of Indo-China on demand. This showed that article 62 of the constitution was decidedly null and void. Furthermore, to what extent was this article 10 compatible with article 14 of the armistice agreement: "Between now and the general elections that will reunite Vietnam the civil administration of each regroupment zone is to be undertaken by the side whose forces are to be re-grouped there under the terms of the present agreement."

53. T. Maulnier entitled his article of August 1954 in *Hommes et Mondes*, "After the Asian Munich". R. Cartier made the same criticism in *Match*. *Rivarol*, which only had a small circulation, was the mouthpiece of a French-style neo-fascist organization. It continually expressed hatred of Mendès and had nothing but ill to say about the agreements.

54. In both cases, the MRP felt itself to be under fire. It bore a large part of the responsibility for the way in which the Indo-China affair had been conducted and its leader, Bidault, had been severely taken to task by Mendès. The majority of the MRP abstained from voting in the debate on the Geneva agreements. The MRP also believed in European mystique and was the only party to be totally in favour of the EDC. So, it never forgave Mendès for the shelving of the project, calling it "the crime of 30 August".

55. See the thesis by François Joyaux entitled *La Chine et le Règlement du premier conflit indochinois* (China and the settlement of the first war in Indo-China), published in 1979. In it, Joyaux made the following analysis of the words of Pham Van Dong and Chou En-lai on their visit to the Chinese capital at the beginning of August 1954: "Certainly, as far as both statesmen were concerned, the accords were only a 'first step on the road'. But, for Pham Van Dong, the way forward consisted of achieving peace in Vietnam by 'fighting resolutely for its unification' while, for Chou En-lai, it meant achieving peace in the world through the continued struggle for international detente. It was also extremely noticeable that all Chou En-lai's speeches repeatedly extolled the unity between China and Vietnam, but never once mentioned the unity of Vietnam itself. There was another remarkable difference in view. Pham Van Dong always associated the Khmer and the Pathet Lao with the struggle of the Vietnamese people. Chou En-lai, on the other hand, only considered Vietnam, showing that China honoured Pham Van Dong as the representative of the Democratic Republic of Vietnam rather than that of the Indo-Chinese revolution as a whole."

56. Besides India, the group consisted of Burma, Ceylon, Pakistan and Indonesia.

CHAPTER 7: FROM ONE WAR TO ANOTHER (PP. 183–201)

1. On this feeling of despair, see B. de Castelbajac, *La gloire est leur salaire*, Édition française et internationale, 1958; or J. Lartéguy, *Les Centurions*, Presses de la Cité, 1960.

2. The minister had a foretaste of this on 4 April 1954. During a ceremony at the Étoile, Pleven and Laniel had been seriously jostled. The demonstration had been punctuated by cries supporting Marshal Juin, who was hostile to the government and was conducting a small-scale war against it simply over the issue of appointing marshals posthumously.

3. In January 1957.

4. Other classics from the libraries of colonels interested in psychological action included *Technique du coup d'État*, by Malaparte, *La Propagande politique*, by Domenach, *Foules en délire*, by P. Félice and *La Psychologie des foules*, by G. Le Bon.

5. The role of *Message des forces armées* as a military magazine should also be mentioned. It strongly influenced the officers of what was then called the young army.

6. In *Défense nationale*, PUF 1958. To show to what extent the command had misunderstood the Vietnamese conflict, Lacheroy, as usual, quoted the coversation of one of his superiors in the article: "You are leaving for Indo-China, that's alright; you are going to do your duty as a superior officer, but listen to what I have to say: with your rank, your age, and your previous background, there is nothing for you to learn out there."

7. In Indo-China, it was only in December 1952 that a general department for psychological warfare was created under the dual direction of France and Vietnam. Colonel Lacheroy became chief of the psychological action and intelligence service of the Ministry of Defence. He was one of the group of "colonels" who, locked into their logic of revolutionary war, opposed de Gaulle.

8. The methods they started using—on a small scale—in Indo-China have often been catalogued. The relocation of populations was begun in 1952 in Cambodia with no small measure of success. The experiment was analyzed in an article by Captain Souyris, "An effective procedure against guerilla action", *Revue de défense nationale*, June 1956.

9. Another soldier who had served in Indo-China, Colonel Trinquier, was recalled to France as a result of his activities in Algeria (July 1960). In 1961, he published *La Guerre moderne* (La Table ronde), the themes of which are those of *Guerre, Subversion, Revolution* (Laffont 1968). Like Lacheroy, he led a revolutionary war for his own benefit, but this one was in Katanga.

10. There were 3,200 dead and missing in 1947, 4,200 in 1954: for the French these years were the most tragic.

11. The Viet Minh increased the number of conditions likely to benefit its military operations, propaganda and reconnaissance. As President of the Republic of Vietnam, Ho Chi Minh had to be informed in writing.

12. In September 1950, fifty-two French hostages captured in 1946 in Hongay were released, followed by servicemen. At the same time, hundreds of Viet Minh prisoners were freed (600 on the occasion of the ordination of a new bishop). Since Figuères's return, the French Communist Party had been conducting a campaign for talks on the exchange of prisoners. The French authorities were thus obliged to make more gestures and offers. On one hand they were hopeful, but on the other they were afraid that more general negotiations would take place as a result of the talks.

13. It is true that in 1950 the measures Chanson took in Cochin-China, and Alessandri took in Tongking, caused the Viet Minh serious food problems. Control of the Red River Delta by the French troops caused near-famine in the Viet Bac. This was the time when the revolutionary authorities launched the slogan: "A grain of rice is worth a drop of blood." Full rations were then only given to fighting men.

14. Consider the role of the SED in the GDR regarding the legionnaires, many of whom were German. Many publications appeared in East Berlin which had been written by former legionnaires, deserters or those converted in the camps. For example: G. Halle, *Foreign Legion*, Berlin, Volk und Welt 1952.

15. The press made Geneviève de Galard, "the only woman in the entrenched camp", one of the heroes of the battle.

16. The military negotiators, Delteil and de Brébisson, were in the mixed military commission.

17. As opposed to 2 per cent for non-Catholics.

18. They were the only bishops to leave. The others obeyed the instructions of the apostolic delegate, Monsignor Dooley. In a letter to the Bishop of Hanoi, he recalled the "special obligations of those who are responsible for leading others". Some 300 priests and 4,000,000 believers also stayed behind.

19. *Australia, New Zealand, United States.* Signed in 1951 the tripartite pact did not imply the automatic involvement of the United States, any more than did the

American-Filipino treaty of the same year.

20. Countries like India constantly denounced the claims of the great western powers that they supervised the affairs of South-East Asia. In some ways, Bandung would appear to have been set up to oppose the Manila pact.

21. South East Asia Treaty Organisation. SEATO was set up at the Bangkok conference of February 1955. No permanent force was made available for it.

22. In a speech to the foreign affairs committee of the House of Representatives (from the *Far East Journal*, 2 January 1955).

23. He inspired Greene's central character in *The Quiet American*. But Lansdale himself was not assassinated.

24. Diem refused the compromise solution which would have kept the principle of monarchy. The idea of making the very Catholic Bao Long, head of state, now or at a later stage, had been rejected.

25. The popular tribunals for agrarian reform could pass the death sentence. "The best estimates give a figure of 50,000 North Vietnamese executed due to agrarian reform and at least twice as many deported to hard labour camps" (B. Fall). This is just one estimate amongst many—it is impossible to give accurate figures. An ex-Viet Minh, Hoang Van Chi denounced the violence and incoherence of agrarian reform in *Du colonialisme au communisme* (Dialogues 1964). The Viet Minh officers who turned nationalist provided the Saigon regime with some of its toughest leaders.

26. The rising ended in the dismissal of the general secretary of the Party, Truong Chinh, and in criticism of the excesses of agrarian reform. Even before these events a campaign had been launched "to correct the mistakes".

27. In February 1956, the official newspaper *Lieng Chuong* was specific: "A deputy will never be allowed to stand up and ask the government to begin talks with the authorities in the North, because of the elections stipulated under the Geneva agreements."

28. Because he was considered a liberal and an advocate of negotiation, some people tried to compromise him during the war. In February 1948, at the instigation of the Minister of French Possessions Overseas, he was arrested and charged with possessing of secret documents relating to the external security of the state.

29. Ely [107].

30. Which allowed the re-establishment of a German army, the Bundeswehr, within NATO.

31. Tran van Huu, who would later appear as leader of the liberal opposition, met Pham Van Dong on 14 July 1954. Buu Hoi and Tran Van Huu paid brief and futile visits to Diemist Vietnam, then returned to Paris.

32. But, apparently, with the help of his assistant, Salan. Ferrandi, who was in the "leader's" entourage, wrote: "There is one intrigue after another. What with the generals of the sects and the special services, General Salan's residence was to some extent a house of intrigue where behind closed doors there was talk of the conditions in which they could rid themselves of the new president" [43]. Salan left Indo-China in October 1954.

33. In the rivalry between Diem and Hinh, the latter was the most powerful. The army was behind its leader, who was also supported by the Binh Xuyen police. There was no need for direct intervention by the expeditionary force for the pro-American group to be eliminated. A go-ahead would have been enough.

34. There were some 200 American officers in Indo-China at the time of ceasefire.

35. It abandoned the franc on 1 January 1956.

36. And American aid decreased proportionally. The United States continued, in fact, to finance the expeditionary force. The Indo-China war was still bringing dollars into France several months after the war ended.

37. Was this increasing military intrusion contrary to the Geneva agreements? The Americans justified themselves by explaining that they were only responding to the aid given to North Vietnam by China.

38. From the end of 1954, *Le Monde* criticised the alignment on the American positions, calling for a rebalancing of French policy in favour of North Vietnam, which should occur as part of the general détente.

39. The vote was 236 for and 0 against. In the same month, the Gaullist group at the French Union assembly tabled a proposal inviting the government "to urgently define the steps that it intends to implement for France's endorsement of the Geneva agreements to be respected, and to ensure the safety of the expeditionary force and the French in Indo-China".

40. "Decent people will believe until their dying day that M. Mitterand betrayed his country, either because he was the source of the leaks, or because he covered up for the real moles" (Fauvet, *Le Monde*, 22 May 1956).

41. "The affair was manipulated against one man, his friends, his politics" (*idem*). It was true from 1954 and for other leaks. The government seized *L'Express* of 29 May at a time when Mendès seemed a likely successor to Laniel. Similarly, the attacks against *L'Observateur*, for which journalist R. Stéphane spent several days in prison at the start of 1955 (for his article outlining the Navarre plan) seemed to be linked to the "Mendès-France phenomenon".

42. It was only in 1966 that Paris accepted the existence of a general delegation from the DRV.

43. "Here is one example out of a hundred: it took three weeks for the wife of one of the French engineers at Hongay suffering from a terrible toothache to obtain a pass to go to Hanoi for treatment" (Sainteny [138]).

44. One of the teachers, G. Tongas, wrote *J'ai vécu dans l'enfer communiste du Nord-Vietnam et j'ai choisi la liberté* (I lived in the communist hell of North Vietnam and I chose liberty), Debresse 1960. Which more or less says it all.

45. Although the kingdom, like its southern neighbour, suppressed any reference to the French Union in its constitution "a free country not having to mention in its constitution the alliances which it might form with any friendly country" (Souvanna Phouma).

46. Although it was now legalized, the Communist Party, alias the Prachacheon (People's Party) only won 4 per cent of the votes.

47. In 1960, the Ministry of Information stated that 50,000 Viet Cong members had been arrested since 1954.

CHAPTER 8: CONCLUSION (PP. 202–205).

The Chinese community of Indo-China hardly participated at all in the armed struggle. Like the majority of the inhabitants, it was content with paying a toll to the Viet Minh to support the revolution. After Geneva, the majority of the Chinese who lived north of the 17th parallel moved south.

Bibliography

GENERAL WORKS

REFERENCE WORKS

1. Auvade R., *Bibliographie critique des œuvres parues sur l'Indochine française*, Maisonneuve et Larose 1965.
2. Descours-Gatin C. and Villiers H., *Guide de recherches sur le Vietnam*, Harmattan 1983.
3. Désiré M., *La Campagne d'Indochine. Bibliographie*, Service historique de l'armée 1971–7.
4. Nguyen The Anh, *Bibliographie critique sur les relations entre le Vietnam et l'Occident*, Maisonneuve et Larose 1967.

BACKGROUND
France

5. Chapsal J., *La Vie politique en France depuis 1940*, PUF, 5th ed. 1979.
6. Elgey G., *Histoire de la IVe République*, Fayard 1965.
7. Fauvet J., *La IVe République*, Fayard 1959.
8. Julliard J., *La IVe République*, Calmann-Levy 1968.
9. La Gorce P.-M. de, *L'Après-Guerre (1944–52)*, Grasset 1978.
10. Rioux J.-P., *La France de la IVe République*, Le Seuil 1981–3.
11. Auriol V., *Journal du septennat*, Armand Colin 1970–80.

The French Union

12. Borella F., *Évolution juridique et politique de l'Union française après 1946*, Librairie générale de droit et de jurisprudence 1958.
13. Girardet R., *L'Idée coloniale en France (1871–1962)*, La Table ronde 1972.
14. Gonidec P.-F., *De l'empire colonial de la France à la Communauté*, Montchrestien 1960.
15. Mitterand F., *Aux frontières de l'Union française*, Julliard 1953.
16. Mus P., *Le Destin de l'Union française*, Le Seuil 1954.

Indo-China

17. Bain C., *Vietnam*, A Spectrum Book 1967.
18. Buttinger J., *Vietnam: A Dragon Embattled*, New York, Frederick A. Praeger 1967.
19. Carrère d'Encausse H. and Schrams S., *Le Marxisme et l'Asie*, Armand Colin 1965.

20. Chesneaux J. et al., *Tradition et Revolution au Vietnam*, Anthropos 1971.
21. Delvert J., *Le Cambodge*, PUF 1983.
22. Deuve J., *Le Royaume du Laos*, École française d'Extrême-Orient 1984.
23. Devillers P. et al., *L'Asie du Sud-Est*, Sirey 1981.
24. Féray P.-R., *Le Vietnam au XXᵉ siècle*, PUF 1971.
25. Isoart P., *Le Phénomène national vietnamien*, Librarie générale de droit et de jurisprudence 1961.
26. Le Bar F. and Suddard A., *Laos. Its People. Its Society. Its Culture*, Newhaven, HRAF 1960.
27. Nguyen Khac Vien, *Histoire du Vietnam*, Éditions sociales 1974.
28. Pirowano Wang N., *L'Asie orientale de 1840 à nos jours*, Nathan 1970.
29. Richer P., *L'Asie du Sud-Est*, Imprimerie nationale 1981.
30. *L'Asie du Sud-Est*, Moscow, Éditions du Progrès 1972.

International relations
31. Duroselle J.-B., *Histoire diplomatique de 1919 à nos jours*, Dalloz 1978.
32. Fontaine A., *Histoire de la guerre froide*, Fayard 1967.
33. Grimal H., *La Décolonisation*, Armand Colin 1965.
34. Grosser A., *Les Occidentaux*, Fayard 1978.
35. Grosser A., *La IVᵉ République et sa politique étrangère*, Armand Colin 1967.
36. Joyaux F., *La Nouvelle Question d'Extrême-Orient*, Payot 1985.
37. Aron R., *La République impériale*, Calmann-Levy 1973.
38. Carmoy G. de, *Les Politiques étrangères de la France*, La Table ronde 1967.

THE INDO-CHINA WARS
39. Cameron A., *Vietnam Crisis*, Ithaca (N.Y.), Cornell University Press 1971.
40. Catroux D., *Deux Actes du Drame indochinois*, Plon 1959.
41. Chaffard G., *Les Deux Guerres du Vietnam*, La Table ronde 1969.
42. Devillers P., *Histoire du Vietnam de 1940 à 1952*, Le Seuil 1952.
43. Ferrandi J., *Les Officiers français face au Viet Minh*, Fayard 1966.
44. Fonde J. and Massu J., *L'Aventure viet-minh*, Plon 1980.
45. Fourniau C., *Le Vietnam face à la guerre*, Éditions sociales 1967.
46. Gras (General), *Histoire de la guerre d'Indochine*, Plon 1979.
47. Karnow S., *Vietnam*, Presses de la Cité 1984.
48. Lancaster D., *The Emancipation of French Indo-China*, Oxford University Press 1961.
49. Marchand (General), *La Guerre d'Indochine*, Peyronnet 1953.
50. Mus P., *Vietnam, sociologie d'une guerre*, Le Seuil 1952.
51. Mus P. and MacAlister J., *Les Vietnamiens et leur revolution*, Le Seuil 1972.
52. Salan (General), *Mémoires*, vol. 2, Presses de la Cité 1971.
53. Saurel L., *La Guerre d'Indochine*, Éd. Rouff 1966.
54. Suant J., *Vietnam 45–72*, Arthaud 1972.
55. Teulières A., *La Guerre du Vietnam (1945–75)*, Lavauzelle 1979.

OTHER WORKS

CHAPTER I
Social and economic accounts of colonial Indo-China
56. Gauthier J., *L'Indochine dans la paix française*, Eyrolles 1949.
57. Gourou P., *Le Tonkin*, Exposition coloniale internationale 1931.

58.   Gourou P., *Les Paysans du delta tonkinois*, Éditions d'art et d'histoire 1936.
59.   Robequain P., *Le Développement économique de l'Indochine française*, Hartmann 1939.
60.   Murray M., *The Development of Capitalism in Colonial Indo-China (1870–1940)*, Berkeley, University of California Press 1980.
61.   Ngo Vinh Long, *Before the Revolution: The Vietnamese Peasants Under the French*, Cambridge (Mass.), The MIT Press 1973.

The Nationalist Movement
62.   Hemery D., *Revolutionnaires vietnamiens et pouvoir colonial en Indochine, de 1932 à 1937*, Maspero 1975.
63.   Marr D., *Vietnamese Tradition on Trial*, Berkeley, University of California Press 1981.
64.   Roussett P., *Communisme et nationalisme vietnamiens*, Galilee 1978.

Ho Chi Minh
65.   Ho Chi Minh, *Œuvres choisies*, Hanoi, ELE 1962.
66.   Ho Chi Minh, *Œuvres choisies*, Maspero 1970.
67.   Pasquel-Rageau C., *Ho Chi Minh*, Éditions universitaires 1970.
68.   Lacouture J., *Ho Chi Minh*, Le Seuil 1977.
69.   Giap (General) et al., *Souvenirs sur Ho Chi Minh*, Hanoi, ELE 1960.
70.   Pham Van Dong, *Le Président Ho Chi Minh*, Hanoi, ELE 1961.
71.   Troung Chinh, *Le Président Ho Chi Minh, leader vénéré du peuple vietnamien*, Hanoi, ELE 1966.

CHAPTER 2
Two essential works
72.   Isoart P. et al., *L'Indochine française (1940–5)*, PUF 1982.
73.   Institut Charles de Gaulle, *De Gaulle et l'Indochine*, Plon 1982.

Memoirs
74.   Gaulle C. de, *Mémoires de guerre*, Plon 1954–9.
75.   Decoux (Admiral), *A la barre de l'Indochine*, Plon 1949.
76.   Boisanger C. de, *On pouvait éviter la guerre d'Indochine*, Maisonneuve 1977.
77.   Gautier G., *La Fin de l'Indochine française*, Société de production littéraire 1978.
78.   Mordant (General), *Au service de la France en Indochine*, Saigon, Imprimerie française d'Extrême-Orient 1950.
79.   Sabattier (General), *Le Destin de l'Indochine*, Plon 1952.

Other works
80.   Bauchar R., *Rafales sur l'Indochine*, Fournier 1946.
81.   Le Bourgeois J., *Saigon sans la France*, Plon 1949.

CHAPTER 3
French views of the years *1945–6*
82.   Argenlieu (Admiral d'), *Chroniques d'Indochine*, Albin Michel 1985.
83.   Célerier P., *Menaces sur le Vietnam*, Saigon, IEP 1951.
84.   Fonde J., *Traitez tout prix*, Laffont 1971.

85.   Hertrich J.-M., *Doc Lap*, Vigneau 1946.
86.   Sainteny J., *Histoire d'une paix manquée*, Fayard, 2nd ed. 1967.

From the other side
87.   Giap (General), *Des journées inoubliables*, Hanoi, ELE 1975.
88.   Truong Chinh, *La Révolution d'août*, Hanoi, ELE 1962.

On Fontainebleau
89.   Azeau H., *Ho Chi Minh dernière chance*, Flammarion 1968.

A Trotskyist analysis
90.   Ahn and Roussel J., *Mouvements nationaux et luttes de classes au Vietnam*, Imprimerie Réaumur 1947.

CHAPTERS 4 and 5
Baodaiste Vietnam
91.   Bao Dai, *Le Dragon d'Annam*, Plon 1980.
92.   Blanchet M.-T., *La Naissance de l'État associé du Vietnam*, Genin 1954.
93.   Dabezies P., *Les Forces politiques au Vietnam*, unpublished thesis, Bordeaux 1955.
94.   Savani A., *Visages et images du Sud-Vietnam*, Saigon, Imprimerie française d'Extrême-Orient 1955.

The other Vietnam
95.   Fall B., *Le Viet Minh*, Armand Colin 1960.
96.   Bach Thai J., *Le Viet Minh face à la France et au nationalisme vietnamien*, unpublished thesis, Paris 1955.
97.   Figuères L., *Je reviens du Vietnam libre*, Paris 1950.
98.   Giap (General), *Guerre du peuple, armée du peuple*, Maspero 1966.
99.   Giap (General), *Guerre de libération*, Éditions sociales 1970.
100.   Ngo Van Chieu, *Journal d'un combattant viet-minh*, Le Seuil 1955.

The French army
101.   Girardet R., *La Crise militaire française, 1945–62*, Armand Colin 1964.
102.   La Gorce P.-M. de, *La République et son armée*, Fayard 1963.
103.   Monteil V., *Les Officiers*, Le Seuil 1958.
104.   Planchais J., *Une histoire politique de l'armée*, vol. 2, Le Seuil 1967.
105.   Chaumont-Guitry G. de, *Lettres d'Indochine*, Alsatia 1951.

De Lattre
106.   Darcourt P., *De Lattre au Vietnam*, La Table ronde 1969.
107.   *Ne pas subir*, Plon 1984.

The opposition to the war
108.   Naville P., *La Guerre du Vietnam*, Éditions de la Revue internationale 1949.
109.   Lacouture J., *Pierre Mendès-France*, Le Seuil 1981.
110.   Moneta J., *Le PCF et la question coloniale*, Maspero 1971.
111.   Lafon M., *La Lutte du PCF contre le colonialisme*, Éditions sociales 1962.

112.   Ruscio A., *Les Communistes français et l'Indochine*, unpublished thesis, université de Paris-I 1984 (adapted version published by Harmattan 1985).
113.   Stalin J., *Le Marxisme et la question nationale et coloniale*, Éditions sociales 1953.

CHAPTER 6
Defence pleadings
114.   Laniel J., *Le Drame indochinois*, Plon 1953.
115.   Navarre (General), *Agonie de l'Indochine*, Plon 1956.

Dien Bien Phu
116.   Rocolle P., *Pourquoi Dien Bien Phu?*, Flammarion 1968.
117.   Bergot E., *2ᶜ Classe Dien Bien Phu*, La Table ronde 1964.
118.   Fall B., *Dien Bien Phu, un coin d'enfer*, Laffont 1968.
119.   Giap (General), *Dien Bien Phu*, Hanoi, ELE 1959.
120.   Grauwin P., *J'étais médecin à Dien Bien Phu*, France-Empire 1956.
121.   Langlais P., *Dien Bien Phu*, France-Empire 1963.
122.   Pouget J., *Nous étions à Dien Bien Phu*, Presses de la Cité 1964.
123.   Roy J., *La Bataille de Dien Bien Phu*, Julliard 1963.
124.   Tran Do, *Récits sur Dien Bien Phu*, Hanoi, ELE 1962.

Geneva
125.   Devillers P. and Lacouture J., *Vietnam: de la guerre française à la guerre américaine*, Le Seuil 1969.
126.   Randle R., *Geneva 1954*, Princeton (N.J.), Princeton University Press 1969.
127.   Chauvel J., *Commentaire*, vol. 2, Fayard 1973.
128.   Eden A., *Mémoires*, vol. 2, Plon 1960.
129.   Text of the agreements: *Notes et Études documentaires*, no. *1901* and *1909*.

CHAPTER 7
The prisoners
130.   Beucler J.-J., *Quatre Années chez les Viets*, 1977.
131.   Jeandel P., *Soutane noire. Beret rouge*, La Pensée moderne 1957.
132.   Moreau R., *Huit ans ôtage chez les Viets*, Pygmalion 1982.
133.   Pouget J., *Le Manifeste du camp n⁰ 1*, Fayard 1969.
134.   Stihle A., *Le Prêtre et le commissaire*, Grasset 1971.

From Indo-China to Algeria
135.   Kelly G., *Lost Soldiers: the French Army and Empire in Crisis, 1947–62*, Cambridge (Mass.), MIT Press 1966.
136.   Paret P., *French Revolutionary Warfare from Indo-China to Algeria*, London, Pall Mall Press 1964.

The French collapse
137.   Ely (General), *L'Indochine dans la tourmente*, Plon 1964.
138.   Sainteny J., *Au Vietnam, face à Ho Chi Minh*, Seghers 1970.

The American dimension

139. Bator V., *Vietnam: A Diplomatic Tragedy*, Dobbs Ferry (N.Y.), Oceana Publications 1965.

140. Scheer R., *How the United States Got Involved in Vietnam*, Santa Barbara (Calif.), CDSI 1965.

141. Schlesinger A. M. Jr, *Bitter Heritage: Vietnam and American Democracy*, London, Sphere 1967.

142. Truman H. S., *Memoirs*, 2 vols, New York, Doubleday 1956.

143. Eisenhower D. D., *White House Years*, 2 vols, New York, Doubleday 1963–6.

144. *Foreign Relations of the United States*, Washington (D.C.), US Government Printing Office 1972–81.

OTHER VIEWS OF THE WAR

OVERVIEW

145. Bodard L., *La Guerre d'Indochine*, 5 vols, Gallimard 1963–7.

NOVELS

146. Axelrad E., *Marie Casse-Croûte*, Lattès 1985.

147. Courtade P., *La Rivière Noire*, Éditeurs français réunis 1953.

148. Delphey R., *Soldats de la boue*, A. Martel 1949.

149. Greene G., *The Quiet American*, London, Heinemann 1961.

150. Hougron J., *La Nuit indochinoise*, 6 vols, Domat 1950–58.

151. Lartéguy J., *Les Centurions*, Presses de la Cité 1960.

152. Lartéguy J., *Le Mal jaune*, Presses de la Cité 1962.

153. Tauriac M., *Le Trou*, La Table ronde 1960.

PHOTOGRAPHY

Dannaud J.-P., *Guerre morte*, Société asiatique d'édition 1954.

CINEMA

Documentary

Antonio, *Vietnam: l'année du cochon*, 1968.

Devillers, Kanapa, Lacouture, *La République est morte à Dien Bien Phu*, 1974.

Turenne, *Vietnam*, 1984.

Feature Films

Bernard-Aubert, *Patrouille de choc*, 1956.

Bernard-Aubert, *Charlie Bravo*, 1980.

Lam Le, *Poussière d'empire*, 1983.

Schoendorfer, *La 317ᵉ Section*, 1964.

Index